VISUAL OBJECT-ORIENTED PROGRAMMING

VISUAL OBJECT-ORIENTED PROGRAMMING

CONCEPTS AND ENVIRONMENTS

EDITORS

Margaret Burnett

Adele Goldberg

Ted Lewis

MANNING

Greenwich

The publisher offers discounts on this book when ordered in quantity for special sales. For more information, please contact:

Special Sales Department
Manning Publications Co.
3 Lewis Street
Greenwich, CT 06830

Fax: (203) 661-9018
email: 73150.1431@compuserve.com

3-22-95- 1820503

Recognizing the importance of preserving what has been written, it is the policy of Manning to have the books they publish printed on acid-free paper, and we exert our best efforts to that end.

Library of Congress Cataloging-in-Publication Data
Visual object-oriented programming: concepts and environments/
  Margaret Burnett, Adele Goldberg, Ted Lewis, editors.
      p.   cm.
  Includes bibliographical references and index.
  ISBN 1-884777-01-5 : $46.00
  1. Object-oriented programming (Computer science)
  2. Visual programming (Computer science)   I. Burnett, Margaret,
  1949– .   II. Goldberg, Adele.   III. Lewis, T. G. (Theodore Gayle), 1941– .
QA76.64.V58   1994 / 1995
005.1'1—dc20   94-16504
                                                         CIP

Manning Publications Co.
3 Lewis Street
Greenwich, CT 06830

Design: Frank Cunningham
Copyediting: Margaret Marynowski
Typesetting: Aaron Lyon

Printed in the United States of America
1 2 3 4 5 6 7 8 9 10 - BB - 98 97 96 95

Contents

v

PART II   LANGUAGES   43

Preface

This book presents the current state of the art and emerging research in combining visual and object-oriented programming. Visual programming is the use of graphical techniques in computer programming. It takes into account the need for programmers to communicate with computers using both graphics and text, and for computers to communicate with programmers. Object-oriented programming (OOP) is the act of modeling systems in terms of objects—software descriptions of the behavior of a part of the system. Message passing is the fundamental way in which objects interact. Researchers and developers are exploring how to combine visual programming with object-oriented programming to improve the ease of systems development, by investigating how the basic concepts of object-oriented programming—data abstraction, instantiation, composition, and specialization—create new opportunities for expressing systems in terms of visual construction.

The material in this book originated in a workshop on visual object-oriented programming that was held as part of the ACM OOPSLA'93 Conference in Washington, D.C. The workshop participants gathered to determine and to advance the state of the art of visual object-oriented programming. Toward this end, participants presented their current research, discussed unsolved problems, and suggested ways to find solutions. The chapters in this book document these presentations and add material on research related to the workshop discussions. We have added an introductory section to survey the basic ideas of both visual and object-oriented programming. We have also included reprints of papers on two classic systems, Prograph and ThingLab II, that set the stage for the practical application of visual techniques in object-oriented programming.

The book is organized in three parts. Although we assume that the reader has a basic understanding of programming language concepts, similar to that provided in an undergraduate computer science course of study, we do not assume knowledge of visual or object-oriented concepts. We provide this introduction in Part I. Basic concepts are defined and illustrated in Chapter 1. We then emphasize the current commercial viability of visual programming systems by describing in Chapter 2 how one organization uses commercially available visual programming languages to develop software for its customers.

Part II is for the language enthusiast. It contains six chapters that describe the languages and language-related goals and techniques of visual object-oriented programming. Specifically, the section covers Prograph from Prograph International and the Technical University of Nova Scotia, VIPR from the University of Colorado, Pursuit from Carnegie Mellon University, ThingLab II from the University of Washington, Vampire from Rensselaer Polytechnic Institute and IBM Federal Systems Company, and Forms/3 from Oregon State University.

The visual context or environment in which programming takes place is the central theme of Part III, whose chapters focus on how to provide an integrated approach to program creation—design, code reuse, and prototyping—when using a visual object-oriented programming system. This section covers the visual environment for Self from Sun Microsystems Laboratories and Stanford University, Vista from Johannes Kepler University, Linz, SPE and Cerno from the University of Auckland, and a visual approach to framework support from Johannes Kepler University, Linz.

We would like to thank Oregon State University, ParcPlace Systems, Inc., and the Naval Postgraduate School for their support of the administrative costs associated with editing this book. We especially would like to thank our publisher, Marjan Bace, who contributed many excellent suggestions. We appreciated both the suggestions and the spirit in which they were given. We also would like to thank Mamdouh Ibrahim, Workshop Chair for OOPSLA'93, for his encouragement of the workshop that led to this book. And finally, we extend our appreciation to the authors who willingly and ably submitted their chapters to a formal review and revision process.

MARGARET BURNETT

ADELE GOLDBERG

TED LEWIS

Contributors

Ed Baroth
Measurement Technology Center
Jet Propulsion Laboratory
California Institute of Technology
4800 Oak Grove Drive
Pasadena, CA 91109

*Visual Programming in the
Real World*

Alan Borning
Department of Computer Science
   and Engineering, FR-35
University of Washington
Seattle, WA 98195

*User-Interface Construction with
Constraints*

Margaret Burnett
Department of Computer Science
Oregon State University
Corvallis, OR 97331

*What Is Visual Object-Oriented
Programming?*

Seven Programming Language Issues

Bay-Wei Chang
Sun Microsystems Laboratories, Inc.
MS MTV29-116
2550 Garcia Avenue
Mountain View, CA 94043

Getting Close to Objects

Wayne Citrin
Department of Electrical and
   Computer Engineering
Campus Box 425
University of Colorado
Boulder, CO 80309

*The Design of a Completely Visual
OOP Language*

P. T. Cox
Technical University of Nova Scotia
Halifax, Canada B3L 4G7

Prograph

Michael Doherty
Department of Computer Science
University of Colorado
Boulder, CO 80309

*The Design of a Completely Visual
OOP Language*

Stephen Fenwick
Department of Computer Science
Australian National University
Canberra, ACT, Australia

Connecting the Pieces

Bjorn N. Freeman-Benson
School of Computer Science
Carleton University
5th floor Herzberg Building
1125 Colonel By Drive
Ottawa, Ontario, Canada K1S 5B6

*User-Interface Construction with
Constraints*

Joachim Hans Fröhlich
Institut fuer Wirtschaftsinformatik
Software Engineering
Johannes Kepler Universitaet Linz
Altenbergerstr. 69, A-4040 Linz, Austria

*Visual Programming and Software
Engineering with Vista*

F. R. Giles
Acadia University
Wolfville, Canada

Prograph

Adele Goldberg
ParcPlace Systems
999 East Arques Avenue
Sunnyvale, CA 94086-4593

*What Is Visual Object-Oriented
Programming?*

John Grundy
Department of Computer Science
University of Waikato
Hamilton, New Zealand

Connecting the Pieces

Chris Hartsough
Measurement Technology Center
Jet Propulsion Laboratory
California Institute of Technology
4800 Oak Grove Drive
Pasadena, CA 91109

*Visual Programming in the
Real World*

John Hosking
Department of Computer Science
University of Auckland
Private Bag 92019
Auckland, New Zealand

Connecting the Pieces

Ted Lewis
Computer Science Deptartment
Code CS, Spangel Hall
Bldg. 232, Rm. 513
Naval Postgraduate School
Monterey, CA 93943-5100

*What Is Visual Object-Oriented
  Programming?*

David W. McIntyre
Morgan Stanley & Co.
1633 Broadway, 35th floor
New York, NY 10019

*Design and Implementation
with Vampire*

John Maloney
Sun Microsystems Laboratories, Inc.
2550 Garcia Avenue
Mountain View, CA 94043

*User-Interface Construction with
Constraints*

Francesmary Modugno
School of Computer Science
Carnegie Mellon University
Pittsburgh, PA 15213

*Interface Issues in Visual Shell
Programming*

Warwick Mugridge
Department of Computer Science
University of Auckland
Private Bag 92019
Auckland, New Zealand

Connecting the Pieces

T. Pietrzykowski
Technical University of Nova Scotia
Halifax, Canada B3L 4G7

Prograph

Wolfgang Pree
C. Doppler Laboratory for Software
  Engineering
Johannes Kepler University of Linz
A-4040 Linz, Austria

*Framework Development and
Reuse Support*

Stefan Schiffer
Institut fuer Wirtschaftsinformatik
Software Engineering
Johannes Kepler Universitaet Linz
Altenbergerstr. 69, A-4040 Linz, Austria

*Visual Programming and Software
Engineering with Vista*

Randall B. Smith
Sun Microsystems Laboratories, Inc.
2550 Garcia Avenue
Mountain View, CA 94043

Getting Close to Objects

David Ungar
Sun Microsystems Laboratories, Inc.
2550 Garcia Avenue
Mountain View, CA 94043

Getting Close to Objects

Benjamin Zorn
Department of Computer Science
University of Colorado
Boulder, CO 80309

*The Design of a Completely Visual
OOP Language*

PART I   ❑ ❑ ❑ ❑ ❑

INTRODUCTION

C H A P T E R   1   ❏ ❏ ❏ ❏

What Is Visual Object-Oriented Programming?

ADELE GOLDBERG, MARGARET BURNETT, AND TED LEWIS

CONTENTS

3

We begin our treatment of visual object-oriented programming with this chapter's description of the basic concepts and terminology used in this book. An introduction to object-oriented programming is followed by an introduction to visual programming. The implications of combining those two technologies are briefly discussed in preparation for the more extensive treatments given in the remainder of the book.

1.1 INTRODUCTION

Visual object-oriented programming is programming that combines both object-oriented and visual programming techniques. Common usage applies this term to two distinct contexts, either to the use of an object-oriented programming language that has a visual syntax, or to the use of an environment with graphical tools to manipulate programs written in a textual object-oriented language. Figure 1.1 relates these two contexts with two others, which we do not consider to be visual object-oriented programming—textual object-oriented programming to produce graphical output and textual object-oriented programming to produce applications without graphics.

1.2 OBJECT-ORIENTED TECHNOLOGY

We program a computer to provide a set of instructions that we expect to use repeatedly. The task of programming consists of selecting a representation for information and specifying the processing of that information. The basic tenets of object-oriented technology are that information is represented as abstract data types and information processing takes place through message passing. Messages are sent from one instance of a data type, called an *object*, to invoke behavior and request data from other instances. The combination of these two powerful ideas— abstract data types and message passing—allows systems to be made up of independently managed parts.

An object is a system part with a well-defined interface that specifies the object's functionality. Any information required to carry out this functionality is private to the object and accessible to other objects only if such access is specified by the interface. The internal details of how an object achieves its functionality are not accessible to other objects, and this means that no object can be dependent on the implementation of another.

The concept of an abstract data type is not new with object-oriented technology. The ability to define new types through record or structure definitions and to define new operations for these new types through procedures has existed for

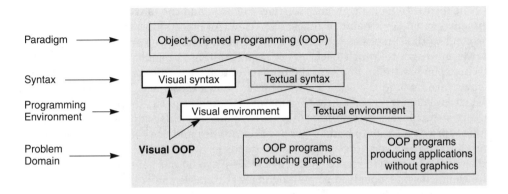

Figure 1.1   Visual object-oriented programming is object-oriented programming using either a language with a visual syntax or a graphical environment for a textual-based language

many years in procedural languages. However, object-oriented technology enforces the rule that it is not possible to circumvent the operations defined for an object to manipulate the information belonging to an object in ad hoc ways.

Most object-oriented programming languages adopt the terminology of classes and instances. A *class* is an abstract description of a set of objects that provide the same functionality but differ according to the values of their private information. Each member of the class that specifies these values is an *instance* of the class. Programming languages that support classes, instances, and message passing are referred to as *object-based languages*. Some languages enhance the notion of classes to permit an inheritance structure whereby one class is defined as inheriting the specification of one or more other classes, called the *superclasses*. The *subclass* refines the inherited specification through provision of implementation details or addition of functionality. Moreover, more than one class can specify identically named functionalities (messages). The object that receives the message determines what should be done—how to respond to the message. Object-based languages that support inheritance are referred to as *object-oriented languages*.

A program in an object-oriented language takes the form of a declaration of *message-sends*. Each message-send can create new objects, or request action or information from an existing object. For example, suppose we wish to create a computer-based card game with a graphical user interface in which the deck of cards and players' hands are displayed on a screen. The game is represented in terms of a deck of cards, players holding onto a subset of the cards, and rules by which players exchange cards, organize cards, and determine a winning position. We put a game object in charge of initiating a round of play. The game's first action is to send a message to the deck object to shuffle the cards. It is the deck's responsibility to determine how to shuffle. The algorithm used to shuffle the cards is private to the definition of the deck.

The next action of the game is to show the deck and the players' hands, opening the current player's hand to full screen view. As objects of different classes can respond to the same message, we can send each element or object of the game a **draw** message, to which each object appropriately responds. For example, the deck responds with an image of the undistributed cards, the current player's hand shown face up, and the other players' hands shown face down. The object sending the **draw** message needs only to communicate the request; the receiving objects are responsible for determining how to respond. In this way, object-based languages provide a way to handle different data types and uses of data without having to explicitly provide a *case* statement or some other test-and-dispatch construct. The objects receiving the **draw** message do not have to be members of the same class, although in some languages the classes have to be defined in the same inheritance hierarchy. The ability of different kinds of objects to respond to the same message is called *polymorphism*.

The code below defines a class Card using a simple pseudo code. The class definition encapsulates both the private information and the behavior of a card. The private information about a card is its suit and number. These are called its *instance variables*, the values for which will be identified with each instance of class Card. The methods specify the functionality of each instance. In the example below, the interface to Card specifies the methods for **draw**, **value**, and **suit**.

```
class Card superclass Stack
instance variables: suit, number
methods:
    draw
        <code implementing the draw method>
    value
        "Access the card's value—Ace, King, Queen, Jack, 2, 3, ..."
        return number
    suit
        "Access the card's suit—heart, club, spade, or diamond"
        return suit
```

1.2.1 Reuse Through Composition and Inheritance

Objects are natural candidates for reuse. Programming becomes largely a matter of composition and specialization—reusing previously existing objects to make new objects.

The values of the instance variables defined for a class are themselves objects. In the card example, one instance variable is an object denoting the suit, and another object denotes the number. The new type of object (the card) is a composition of two existing types of objects (suits and numbers). To draw the image of a card, Card can delegate part of the drawing effort to its parts, sending a message to the suit and the number to draw themselves at a designated position on the screen. Such delegation is one way in which to reuse an object's functionality.

Inheritance offers another form of reuse. Class hierarchies are structured around similarity of function. Each subclass inherits the specification of its super-

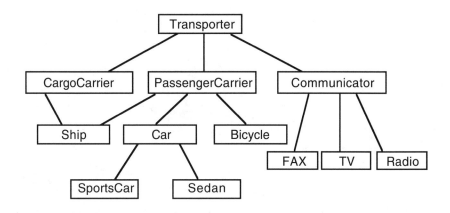

Figure 1.2   This class hierarchy distinguishes the abstract notion of a transporter of something from specific kinds of elements that may be transported—cargo, people, or digitized information. The hierarchy further distinguishes the kind of vehicles that can be used to transport these elements. Note that Ship is defined as multiply inheriting from CargoCarrier and PassengerCarrier.

classes. Some object-oriented languages allow only a single immediate superclass, while others permit multiple superclasses and define how to resolve the ambiguities that can arise when two superclasses specify the same function. Mostly by convention, a subclass is more concrete than its superclass. Sample class hierarchy is shown in Figure 1.2, whereby the class structure is used to support the requirements of the application to distinguish among the different kinds of content that can be transported—cargo, people, or digitized information.

A class hierarchy defines an application-independent description of data types. Applications are defined by creating instances of these data types and specifying the application-specific use of the functionality. The objects specified by the data types of Figure 1.2 could be used to create a simulation of road traffic, to create a control system for cargo transportation, to specify the inventory of a superstore for transporters, to create a decision-support system for determining optimal ways to transport information, and so on.

A subclass reuses the functionality specified by the superclasses. In some object-oriented languages, it is also possible for the subclass to reuse the implementation details of the superclasses—the instance variables and methods. The subclass can be extended to support new functions or to provide alternative implementations for inherited functions. For example, suppose **RaceCar** is a subclass of **SportsCar** that has to provide for immediate maintenance during a race. The functions associated with race maintenance could include use of a personal maintenance crew. Both an instance of **SportsCar** (or any car) as well as of **RaceCar** might respond to messages to refill the gas tank or to change tires, but the **RaceCar** instance would provide instantaneous response, backed up by the personal maintenance crew.

Another example class hierarchy, shown in Figure 1.3, contains the components of a graphical user interface (GUI) based on a framework called Objex [Keh and

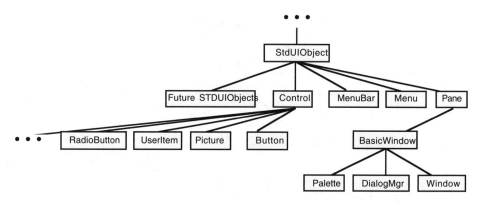

Figure 1.3   A portion of the class hierarchy of Objex for creating graphical user interfaces

Lewis 1991]. The Objex classes specify typical GUI functionalities and serve as the
initial components for the user interface portion of an application. For example,
suppose we would like to add two buttons to the card game application discussed
earlier, one to start playing the game and one to quit.* To do this, we create two
new subclasses that specialize the Objex **Button** class, supplying only the code
needed to start or quit the game in the event of mouse button presses. All the
remaining functionality needed by buttons, such as the ability to draw themselves
on the screen or to work in a window and in a palette, is provided by the existing
Objex classes. The new class **QuitButton** could be defined as follows, assuming
that **Button** defines the method for **setButtonLabel**, that self refers to the current instance, and that **System** is an object known to all instances of **Button** and
is able to respond appropriately to the message **exit**:

```
class QuitButton superclass Button
methods:
        initialize
               self setButtonLabel: Quit
        doMouseDown
               System exit
```

C++ [Stroustrup 1992] and Smalltalk [Goldberg and Robson 1986] are two popular object-oriented programming languages that take a class-and-instances
approach to the definition and use of objects. In C++, subclasses are called *derived
classes*. In contrast, Self [Ungar and Smith 1987] is an example of classless object-
oriented language. To program in Self, you describe a specific object. If you wish to
reuse the behavior of an object, you clone it and then describe any refinements.
The original object serves as a *prototype* for cloning new objects.

---

* This example borrows from Budd's game of Solitaire, created by specializing a hierarchy of
GUI components [Budd 1990].

1.2.2 Objects and Granularity

Objects, as system parts with well-defined interfaces, represent different levels of detail. At the finest granularity are primitive data types such as numbers and characters. Data structures that combine these primitives are also objects, such as the hand of cards in the card game example. Entire applications are also objects, such as the card game object. There are also objects that represent entire groups of applications, called *application frameworks*. An application framework is a set of objects that interact to provide the basic structure and processing of applications within a given domain. The objects that provide the general behaviors required by the framework are called *components* of the framework. The framework defines the order in which messages flow between components.

A framework is used to create a specific application by combining selected components with the basic framework. For example, suppose we have a framework for payroll systems. The kinds of components of a payroll system are employees, pay scales, taxes and other withholding policies, and pay periods. The framework includes the processing structure that combines descriptions of specific employees, pay scales, and policies to form the payroll for a specific organization. Another example is a framework for coordinating the transportation of cargo. The framework provides the structure for combining individual carrier cargo capacity, routes and prices; a specific trucking company creates its transportation system by specifying the trucks it has available, the routes it can take, and its prices. The computation of cargo loading and route optimization is inherited from the framework.

A framework is extended by creating new components, such as new payroll policies or new cargo carriers. And a framework is modified by refining the methods it uses to provide the general behaviors. The payroll framework could be modified to supply new kinds of basic reports. The transportation framework could be modified with a new route optimization algorithm.

1.2.3 Designing Systems Using an Object-Oriented Approach

Object-oriented design models systems as dynamic networks of interacting objects, each of which is responsible for carrying out the functions requested by other objects. The goal of object-oriented design is to define independent system parts that exhibit a high degree of internal cohesion, that are then loosely coupled through message passing and shared message naming, parts composition and delegation of responsibility, and inheritance. Another goal is to retain a close mapping between the description of the problem domain and that of the computer representation of a solution. Designing systems using an object-oriented approach involves:

- Finding the objects in the problem domain, and constructing the relations among the objects
- Selecting the vocabulary of object names and messages as used in the language of the problem domain
- Structuring objects so that their functionality is assigned in a way that leads to clear delegation of system capabilities, factored for ease of reuse

Each of these three tasks is difficult to do well. A number of techniques have been proposed to assist analysts and designers. These techniques are augmented by special notation for object diagrams, interaction diagrams, and so on, to describe the resulting object models in an implementation-independent way. One approach to finding objects is to create scenarios for using the proposed system. An analyst selects use scenarios that fulfill system objectives. For example, scenarios for an organization's payroll system might include: create a paycheck for an employee, compute withholding tax for an employee, and compute an employee's vacation benefits. By scripting each of the steps needed to fulfill the system objective, naming the participants in each step and what actions must be supported, the analyst determines system roles and responsibilities. Roles are assigned to objects, so that the responsibilities translate to the functionality these objects must be able to carry out. The scenarios further help define the system dynamics—how individual objects interact to fulfill the system objectives. In the process of creating the scenarios, the analyst works with problem-domain experts to select the vocabulary of the participants and actions that will map to the names of objects and messages. The designer can then refine the initial analysis object model to account for various implementation-related issues, such as choice of external information storage, preferred style of the user interface, or requirements to exchange information with other systems. This refinement may lead to additional (design-specific) objects, determined by refactoring or generalizing the objects derived from the analysis.

1.3 VISUAL PROGRAMMING

Visual programming is distinguished both by what is described and how it is described. What is described are programs, expressed in terms of the syntax and semantics of the programming language. When at least some of the terminals of the language grammar are graphical, such as pictures or forms or animations, we say that the language has a *visual syntax*. A visual syntax may incorporate spatial information such as containment or connectedness (relationships), and visual attributes such as location or color. Text can also be a part of a visual syntax. Examples of text in a visual syntax are textual comments and textual labels that name icons. Examples of languages with visual syntax include many kinds of diagrammatic languages, such as dataflow languages or state-transition languages, in which nodes and arcs are the terminals. Other examples include iconic languages in which spatial composition of icons are the terminals used to specify the composition of tokens or the preconditions and postconditions of action rules. We use the term *visual programming language* (VPL) to mean a language with a visual syntax.

The form in which the programmer works to create, modify, and examine programs is defined by the programming environment. The environment consists of a set of tools and a user interface for accessing the tools. We say that the system has a *visual environment* when the tools are graphical, using graphical techniques for manipulating pictorial elements and for displaying the structure of the program, whether it was originally expressed textually or visually. Sample techniques for constructing a program in such an environment include point-and-click for action invocation or selection, and *wiring*, whereby objects are selected and related to one another by drawing a line from one to the other. The lines specify message-sends or other relationships. An example for visually displaying program information in a visual environment is a drawing, such as a dataflow diagram, a dependency graph, or a state transition diagram.

Both forms of visual programming systems—visual programming languages and visual environments—aim to improve how programmers express information representation and processing so that it is easy to understand and to modify logical connections and results. Visual language researchers seek new programming languages with new visual representations. Examples include languages in which the programmer explicitly diagrams relationships among data, very simple languages aimed at domain experts who are not professional programmers, and languages in which the programmer can include sample values or even sample executions to specify or document a program. Environments researchers study work flow, information exchange and presentation, tools, tool integration, user interaction, and how these can be designed in a manner that is consistent with the underlying programming languages.

In practice, VPLs are usually embedded in and tightly integrated with visual environments. Because of this, a VPL is often characterized by attributes of both its syntax and its environment. One such attribute is the level of immediate visual feedback provided. In some VPLs, every time the programmer makes an edit, the system responds by automatically updating any related display information. The degree to which a VPL provides immediate feedback is called its *liveness* level [Tanimoto 1990].

Concreteness is an attribute of some visual languages and environments. We are concrete when we use specific values, rather than a description of possible values. Concreteness may be used in two ways—to provide feedback or to specify part or all of a program. Garnet's C32 [Myers 1991] is an example of a VPL that uses specific values to provide concrete feedback. In C32, the programmer enters formulas in a manner similar to programming a spreadsheet, and then can add specific values to test these formulas. For example, the programmer might enter formulas for **Tax** calculation (**Gross** − (**Deductions** × 100) − **Credits**) × .3333 and **Net** revenue (**Gross** − **Tax**). To test **Net**, the programmer can provide a specific value for **Tax**, rather than calculating **Tax** based on suggested values for all the parameters that appear in the tax formula.

PT [Ambler and Hsia 1993] is an example of a VPL that supports concreteness in program specification. The PT user programs by demonstrating—through point-and-click user interface techniques—the step-by-step use of specific values. The programmer also provides the abstract information that distinguishes the values. For example, the programmer defines a selection sort by creating a group containing specific (unsorted) values and an empty group to hold the sorted values. After responding to the prompt for the new procedure's name, the programmer presses a button to notify the system that the upcoming demonstration applies only in a certain situation, when the group of unsorted values is not empty. The

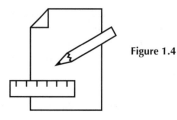

Figure 1.4   Message passing in HI-VISUAL uses a visual syntax. A pencil icon on top of a paper icon sends the *draw* message to the paper. By attaching a ruler to this combination, a more specialized version of *draw* to draw a table is invoked. (Adapted with permission from [Hirakawa et al. 1991] © 1991 IEEE)

programmer then demonstrates the solution by selecting the smallest value from the group of unsorted values, notifying the system that the selection represents the smallest value, moving it into the group for sorted values, and requesting a replay on the remaining values. The system takes over the demonstration, replaying the actions on the specific values until the situation test fails, that is, until the unsorted group has become empty. The programmer takes over the demonstration to end the program when this situation occurs, with the desired result in the group of sorted values.

1.3.1 Examples of Visual Programming Languages

An example of the VPL HI-VISUAL [Hirakawa et al. 1991] is shown in Figure 1.4. In HI-VISUAL, icons are used to represent everyday entities such as paper and rulers, and application-specific entities such as sales books, companies, and departments. The visual syntax of HI-VISUAL describes the way in which objects interact. It uses textual expressions to define object functionality. For example, a message-send is denoted as overlapping icons, each icon representing a potentially interacting object. Rules are used to interpret which object is the sender, what message is to be sent, and which object is the message receiver. HI-VISUAL's rules match patterns of spatial arrangements of the icons and bind these to legal object interactions. In Figure 1.4, the pencil is on top of a paper icon, indicating that a message should be sent from the pencil to the paper. Because the pencil is capable of sending **draw** messages, and because the paper is capable of understanding **draw** messages, the message sent will be a **draw** message. The ruler icon serves as a restrictor with which the pattern matcher selects the appropriate **draw** message to send. When more than one pattern match is found, a decision is made based on a prioritized pattern-matching scheme.

Another example of a VPL is ObjectWorld [Penz 1991]. In ObjectWorld, a program is created by manipulating textually-labeled visual objects shown on the screen or *object workbench*. The syntax incorporates spatial relations, pictorial tokens, and textual tokens. Objects can be gathered together through a point-and-click technique, to form new composite objects. Each object is declared to be public or private, and all public objects appear in a special menu. Selecting an object from this menu causes an **evaluate** message to be sent to the object. Other editing facilities of the visual environment let the user resize objects, add textual labels, and rearrange spatial relations.

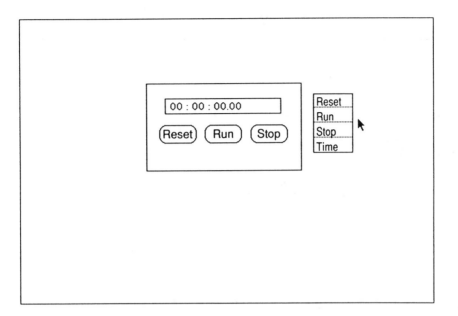

Figure 1.5   The public parts of the stopwatch program. (Reprinted from [Penz 1991] with permission of Franz Penz and Academic Press)

Figure 1.5 shows a stopwatch object in ObjectWorld. The view is of the interface or the *outside of the box* in ObjectWorld terminology, the aspect of the stopwatch that users are allowed to know about. Figure 1.5 shows both the public aspect of the program and a sample execution, because the objects are both the data and the definition. This concreteness and intertwining of execution with programming for immediate visual feedback are common in VPLs. The *inside of the box,* as shown in Figure 1.6, is used by the implementor to create the stopwatch. The syntax of the methods corresponding to the messages is largely textual, but also includes visual objects as tokens (such as the **Time** object in the figure). The process of creating a program is interactive, incorporating techniques such as direct manipulation, pop-up dialog boxes, and immediate feedback.

1.3.2 Examples of Visual Environments

Popular commercial examples of visual environments for textual programming languages are OpenStep (for Objective C), Visual Basic (for Microsoft Basic), and VisualWorks (for ParcPlace Smalltalk). OpenStep creates applications out of existing objects using the wiring technique. The line connecting two objects, *A* and *B,* is labeled by selecting a legal message from a menu of messages that can be sent to object *B*. VisualWorks is a programming environment for Smalltalk that incorporates a painting tool, whereby visual widgets and visual decorations are selected from a palette and placed on a canvas. The elements on the canvas can be named, and linked to one another and to underlying application objects. The act of

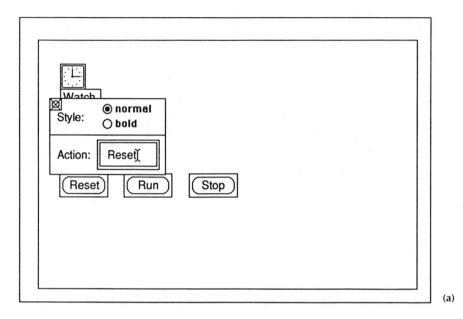

(a)

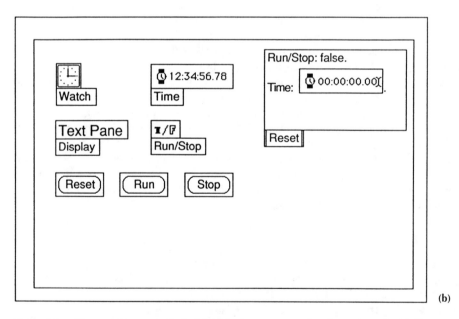

(b)

Figure 1.6   **Steps used to create the inside of the box correspond to those shown in this figure: (a) The programmer specifies that when the *Reset* button is pushed, the message *Reset* is to be sent. This specification is done by filling in the empty *BlockObject* displayed next to *Action:*. (b) *Reset MethodObject* is defined. It contains a line of text and a *TimeObject* initialized to 0. (Reprinted from [Penz 1991] with permission of Franz Penz and Academic Press)**

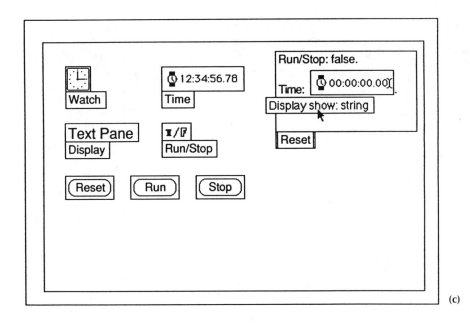

(c)

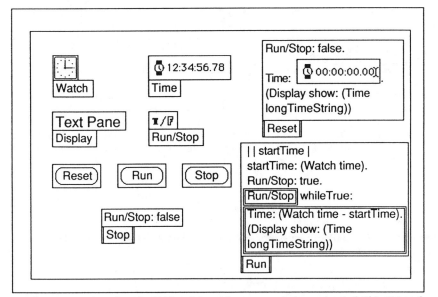

(d)

Figure 1.6 (*continued*) (c) The *show: string* message is dragged out of *ObjectMenu* for the *Display* object and dropped into (added to) *Reset MethodObject*. (d) *Run MethodObject* is defined similarly. (Reprinted from [Penz 1991] with permission of Franz Penz and Academic Press)

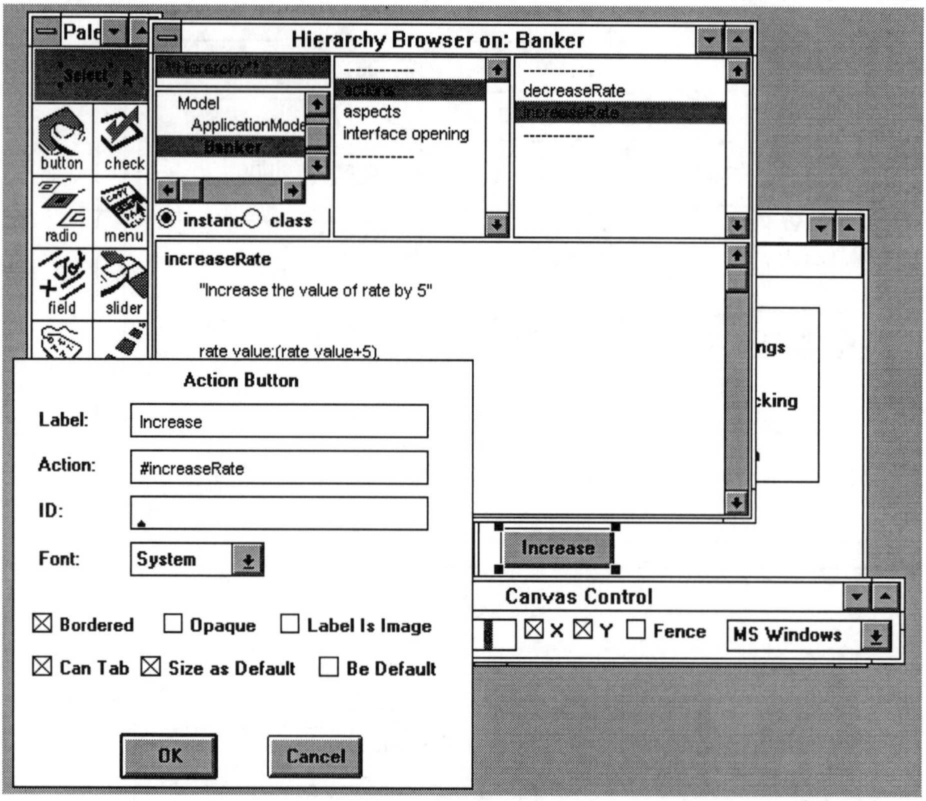

Figure 1.7   Example use of ParcPlace VisualWorks display screen. The user is incorporating a button into an application. To do so, the user selects the button from a palette and fills out the form with appearance specifications and the message that is to be sent to the button when it is pressed. The user programs methods implementing this message in Smalltalk, as seen in the Smalltalk Code Browser in the figure. (Reprinted with permission from Parc-Place Systems)

constructing the canvas is to specify the screen elements and layout. This specification is combined with a user interface look-and-feel policy (such as Windows or Motif) to generate the executable system. Figure 1.7 shows a sample VisualWorks screen.

VisualWorks and OpenStep are both examples of multilayered programming environments. On one layer is a visual environment with a textual programming language (Smalltalk and Objective C, respectively). The visual environment consists of browsers, explainers, inspectors, and visual tracers for debugging. A special set of tools is then created using the first layer that offers assistance in creating certain kinds of applications, notably ones that incorporate a GUI. This set of tools consists of a visual environment (using direct manipulation construction techniques) and a visual syntax made up of user interface widgets, connections among the widgets, and spatial layout information. Other layers, each consisting of a special purpose visual environment and visual syntax, are provided by the vendors of these systems. VisualWorks, for example, provides a database application framework in which the visual environment allows the user to draw (as the way to define) the relationships between objects and the rows and columns of tables in a relational database, and to generate the initial data-access forms derived from these relationships.

1.4 VISUAL OBJECT-ORIENTED PROGRAMMING

Visual object-oriented programming refers either to a VPL that supports the object-oriented programming paradigm, or to the use of a visual environment for a textual object-oriented language. In both cases, the languages support the ability to describe system functionality in terms of responsible objects and information processing via message sending. Visual object-oriented systems also provide ways to reuse function through, for example, classes and their instances.

The goal of visual object-oriented programming is to combine the advantages of each approach—the reusability and extensibility of object-oriented technology, and the accessibility of visual programming. The advantages of such a combination seem obvious. For example, the factoring of functionality supported by object-oriented technology enhances the ability to create visual environments. Every kind of object can have one or more complementary objects that provide visualizations of the capability and status of the object. Individual pictorial representations can display the functions an object supports, and tools (such as diagrammers) can be used to draw the links among objects. The ParcPlace Smalltalk system leverages this idea by providing a framework of views (kinds of presentations) and controllers (kinds of interactions) that can be paired with objects that are the underlying models of an application. Commonly referred to as the MVC framework (model-view-controller), this particular architecture has been adopted by designers of many software systems.

Even though, on the surface, visual techniques seem ideally matched to object-oriented technology, there are several research issues in how best to combine them. These research issues arise from apparent mismatches between some characteristics of object-oriented programming and of visual programming.

One of these apparent mismatches is the size of the software system that the technology can best express. While object-oriented programming has been most successful in the design and implementation of large systems, visual programming has historically been most successful when applied to small programs. However, there is recent commercial interest in components-based programming, whereby existing objects are combined using various visual techniques for end-user programming of small applications. The additional end-user opportunity for visual programming-by-demonstration is another recent example of visual programming's success with small applications [Cypher 1993]. In end-user programming-by-demonstration, users create small programs by visually demonstrating what the program should do. A key to many of the successes in small-scale end-user programming so far has been using approaches that limit the number of different objects visible and available to the end user.

Scaling-up visual programming to build large systems challenges the language designer's ability to maintain design goals such as concreteness, explicitness, or liveness, and still be able to express and manage quantitatively large amounts of information, computation, and relationships among system elements. Directions and recent progress in the components of the scaling-up problem have been surveyed by Burnett and others [Burnett et al. 1995], and include new approaches to traditional programming language features, such as abstraction, types, and persistence; new visual representations and navigation techniques to present a visual program's semantics effectively; and display techniques that are efficient enough even for environments that feature continuous redisplay. These research initiatives are making progress in improving the effectiveness of visual programming for industrial-strength software, as evidenced by reports now emerging from industry of successfully using VPLs for production programming. (See, for example, the report in [Baroth and Hartsough 1994].)

Another research issue in combining object-oriented technology with visual programming concerns how techniques widely used in visual programming—such as concreteness and explicitness—can be combined with object-oriented technology. These techniques assume that the elements of the programming language can be expressed in singular or tangible ways. But one of the strengths of object-oriented languages is their support for abstract specification in terms of classes and hierarchies of classes. Moreover, most objects are implicitly defined by their relationships with other objects, through inheritance, composition, or delegation. Polymorphism also adds to the problem of applying visual techniques to programming based on object-oriented technology because the static program description does not explicitly state which object will receive a message, and therefore which method will be executed in response to a message.

1.5 SUMMARY

Visual object-oriented programming is an emerging area that combines the features of object-oriented technology with visual programming techniques. One goal of such a combination is to improve the quality and accessibility of information exchange between programmers and the computer, while at the same time supporting programs that solve large and complex problems.

The ability to write understandable software systems that solve complex problems is a key contribution of object-oriented technology. The object-oriented approach encourages a style of programming that leads to modular architectures, which in turn promotes reliability and reusability, two attributes needed for large-scale programming. The specification of what an object can do is separated from how other objects make use of it. Consequently, several kinds of programmers can reuse the same underlying object semantics, but can approach the programming task differently. These programmers effectively use different language "dialects" in the sense that they use a subset of the existing objects or a subset of the objects' functionality. Because an object can have multiple visual representations, programmers can even use different syntaxes—some visual and some textual—to invoke the same object capabilities.

Visual programming is a relatively new research and development area. Visual languages and visual environments aim to improve the programming process in different ways, but they both incorporate visual techniques as part of a strategy to achieve their goals. There is still much to learn about how to effectively use visual techniques to facilitate software development. So far, the most commercial successes have been in designing tools and visual techniques for constructing and navigating systems written in textual languages. The chapters in this book address the next steps towards successfully applying visual techniques to object-oriented software development.

Those interested in more extensive coverage of object-oriented programming may wish to consult [Budd 1990], [Cox 1986], or [Korson and McGregor 1990]. Additional sources about visual programming languages and environments are [Ambler and Burnett 1989] and [Glinert 1990].

ACKNOWLEDGMENTS

The authors would like to thank John Atwood, John Bruzas, Paul Carlson, Sherry Yang, and the referees for their suggestions and help.

REFERENCES

[Ambler and Burnett 1989] A. L. Ambler and M. M. Burnett, "Influence of Visual Technology on the Evolution of Language Environments," *Computer*, Vol. 22, No. 10, Oct. 1989, pp. 9–22.

[Ambler and Hsia 1993] A. Ambler and Y.-T. Hsia, "Generalizing Selection in By-Demonstration Programming," *Journal of Visual Languages and Computing*, Vol. 4, No. 3, September 1993, pp. 283–300.

[Baroth and Hartsough 1994] E. Baroth and C. Hartsough, "Visual Programming in the Real World," in *Visual Object-Oriented Programming: Concepts and Environments*, M. M. Burnett, A. Goldberg, and T. Lewis, Eds., Prentice-Hall, Englewood Cliffs, 1994.

[Budd 1990] T. Budd, *An Introduction to Object-Oriented Programming*, Addison-Wesley, Reading, 1990.

[Burnett et al. 1995] M. Burnett, M. Baker, C. Bohus, P. Carlson, S. Yang, and P. van Zee, "The Scaling-Up Problem for Visual Programming Languages," *Computer*, March 1995, to be printed.

[Cox 1986] B. Cox, *Object-Oriented Programming: An Evolutionary Approach*, Addison-Wesley, Reading, 1986.

[Cypher 1993] A. Cypher, Ed., *Watch What I Do: Programming by Demonstration*, MIT Press, Cambridge, 1993.

[Glinert 1990] E. P. Glinert, Ed., *Visual Programming Environments: Paradigms and Systems* and *Visual Programming Environments: Applications and Issues*, IEEE Computer Society Press, Los Alamitos, 1990 (two volumes).

[Goldberg and Robson 1986] A. Goldberg and D. Robson, *Smalltalk-80: The Language,* Addison-Wesley, Reading, 1986.

[Hirakawa et al. 1991] M. Hirakawa, Y. Nishimura, M. Kado, and T. Ichikawa, "Interpretation of Icon Overlapping in Iconic Programming," *Proceedings of the 1991 IEEE Workshop on Visual Languages*, Kobe, Japan, Oct. 8–11, 1991, pp. 254–259.

[Korson and McGregor 1990] T. Korson and J. D. McGregor, "Understanding Object-Oriented: A Unifying Paradigm," *Communications of the ACM*, Vol. 33, No. 9, Sep. 1990, pp. 40–60.

[Keh and Lewis 1991] H. C. Keh and T. G. Lewis, "Direct-Manipulation User Interface Modeling with High-Level Petri Nets," *Proceedings of 19th ACM Computer Science Conference*, San Antonio, Texas, March 1991, pp. 487–495.

[Myers 1991] B. Myers, "Graphical Techniques in a Spreadsheet for Specifying User Interfaces," *CHI'91 Proceedings*, New Orleans, Louisiana, April 27–May 2, 1991, pp. 243–249.

[Penz 1991] F. Penz, "Visual Programming in the ObjectWorld," *Journal of Visual Languages and Computing*, Vol. 2, No. 1, March 1991, pp. 17–41.

[Stroustrup 1992] B. Stroustrup, *The C++ Programming Language, Second Edition,* Addison-Wesley, Reading, 1992.

[Tanimoto 1990] S. L. Tanimoto, "Towards a Theory of Progressive Operators for Live Visual Programming Environments," *Proceedings of the 1990 IEEE Computer Society Workshop on Visual Languages*, Skokie, Illinois, October 4–6, 1990, pp. 80–85.

[Ungar and Smith 1987] D. Ungar and R. Smith, "Self: The Power of Simplicity," *ACM SIGPLAN Notices* (proceedings of the ACM OOPSLA'87), Vol. 22, No. 12, 1987, pp. 227–242.

CHAPTER 2 ❏ ❏ ❏ ❏

Visual Programming in the Real World

ED BAROTH AND CHRIS HARTSOUGH

CONTENTS

21

As the previous chapter pointed out, the *visual* part of the term *visual object-oriented programming* refers to visual environments or to visual programming languages. Of these two possibilities, visual programming languages represent the biggest departure from traditional programming approaches, and because of this, less is known about them. Many are still in the research prototype stage. This fact has made it hard to predict just how suitable visual programming languages will be for practical use.

This chapter sheds some light upon this question. It contains one of the first reports to appear of experience using visual programming languages for real software development. The experiences of MTC provide some evidence of the viability of visual programming languages for practical use. Insights are also provided into some of the ways in which this real-world organization finds visual programming to be the most valuable.

2.1 INTRODUCTION

This chapter reports direct experience with two commercial, widely used visual programming environments. This experience has shown that it is possible to use visual programming for realistic programming applications. Because little proof of this exists in the literature, we feel this is an important contribution and that others may gain from our experience. This chapter reports how visual programming has been successful for real applications by providing a common 'language' that facilitates communication between the customer, the developer, and the computer. Visual tools have transformed the development process, and indicate a direction for visual object-oriented tools to follow. Designers of visual object-oriented programming should keep this in mind when designing their languages.

Our use of visual tools for real-world applications has exposed a perhaps unexpected effect of the systems development environment: the most dramatic gains in productivity can be attributed to the communication among the customer, the developer, and the computer, facilitated by the visual syntax of the tools. If a similar level of communications support can be achieved in the visual object-oriented programming environment, there may be productivity gains available from two sources, the advantages of the object-oriented paradigm and those of the communications support. While any language that facilitates communication will help productivity, ultimately one is limited by the underlying paradigm. This limitation is without regard to the language representation. For example, no matter how good the communications forms are, the paradigm of four elements (earth, fire, water, air) has intrinsic limitations. The object-oriented paradigm is intrinsically

The work described in this chapter was carried out by the Jet Propulsion Laboratory, California Institute of Technology, under a contract with the National Aeronautics and Space Administration.

more powerful than other programming paradigms, including both visual programming environments discussed.

This chapter also compares visual programming with text-based programming in the environment of *test and measurement*. In this environment, visual programming currently provides productivity improvements of 4 to 10 times, compared to conventional text-based programming.

Two examples of applications created using visual programming tools will be discussed. The first is an application created as the result of parallel development between a visual programming team and a text-based (C) programming team. Although not a scientific study, it was a fair comparison between different development methods and tools. With approximately eight weeks of funding over a period of three months, the visual programming effort was significantly more advanced, having gone well beyond the original requirements, than the C development effort, which did not complete the original requirements. As a result of this application, additional work was awarded to the visual programming team. The second application involved ground test and characterization of two aspects of a large space-based instrument. A flexible and reliable method was developed to write the test sequences that coordinate commands to and data from the instrument and the test equipment.

2.2 BACKGROUND

The Measurement Technology Center (MTC) evaluates commercial data acquisition, analysis, display, and control hardware and software products that are then made available to experimenters at the Jet Propulsion Laboratory. MTC specifically configures and delivers turn-key measurement systems that include software, user interface, sensors (e.g., thermocouples, pressure transducers), and signal conditioning, plus data acquisition, analysis, display, simulation, and control capabilities [Baroth et al. 1992a, 1992b].

Visual programming tools are frequently used to simplify the development (compared to text-based programming) of such systems, specifically National Instruments' LabVIEW and Hewlett Packard's Visual Engineering Environment (VEE). Employment of visual programming tools that control off-the-shelf interface cards has been the most important factor in reducing the time and cost of configuring these systems. MTC consistently achieves a reduction in software/system development time by at least a factor of 4, and up to an order of magnitude, compared to text-based software tools tailored specifically to our environment [Wells and Baroth 1993, Bulkeley 1993, Puttré 1992]. Others in industry are reporting similar increases in productivity and reduction in software/system development time and cost [Kent 1993, Henderson 1993, Jordan 1993].

Our use of visual programming provides an environment where programs (not simply user interfaces) are produced by creating and connecting icons, instead of by traditional text-based programming. The icons represent functions (subroutines) and are connected by "wires" that are paths which variables travel from one function to the next. Visual "code" is actually the diagram of icons and wires rather than a text file of sequential instructions. Previous terms for this type of environment have included diagrammatic, iconic, or graphical programming. The tools discussed here are based on the dataflow diagram (DFD) paradigm [Kodosky et al. 1991]. Visual programming is not synonymous with visual object-oriented programming, nor does it imply object-oriented programming. From our perspective, however, the merging of visual and object-oriented programming technologies offers the largest possible productivity and reliability gains.

Both systems discussed share salient characteristics, and the results from using both systems are comparable. Those results include increased productivity and customer acceptance of both our products and processes. It is felt that the key features of LabVIEW and VEE illuminate a direction that visual object-oriented programming systems of the future could follow. The key feature of both systems is that they implement a visual syntax. LabVIEW and VEE blend the visual syntax's of dataflow diagrams and flow charting; they also include (or are strongly influenced by) Hierarchical Input Process Output (HIPO) charting and, for VEE at least, some decision tables. Both systems support the use of text for labels, notes, and expressing mathematical formulas.

The visually based syntax is the key factor in the acceptance of the tool by our customers. Our experience is that the development paradigm of a *requirements* definition followed by an implementation phase is obsolete in our test and measurement environment. The process now more closely represents rapid applications development (RAD) [Yourdon 1992], and eliminates a separate implementation phase, because in general, when the requirements definition has been completed, so has the system. Traditionally, the requirements definition is part of the communications chain that ultimately ends with the developer coding at the computer. Using these tools shortens the communications chain between the customer, the developer, and the computer, because coding usually is implemented interactively, with the customer and the developer together at the computer.

Our evidence shows that these tools facilitate communications because they provide a common expression that can be read by our customers, the developer, and the computer. There are different details of each syntax that facilitate communication, but the details are unimportant: what is important is the transformation of requirements from a statement to a dynamic conversation, with the results that system components emerge as a natural outcome of the process.

2.3 VISUAL PROGRAMMING ENVIRONMENTS IN THE MTC

Our entry into the visual programming environment came through vendors of test equipment. We began using these tools simply as a better way to meet our customers' needs. Since our initial uses, we have become aware of more general uses of the paradigm, and are now expanding our use of these tools and investigating the applicability of other visual and object-oriented programming environments (e.g., Prograph). We recognize that these are not the only visual programming environments, but these are the two with which we have had extensive experience to date.

For those interested in developing commercial visual object-oriented programs for this market, see Baroth et al. [Baroth et al. 1993a] for the criteria for tool selection considered relevant for providing the service of configuring measurement systems.

2.3.1 National Instruments LabVIEW

LabVIEW is a graphics-based language environment for developing, debugging, and running programs. Initially designed to work with National Instruments' data acquisition and control boards that plug into a Macintosh, it has now been extended to the PC and Sun platforms. Because it is closer to a general purpose language, however, it can and has been used for many different types of applications, including simulations and pure data processing and analysis. The first version of LabVIEW appeared in 1986 and was interpreted and monochrome. The LabVIEW 2 compiler was released in 1990 and supports color. LabVIEW 3.0 supports cross-development between the Mac, Sun, and PC, and looks and operates essentially the same way on all three platforms. While LabVIEW itself is not an object-oriented programming environment, the implementation of LabVIEW by National Instruments is very much object oriented [Dye 1989].

LabVIEW is used to create and run LabVIEW document files that are called VIs (Virtual Instruments). The front panel of the VI appears in a window when opened and may contain an assortment of input and output objects, such as knobs, dials, meters, charts, animated graphics, and text boxes. Inputs are called *controls* and outputs are called *indicators*. The front panel may also contain passive graphics and text (Figures 2.1 and 2.2).

Associated with the VI is an icon that can be any small graphic image. "Behind" the icon is a connector pane that can have an active region associated with each control and indicator on the front panel.

In addition to the front panel of each VI, a diagram appears in another window when opened. The diagram contains an icon for each control and indicator. These icons are 'wired' together, to other built-in icons representing various functions and structures, or to other VI files that have previously been 'collapsed' into their own icons and are referred to as subVIs (subroutines).

The process of developing a VI starts with creating a front panel with the required controls and indicators. If the intent of the VI is to function as a user interface, then emphasis may be placed on visual impact and usability. If the VI will be used primarily as a subVI, with parameters passed to and from it by other VIs, then simple numeric controls and indicators may be used instead.

The programmer then typically works in the diagram window, developing the overall structure of the program using the built-in icons. Many of these icons are dynamic, in that they can be expanded to accommodate more inputs or outputs, or resized to provide more area for other icons and wires (Figure 2.3). Other icons can be added as needed, and those that represent subVIs that haven't been developed yet can also be included as dummy functions that will automatically switch over to

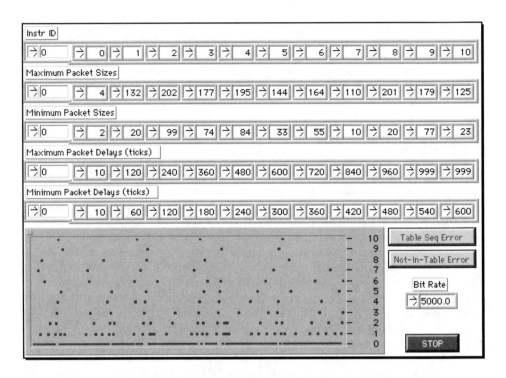

Figure 2.1   Telemetry generator user interface (example of LabVIEW front panel)

the actual subVIs as they become available. This feature can also be used to simulate hardware functions in the early stages of programming and then switched over to the actual hardware interfaces.

At any stage of the programming process, if the *RUN* icon for the VI does not appear broken, the programmer can test the VI. LabVIEW will automatically compile and execute the VI. After each test, changes can be made on the front panel or the diagram or to any subVIs. Most LabVIEW programming is done with the mouse rather than the keyboard. [For more details on the LabVIEW environment, see Small 1991, Evaluation Engineering 1992, Baroth et al. 1993b, National Instruments 1994.]

2.3.2 Hewlett Packard Visual Engineering Environment (VEE)

VEE is HP's visual programming tool for test engineering data acquisition and analysis. It provides the ability to gather, analyze, and display data without conventional (text-based) programming. This iconic application was targeted for engineers and scientists or test and measurement professionals. Version 1.0 was released in 1991, and Version 2.0 extends its capabilities.

Dataflow diagrams, or models, are created in VEE by selecting and placing graphical objects on the screen and connecting them with lines or information paths. These models are built, modified, and run by selecting options from the menus.

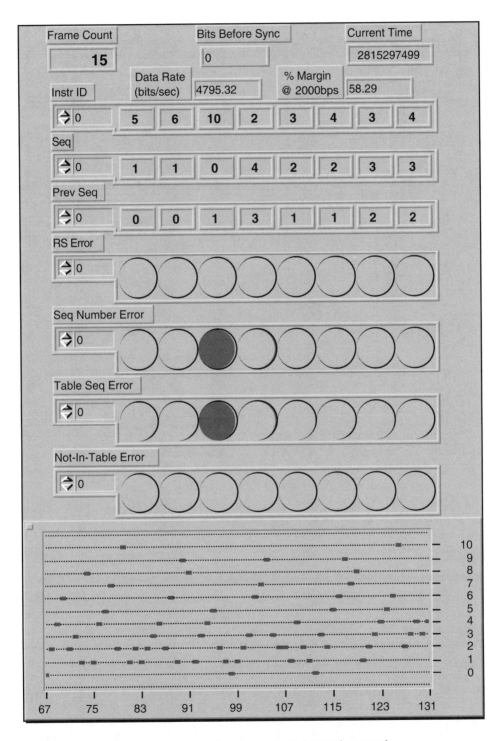

Figure 2.2   Telemetry analyzer user interface (example of LabVIEW front panel)

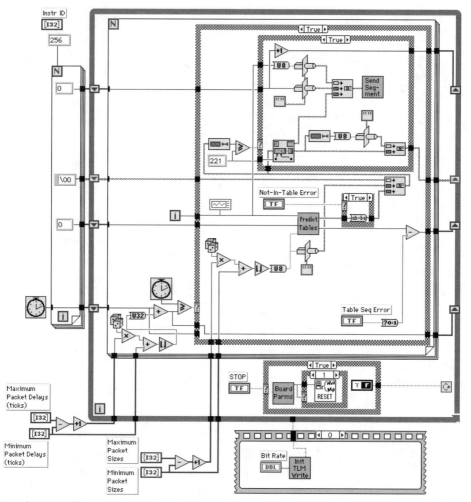

Figure 2.3   Telemetry generator program (example of LabVIEW diagram)

Menu options are accessed by clicking and dragging the mouse. Design elements are easily manipulated in the same manner and can be collapsed into icons or double-clicked to reveal their Open views, which allow the user to view and edit a components configuration. For instance, the number of input or output terminals may be set from a component's Open view.

VEE is similar to LabVIEW in that the customer and the developer see a cross between a drawing program and a computer-aided design (CAD) package. In VEE there is a Detail View and a Panel View. These correspond, roughly, to the LabVIEW front panel and diagram windows. With VEE, however, the Detail View contains all the information, and the Panel View has selected controls and display with none of the interconnecting wires. In LabVIEW there is no synoptic view.

Where LabVIEW provides subVIs, VEE has UserObjects and UserFunctions. A UserFunction most closely corresponds to a subroutine, and a UserObject is a convenient method of encapsulation and information hiding. (UserObjects often become a raw materials source. As a matter of practice, developers will copy a UserObject and modify it rather than start from scratch. While not exactly inheritance, this is a form of reuse.) Like LabVIEW subVIs, each VEE block can be opened and closed. In this way, information can be hidden and accessed in the hierarchy with a few mouse clicks. Debugging and execution are nearly identical. Several simple-to-use and powerful tools support debugging. Breakpoints, data probes, highlighted execution display, and animated data flows are all available. In addition, because of the close linkage of most VEE applications with noncomputer elements (e.g., test equipment), monitors of I/O traffic are provided.

A major difference between VEE and LabVIEW is the form of execution. With VEE, there is no compile step. VEE is not an object-oriented system for the developer; however, the underlying implementation is object-oriented programming (Objective C). When a VEE model is created, a large collection of objects are incarnated and interact in standard object-oriented fashion. [For more details on the VEE environment, see Helsel 1994, Baroth et al. 1993b, and Hewlett Packard 1991a, 1991b, 1991c.]

2.4 CASE STUDIES

2.4.1 Galileo Mission Telemetry Analyzer

MTC is currently supporting the redesign of the computer data system for NASA's Galileo mission to Jupiter. LabVIEW is being used to assist in the ground test of the flight software redesign as one of a series of tools used to configure measurement systems.

MTC was approached to create a telemetry analyzer. A similar task was given to another group using text-based coding (C) on a Sun workstation and a single-board computer. Both groups were given equal time and funding. The purpose was to determine if the LabVIEW software environment could perform telemetry stream decommutation and decoding, and to verify advantages of visual over text-based programming in the time needed to create and modify code.

Two Macintosh computers were used, a Mac IIfx and a Quadra 950. The Mac IIfx was used to generate the telemetry stream using an interface board's digital-to-analog channels. The Quadra 950 functioned as the telemetry analyzer using the analog-to-digital converter on a similar board to capture a data channel triggered by a clock channel.

The original requirement and expectation for the task was to use one computer for simulation and analysis of the telemetry channel (using global variables), but because that requirement was met long before the deadline, the actual generation of the telemetry channel was accomplished. The separation of the generator and analyzer into two separate computer systems was performed to approximate more closely the real environment and to allow more precise measurement of performance parameters.

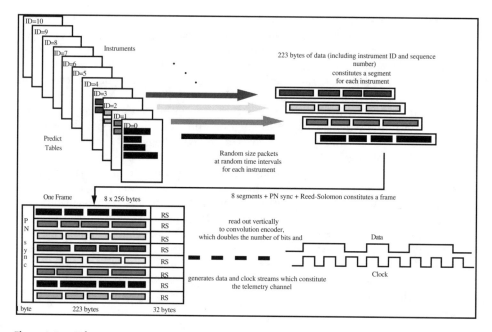

Figure 2.4   Telemetry generator sequence

The telemetry data stream consists of a two-line serial interface (data and clock). Although it needs to operate only at 200 bits per second, it was tested at up to 5000 bits per second to measure the CPU margin.

Telemetry Generator   There was no actual requirement for a telemetry generator, only an analyzer. The generator was created to test the analyzer. Figure 2.4 is the telemetry generator sequence. The source of the data is a set of predetermined *Predict Tables* containing random bytes. For each instrument there is a separate table. These tables are stored in both the generator and the analyzer computers. The overall approach is that each instrument sends packets of up to 220 bytes at random intervals of time and eventually these packets are picked up by the analyzer and verified in its Predict Tables. Packets that are received out of sequence or that are not present in the Predict Tables will be registered as errors. This is a verification of the transmitting and receiving process, not of the data itself.

The entire telemetry scheme can be thought of as having an independent channel for each instrument. Packets from an instrument are not actually sent until enough are received to fill a segment of 223 bytes (including some overhead). A Reed-Solomon error-correcting code of 32 bytes is appended to each segment, and when eight segments are assembled (not necessarily from the same instrument), an eight-byte PN (pseudo-number) Sync word is attached. The bytes are sent, starting with the PN Sync word, and continue through the first byte of each segment, followed by successive bytes of each segment. Before being sent over the telemetry channel, the stream is run through a convolution algorithm that provides additional error-correcting capabilities but doubles the number of bits.

The implementation of the various algorithms (e.g., Reed-Solomon and Convolution Coders) has traditionally been done in hardware using shift-registers, ex-OR gates and counters. The close analogy of LabVIEW's icons to actual circuitry has enabled easy and straightforward implementation of otherwise complex coding.

Figure 2.1 is the user interface (LabVIEW Front Panel) for the telemetry generator. The range of packet sizes and time intervals can be specified for each instrument, as well as the data rate. As each packet is generated, it is displayed on the strip chart as a dot. For example, instrument (Instr ID) = 0 attempts to output a packet of between 2 and 4 bytes every 1/6 of a second (1 tick = 1/60 second), while ID = 1 attempts to output packets containing between 20 and 132 bytes every 1 to 2 seconds. These rates are adjusted by simply clicking on the up or down arrows, but are limited by the Bit Rate set on the front panel. Two types of errors can also be created to test the diagnostic capabilities of the analyzer. They are initiated by clicking the buttons.

Figure 2.3 is the actual program (LabVIEW diagram) for the telemetry generator. It is responsible for temporarily storing the packets from each instrument until enough are available for a segment. A detailed explanation of the diagram is given in the Appendix.

After a complete telemetry frame is assembled, the bits are passed through a convolution coder that doubles the number of bits. The bits are eventually doubled again (so that each bit is present for two clock times) and used to control two voltage levels (0 and 5 volts) on one channel of the double-buffered digital-to-analog converter. The other channel generates an alternating bit pattern to form the clock.

Telemetry Analyzer   The telemetry analyzer uses the double-buffered analog input with samples taken on each falling edge of the clock. Each analog sample is immediately converted to a Boolean value by a simple comparison test and passed through the convolution decoder.

The remainder of the telemetry analyzer basically performs the same functions of the generator, but in the opposite order. The same Reed–Solomon calculations are done on each segment, but instead of correcting errors they are simply flagged on the analyzer user interface (LabVIEW front panel, Figure 2.2). The header information from the packets is then stripped away, the data are compared to the Predict Tables, and appropriate error flags are set. With the front panel logging turned on, the status at each frame can be saved to disk. Each frame will have status information for eight segments, including the Instrument ID, the current sequence number, the previous sequence number, error flags to indicate if the Reed-Solomon code is incorrect, if the sequence is not properly incremented, if the packet bytes were found in the Predict Tables but not in the proper place, and if the packet bytes were not found in the Predict Tables. The strip chart indicates which Instrument IDs go with each of the eight segments, but it is not useful for data logging since only the last segment of each frame will be logged. Several other parameters relating to the frame itself are also indicated at the top of the front panel, including the frame count, the number of bits found before the PN Sync code (which should always be 0 after the first frame), the current time, the actual data rate, and finally the percentage margin, assuming a data rate of 2000 bits per second. All testing was done at 10 times the targeted rate to save testing time.

Several utility programs were created to read the previously logged data, even while logging is in progress. Among these is a monitor to graph any of the parameters on the front panel against any of the others, e.g., to plot the bit rate against the frame count; a monitor to indicate Instrument ID utilization in the form of a bar graph; and a scrolling graph to display Instrument IDs as a function of real time.

With approximately eight weeks of funding over a period of three months, the visual programming effort was significantly more advanced, having gone well beyond the original requirements, than the C development effort, which did not complete the original requirements. The visual programming team worked in a very interactive mode with the customer, meeting frequently and actually coding together at the computer. At times, coding of the task was ahead of the requirements discovery. The text-based team took the initial requirements and did not meet the customer again until their demonstration at the end of the task.

LabVIEW was able to perform advanced data analysis tasks such as telemetry stream emulation and monitoring plus display. This proved that it is possible to use visual programming for realistic programming applications. This task succeeded in convincing people in our organization that visual programming can significantly reduce software development time compared to text-based programming. As a result of this demonstration, additional work was awarded to the visual programming team.

2.4.2 Flight Test for NASA Scatterometer Instrument

To support the test of the flight electronics for the NASA Scatterometer (NSCAT) instrument, a software application to coordinate the activities of the flight instrument and a suite of 15 test instruments and software interfaces was required. Since the test engineers did not know (in fact could not know) the details of the tests until just before they began (sometimes five minutes before), a very reliable yet flexible system was required. What was delivered was a very simple language processor for commanding the system elements. This processor was used to sequence predebugged routines in flexible ways. Intentionally, there was little flexibility in the language, as both the software and scripts were debugged with the flight instrument. Operations support was provided through a control panel that not only informed the operations team of the current activity but also allowed the operations team to run, pause, abort, or step through the current test. Operations flexibility was further managed by having a set of standard scripts readily available as utilities, e.g., power on, power off, and data delivery.

The system was developed, in VEE, from scratch in three months. Requirements were limited to a few sheets of paper that said, in effect, "We need drivers for these test instruments: ." A senior designer/analyst/programmer and two knowledgeable test analyst/engineers produced two versions in the three-month period. Surprisingly, there were only two days devoted to fixing bugs after the development team said the system was ready for operation. Since these deliveries, this program has undergone nearly continuous revision and upgrading.

For the same project, NSCAT, another completely different application was also created using VEE. This application required the real time collection of data from a receiver as an antenna was turned, or as a radiofrequency probe was moved. In addition, the use of a laser range finder had to be coordinated with the movement of the antenna. The data formats for the output were already defined by an existing set of FORTRAN programs, and VEE reproduced this format. To satisfy the requirements, a classic Structured Design approach was taken, and it was both adequate and successful. Real time performance was isolated to two modules, one for antenna movement, one for probe movement. Adequate performance was provided from VEE and coding the real-time modules in C was not required.

As a result of these efforts, there are laurels for VEE, most notably the speed and reliability that VEE enables in system implementations, and the reliability of VEE in operation. There are a few problems, notably the overall execution performance and use of screen real estate. VEE has some quirky behavior, notably the suspension of all activity when the console is supplying data and the suspension of internal multitasking when executing a UserFunction. These are being addressed by Hewlett Packard.

2.5 REAL-WORLD GAINS

The advantages and disadvantages of any programming environment depend on the context in which the environment is being used. Our specific environment is the production of measurement systems, usually under schedule pressure. In three years, MTC has created over 40 applications, from the intended uses of data acquisition and control, to areas not originally intended, including simulation, analysis, telemetry, training, and modeling. We have found productivity increases (compared to text-based tools) in all applications, domain specific or not.

It is important to understand that MTC is not, in general, a center for software research or general purpose development. As such, the software used to create these systems is simply a tool, not a language on which to conduct studies. In the areas of data acquisition, analysis, display, and control, using visual programming tools simply allows MTC to perform its function more effectively than using text-based tools [Wells and Baroth 1993, Baroth et al. 1993b, Breeman 1993]. While MTC has not yet used a visual object-oriented programming tool to provide a deliverable application, it has delivered text-based object-oriented applications.

It is significant to note that the productivity gains are not the result of a basic paradigm shift. As stated, both LabVIEW and VEE directly implement hybrids of the dataflow diagram paradigm. Both tools, in effect, collapse the phase called *coding* because the diagram executes. Programming, of course, is still taking place, but there is no isolated programming activity, as it is integrated with the requirements discovery and systems design process. Keeping a well-known paradigm has both positive and negative effects. In the plus column are ease of learning, ease of communication with the user, speed, and adaptability. In the minus column are mostly implementation effects, excluding the major limitation: the underlying paradigm. The quibbles are a lack of effective *find* utilities in the graphic environ-ment, a lack of zoom capability, and small idiosyncratic details that are always in newer products. Quibbles aside, without any paradigm shift, these tools have transformed system development in MTC.

There have been few studies comparing visual programming with other types of programming, and those that exist have focused on aspects that do not seem to correspond with our use of visual programming in the real world. The study by Green et al. [Green et al. 1991] compared the readability of textual and graphical programming (LabVIEW). Their clear overall result was that graphical programs took longer to understand than textual ones. The study by Moher et al. [Moher et al. 1993] essentially duplicated the former study, but compared petri-net represen-tations with textual program representations. Moher et al. duplicated some of the earlier results, but found areas where the petri-net representation was more well suited, albeit with reservations.

Both studies focused on experienced users of visual or textual code. In neither study was the time to create or modify the programs discussed. It is in these areas—that of user (not programmer) experience and time needed to create and modify programs—that we find advantages in visual over textual programming. In addition, both studies used only static visual representations, whereas in real-world systems, customers and developers get to interact with the program while trying to understand it.

Our customers are mostly engineers and scientists, with limited programming experience with either visual or text-based code. Most, if not all, understand data-flow diagrams, so the question becomes one of which representation is easier to understand with little or no prior experience. We have consistently found users with little or no experience in LabVIEW or VEE could understand at least the pro-cess, if not the details, of the program. In fact, we usually program together with the customer at the terminal, and they follow the dataflow diagrams well enough to make suggestions or corrections in the flow of the code. It is difficult to imagine a similar situation using text-based code, where someone with little or no under-standing of C could correct a programmer's syntax or flow. Actually, it is difficult to imagine anyone watching someone else program using text-based code at all.

The study by Pandey and Burnett [Pandey and Burnett 1993] compared time, ease, and errors in constructing code using visual and text-based languages. The programs chosen were on the level of homework-type tasks, certainly not real-world problems, but even at that level they found evidence that matrix and vector manipulation programs were more easily constructed and had fewer errors using visual programming.

Using visual programming at this last stage of the coding process, however, removes much of the advantages we've seen. Once specifications are determined, it simply becomes a race to see who can type faster or who has access to more or bet-ter libraries of code or icons. The real benefit we find in using visual programming is the flexibility in the design process, before requirements have been determined. Communication between the user, the programmer, and the computer is substan-tially improved because of the speed at which modifications can be made.

None of the existing studies have dealt with the ability of visual or text-based programming to solve real-world problems, i.e., to determine specifications, and create and modify code and user interfaces, as well as train inexperienced users to operate and modify systems. Studies need to be done which allow creativity in constructing, testing, and modifying models using visual and textual programming.

The most important advantage MTC has found in using visual programming is the support for communications among the customer, the developer, and the hardware that visual programming enables. This ease of communication provides the ability to go from conception, to simulation of components, subsystems, and systems, to testing of actual hardware and control functions using a single software environment (on multiple platforms). Modules or icons that represent simulations of instruments, processes, or algorithms can be easily replaced with the actual instruments or components when they become available. In our opinion, object-oriented programming provides the technical ability mentioned, but without the visual component, the support for communications is not present. Visual object-oriented programming systems need to do both to be truly effective.

A limitation of the discussed visual programming tools is they are based on the dataflow diagram paradigm. For problems that won't yield to a dataflow diagram analysis, these tools are not particularly useful. Neither tool produces a conventional text-based programming language representation of the model. For many programmers, this is perceived as a major disadvantage, and in some cases precludes acceptance. The authors have not found this to be a problem in our use of the tools.

Regarding training, MTC personnel, including newly hired individuals, coop and summer students (in mechanical, aerospace, or electrical engineering) have learned to program in about a month, and within two months have delivered working programs to customers.

The fundamental limits of these tools are scaling and maintenance. MTC has produced real systems of moderate scope. We have not hit the scaling limit yet, but it is clearly present. Our systems have short to intermediate lifespans, a few weeks to a few years. Our customers tend to maintain the systems we develop for them, but have not attempted major revisions without the support of the original authors. If these systems had to be maintained over ten years, we're not certain that our current implementation techniques would be adequate.

These tools are best used on problems that are functionally intensive, not data intensive. These systems excel in the transformation and display of volatile data sources, as opposed to the maintenance of large data repositories. Currently, they are not appropriate for image data, although they could be extended into that arena comfortably. Beyond this, we are reluctant to bias a reader away from any area: we've been successful many times in areas that were purported to be inappropriate.

2.6 VISUAL, COUPLED WITH OBJECT-ORIENTED PROGRAMMING

The customer's ability to interact with the model as it's being developed needs to be present in a visual object-oriented programming system. Our customers are typically engineers and scientists with training in FORTRAN, BASIC, and (recently) C. Few are comfortable with the details of a full object-oriented analysis (OOA), design (OOD), and programming language (OOPL) paradigm, while almost all have experience or exposure to dataflow diagrams or flowcharts. Much of their training relies on the extensive use of diagrams, charts, etc. As a result, these customers are comfortable with graphical representation of information. Yourden asserts that the object-oriented community does not yet have a generally agreed upon graphical syntax. Further, he states (page 125): "If you can't draw a precise picture of the pattern, it doesn't exist. In an OOPL environment, the problem vocabulary and the implementation vocabulary are close enough that we might consider using the same graphical notation for OOA and OOD." Should a visual object-oriented programming tool become available that is familiar to our customers, MTC would embrace it without reservations.

In a sense, the commercial visual programming tools discussed here have the same graphical notation for analysis, design and implementation. That commonality supports communication, and the interactive process supported by that communication allows increases in productivity. In that regard, the visual programming tools discussed can illuminate a path for substantial gain in a visual object-oriented programming environment. While it is certainly possible to have productivity improvements without visual syntax, or even without object-oriented programming, if the customer cannot understand the coding language, then the interactive and dynamic advantages witnessed using visual programming are substantially diminished. Visual object-oriented programming needs to be more than text-based object-oriented programming made visual. It needs to be understandable, or at least readable, by the customer.

The combination of a graphical syntax, diagrams, and patterns, specifically tailored to object-oriented programming systems and accessible to the "average" customer, supported directly by a tool, has the potential to produce improvements in productivity and accuracy greater than the sum of the improvements currently available from visual programming and object-oriented programming individually.

2.7 CONCLUSIONS

Both visual programming tools we have used provide comparable productivity improvement. The dataflow diagram environment (not simply one program from one developer) has shown real capability of reducing software development time in areas that are not domain specific. This productivity improvement is due primarily to the improved communication between the customer, the developer, and the computer that the visual syntax provides. If the visualization component of a visual object-oriented programming system does not support communication between the customer, the developer, and the computer, the productivity improvements associated with LabVIEW and VEE will not be present.

Existing system development methodologies are inadequate in this new environment. Because existing system development methodologies presume the existence of one or more coding phases, and because these phases are conducted outside the presence of the customer, they do not address the work environment in which we find ourselves. The lack of viable methodology is not a simple issue. If you simply compare coding time between a visual and textual language you miss the point. Using these systems essentially blurs the requirements, design, and coding phases into a single activity. In many cases, MTC has found that it is faster to build the system using informal specifications than to write a formal requirements document.

The environment of visual programming has changed the communication between the developer and the customer. Instead of communicating in writing or meetings, the definition of requirements takes place using visual programming while the code is being diagrammed. Development becomes a joint effort between the developer and the customer. In these working sessions, the developer often waits while the customer considers what is wanted or what next needs to happen. Some development still occurs without the customer's participation, e.g., questions concerning the operating system interfaces, or issues on which no immediate feedback from the customer is required.

What to do with these patterns in the context of a conventional development model is unclear. This is a serious issue. There are almost no predictors of job resource requirements: by the time the traditional measures are available, the job is nearly done. It is difficult to manage these projects because there is no realistic model against which to measure progress. So far, the only measures we use consistently are measures of system behavior.

We are doing tasks that are not small, but not very large either. When we scale up for larger projects, issues of predictable methods will become more serious.

The visual aspect of these tools is not an add-on, but is integral to the underlying method of expression. Both LabVIEW and VEE are tools that automate a graphic syntax already in common use. Within both are features that have been adapted from text paradigms. Where the text form is imported directly, e.g., FORTRAN or C equation expressions, it works well. When a basic text construct such as data structure has graphics components appended to a well-understood text syntax, the whole thing falls a bit flat. Some attempts to put object-oriented features in a graphical language have had some of the same problems; i.e., graphics were simply added and were not part of an underling graphical syntax. This is not to say that the graphics don't help; they do. It is just that the results are not as dramatic as automating graphic syntax directly.

Without the visualization component of these tools in viewing program execution, the tools would be of limited or no value. Visualization in this context is the ability to graphically communicate the state of execution of a system to the customer. This capability to see directly what the code is doing is of inestimable value. The graphics description of the system without the animation would be not much more than a CASE tool with a code generator; with the animation, the boundaries between requirements, design, development, and testing appear to collapse. Seamless movement from one activity focus to another makes the development different in kind, not degree. This is because we can sustain the communication among the customer, the developer, and the computer. If there were substantial time lags in changing tools (e.g., conventional debuggers), the conversational environment would break down.

Failure to incorporate standard hardware drawing control capabilities places a burden on the memory (mental and paper) of the developers and maintainers of very large systems. Managing large sets of drawings using parts lists and reference designators is not new. Configuration management support in visual languages is not yet present. The single largest problem we face in scaling up the use of these tools into larger systems devolves to configuration management. Presently, there is no clear answer to this problem.

The tools facilitate; they don't provide the solutions. In the hands of an expert (in both development and problem domains), these tools provide tremendous leverage on time and efficiency. In the hands of a novice (in either area), you still have a novice. Part of being an expert is knowing when to switch tools.

These applications, plus an additional 40 or more, have convincingly demonstrated to us and our customers that visual programming significantly reduces system development time. The two tools discussed are effective and real. MTC consistently finds that visual programming reduces development time by at least a factor of 4, and up to an order of magnitude.

As stated, the most dramatic productivity increases we've observed occur when the communication between the customer, the developer, and the computer is facilitated by the tools. With this communication, the boundaries between requirements, design, development, and testing appear to collapse. It is in this regard that the visual programming tools discussed here can illuminate the path for substantial gain in a visual object-oriented programming environment. If the customer cannot understand the coding language, than the interactive and dynamic advantages witnessed using visual programming are substantially diminished. Visual object-oriented programming needs to be more than text-based object-oriented programming made visual. It needs to be understandable, or at least readable, by the customer.

ACKNOWLEDGMENTS

The authors wish to acknowledge the contributions of George Wells toward the writing of this chapter.

REFERENCES

[Baroth et al. 1992a] E. C. Baroth, D. J. Clark, and R. W. Losey, "Acquisition, analysis, control, and visualization of data using personal computers and a graphical-based programming language," in *Conference Proceedings of American Society of Engineering Educators (ASEE)*, Toledo, June 1992, pp. 1447–1453.

[Baroth et al. 1992b] E. C. Baroth, D. J. Clark, and R. W. Losey, "An adaptive structure data acquisition system using a graphical-based programming language," in *Fourth AIAA / Air Force / NASA / OAI Symposium on Multidisciplinary Analysis and Optimization,* Cleveland, September 1992.

[Baroth et al. 1993a] E. C. Baroth, C. Hartsough, L. Johnsen, J. McGregor, M. Powell-Meeks, A. Walsh, G. Wells, S. Chazanoff, and T. Brunzie, "A survey of data acquisition and analysis software tools, part 1," *Evaluation Engineering Magazine*, October 1993, pp. 54–66.

[Baroth et al. 1993b] E. C. Baroth, C. Hartsough, L. Johnsen, J. McGregor, M. Powell-Meeks, A. Walsh, G. Wells, S. Chazanoff, and T. Brunzie, "A survey of data acquisition and analysis software tools, part 2," *Evaluation Engineering Magazine*, November 1993, pp. 128–140.

[Breeman 1993] D. Breeman, "Jet propulsion lab aids in space craft project," *Scientific Computing and Automation*, November 1993, pp. 26–28.

[Bulkeley 1993] D. Bulkeley, "Today's equipment tests tomorrow's designs," *Design News Magazine*, May 1993, pp. 82–86.

[Dye 1989] R. Dye, "Visual object-oriented programming," *Dr. Dobb's Macintosh Journal*, Fall 1989.

[Evaluation Engineering 1992] "Graphical programming for Windows/Sun," *Evaluation Engineering Magazine*, September 1992, pp. 60–63.

[Green et al. 1991] T. R. G. Green, M. Petre, and R. K. E. Bellamy, "Comprehensibility of visual and textual programs: A test of superlativism against the 'match-mismatch' conjecture," in *Fourth Workshop on Empirical Studies of Programmers*, New Brunswick, December 1991, pp. 121–146.

[Helsel 1994] R. Helsel, *Cutting Your Test Development Time With HP VEE*, Prentice Hall Inc., Englewood Cliffs, 1994.

[Henderson 1993] J. R. Henderson, "Sequential file creation for automated test procedures," in *Proceedings from NEPCON West '93*, Anaheim, February 1993, pp. 1065–1077.

[Hewlett Packard 1991a] "VEE visual engineering environment," technical data, 5091-1142EN, 1991.

[Hewlett Packard 1991b] "Complete data acquisition solutions with HP VEE-Test," application note, 1206-01, 5091-1139E, 1991.

[Hewlett Packard 1991c] "Design characterization using HP VEE-Test," application note, 1206-02, 5091-1140E, 1991.

[Jordan 1993] S. C. Jordan, "Cutting costs the old fashioned way," in *Proceedings from NEPCON West '93*, Anaheim, February 1993, pp. 1921–1931.

[Kent 1993] G. Kent, "Automated RF test system for digital cellular tele-phones," in *Proceedings from NEPCON West '93*, Anaheim, February 1993, pp. 1055–1064.

[Kodosky et al. 1991] J. Kodosky, J. MacCrisken, and G. Rymar, "Visual pro-gramming using structured dataflow," in *Proceedings of the 1991 IEEE Workshop on Visual Languages*, Kobe, Japan, October 1991, pp. 34–39.

[Moher et al. 1993] T. G. Moher, D. C. Mak, B. Blumenthal, and L. M. Lev-enthal, "Comparing the comprehensibility of textual and graphical pro-grams: The case of petri nets," in *Fifth Workshop on Empirical Studies of Programmers*, Palo Alto, December 1993.

[National Instruments 1994] *National Instruments Catalog*, pp. 17–112, 1994.

[Pandey and Burnett 1993] R. Pandey and M. Burnett, "Is it easier to write matrix manipulation programs visually or textually? An imperical study," in *Proceedings of the 1993 IEEE Symposium on Visual Languages*, Bergen, Norway, August 1993, pp. 344–351.

[Puttré 1992] M. Puttré, "Software makes its home in the lab," *Mechanical Engineering Magazine*, October 1992, pp. 75–78.

[Small 1991] C. H. Small, "Diagram compilers turn pictures into programs," *EDN Magazine Special Software Supplement*, June 1991, pp. 13–20.

[Wells and Baroth 1993] G. Wells and E. C. Baroth, "Telemetry monitoring and display using LabVIEW," in *Proceedings of National Instruments User Sym-posium*, Austin, March 1993.

[Yourdon 1992] E. Yourdon, *Decline and Fall of the American Programmer*, Yourdon Press, Prentice Hall Inc., Englewood Cliffs, 1992.

APPENDIX: DESCRIPTION OF FIGURE 2.3

Figure 2.3 appears exactly as it does in the VI's diagram (program) win-dow. Each of the controls and indicators on the front panel (user interface) has a corresponding icon in the diagram. The strip chart's icon, for example, appears near the center of the diagram and looks like a miniature strip chart. All of the controls' icons are of similar size, and can be identified by labels next to them cor-responding to their labels on the front panel. These icons disclose the type of each input: TF for Boolean, DBL for double-precision floating-point number, and [I32] for an array of 32-bit integers.

All four LabVIEW structure types are also shown in Figure 2.3. First, there are two **FOR** loops (which look like a stack of papers with an **N** icon in the upper left corner). The tall narrow **FOR** loop on the left side of the diagram is hardwired to iterate 256 times. It generates four arrays of 256 elements each. Note how the wires get thicker as they exit the **FOR** loop along its right edge to indicate that they carry arrays rather than scalars. The iteration **i** icon shown near the bottom is not wired.

The second structure type is the **WHILE** loop (which appears as a large square box formed by a thick arrow encircling it in a counter-clockwise direction). Everything inside this box will continue to execute until the small icon with the circular arrow in the lower right corner receives a false value (which is the state shown in the figure). This **WHILE** loop contains four shift-registers that are two-part devices shown by the small rectangular boxes embedded along the left and right sides of the loop. The ones on the right side are the inputs to the shift-registers and have small arrowheads pointing up to indicate that the values wired into them will propagate around the loop, on the next iteration, to their corresponding outputs on the left side (arrowheads pointing down). The values available from the outputs on the first iteration of the loop are wired into them from the left side of the loop. The iteration **i** icon in the lower left corners of this **WHILE** loop is not wired.

The third structure type is the **Sequence** structure, and appears as a frame from movie film. An example appears near the bottom of the figure, and shows its first frame (numbered **0**). A sequence structure can have any number of frames, although only one appears on the diagram. The programmer can display any frame with the controls at the top, but all of them will execute in order when the program is run. Since this **Sequence** structure is used to initialize the telemetry channel, an arbitrary output from it is wired to the border of the **WHILE** loop above it to guarantee that the **Sequence** structure will finish executing before the **WHILE** loop begins. This illustrates the data dependency inherent in LabVIEW; i.e., no structure or icon will begin to execute until all the data wired into it is available.

The fourth structure type is the **Case** structure which can also have any number of frames. Only one of them will execute, depending on the value wired into the **?** icon on the left border. There are five **Case** structures shown in the diagram. Most of them are controlled by Booleans and will have only two cases, TRUE and FALSE. The one near the bottom of the large **WHILE** loop is controlled by the **STOP** button on the front panel and shows what happens when the user presses it with the mouse. In addition to resetting the board used for generating the telemetry signals, it provides a FALSE constant that stops the loop from iterating again. The other frame supplies a TRUE constant to allow the **WHILE** loop to continue to iterate. A small amount of arithmetic is done on arrays of numbers (indicated by the thicker lines) outside the structures in the lower left corner of the diagram. This demonstrates the polymorphism of many of LabVIEW's built-in icons; i.e., the same icon can operate on different data types.

The major portion of the processing to assemble packets into segments is done in the large **FOR** loop just inside the **WHILE** loop. Note that this **FOR** loop does not have a constant wired to its **N** icon. Instead, it determines the numbers of times to iterate based on the sizes of the arrays brought into it. Although the four arrays coming into the loop from the left side have 256 elements, the four coming into the bottom only have eleven elements because the customer set them up that way, and so the loop executes eleven times, once for each instrument.

The watch, dice, and arithmetic icons in the lower left corners of the **FOR-loop** determine whether it is time for a given instrument to generate another packet as indicated by the TRUE state of the largest case structure. The FALSE state simply passes the outputs from the shift registers (on the left side of the **WHILE** loop) to their inputs (on the right side).

Whenever the TRUE case is executed for a given instrument, a random number of characters is selected from its Predict Table and concatenated with any previously collected characters, along with a byte containing the length of the character string. The **Predict Table** icon is a previously written subVI (subroutine) that has three inputs (on the left) and two outputs (on the right). The top input is the instrument number and comes from the iteration **i** icon of the **FOR-loop**. The middle input is an index into the **Predict Table** for that instrument. The bottom input is the number of characters to return. The characters come out of the top output, and the bottom output is the new index. Note that the new index becomes the index input the next time this instrument generates a packet. Since the number of characters is a numeric type, it is first converted to an unsigned byte (the **U8** icon) and then is typecast to a string character type with the icon that looks like a square peg being forced through a round hole.

After the three character strings are concatenated together, the total length is compared to 221. If it is at least that long, the string is split into two parts: one that is 221 bytes long and another comprising whatever is left over. The leftover part is concatenated with a byte specifying its length, and the result is sent to the shift register. (The entire original string is sent to the shift register in the other frame of the case structure if its length is 221.) The part that is exactly 221 bytes long has two more bytes concatenated in front of it specifying its instrument number and its pocket number, and the final 223 byte string is sent to the previously written **Send Segment** subVI.

Because LabVIEW does not publish text-based code, there is no way to determine how much C code this diagram is equivalent to without actually writing the code.

PART II   ❑ ❑ ❑ ❑ ❑

LANGUAGES

CHAPTER 3   ❐ ❐ ❐ ❐

Prograph†

P.T. COX, F.R. GILES, AND T. PIETRZYKOWSKI

CONTENTS

We begin Section II on visual object-oriented programming languages with a discussion of Prograph, one of the first such languages to be commercially successful. Prograph combines the object-oriented paradigm with the dataflow paradigm, resulting in an approach that is sometimes termed *object-flow*.

Prograph originated as a research project at the Technical University of Nova Scotia. This chapter describes the Prograph language from the perspective of the motivations and design goals of the researchers who developed it.

3.1 INTRODUCTION

Our purpose is to investigate the contributions that visuality can make to the programming environment as a whole, rather than just to programming languages. We must divide the uses of visuality into two categories: general uses such as windows and menus, and specific ones, such as representing algorithms and data with pictures rather than text. To this end we will first investigate the origins of textual programming, and attempt to identify appropriate and inappropriate uses of text. We will propose pictorial alternatives to the latter, illustrated by the pictorial programming language Prograph, implemented in a rich software development environment.

The development of textual programming languages and environments has paralleled that of computer hardware, and therefore has been influenced by the organisation of this hardware. As a consequence, languages tend to be oriented towards simple, character-based input and output, and to be sequential in structure. They also rely on a combination of mathematical formalisms and natural languages, with the result that their syntax is complex and unforgiving, enforcing restrictive structure on algorithms. In recent years, user interfaces have been revolutionised by the advent of sophisticated high resolution graphics, providing possibilities for rich interactions with the user. Existing textual languages and environments are deficient for such hardware for two reasons: first, they do not facilitate the design and programming of pictorial interfaces, and second, they do not take advantage of pictures to represent algorithms and data. On the other hand, for some uses text is superior to pictures: namely, for comments, identification of program elements and certain algebraic formulae.

This research was supported by Operating Grants from the Natural Sciences and Engineering Research Council of Canada.

3.2 EVOLUTION OF PROGRAMMING ENVIRONMENTS

3.2.1 Textual Programming

Textual programming languages developed from a desire to make the representation of algorithms precise and readable. Therefore they have been influenced by languages used for other purposes, namely natural languages and mathematical formalisms such as algebra, first order predicate calculus, and lambda calculus. A further influence on the development of textual programming languages stemmed from the computing hardware and operating environments available for executing algorithms. The hardware imposed a certain structure on languages because of its von Neumann archtecture, while operating environments were very crude, providing only the simplest character-oriented input and output facilities.

The natural language component of programming languages originated in attempts to describe the functions of the hardware. For example, variables were used to symbolise addresses, keywords such as **goto** and **if-then** were used to describe unconditional and conditional branches. Later, some higher level languages discarded natural language structures in favour of mathematical formalisms, like lambda calculus in Lisp and predicate calculus in Prolog.

This historical development of programming languages has several unfortunate consequences. The facilities these language provide for describing algorithms correspond more closely to how computers operate than to the cognitive or perceptual processes of the programmer. Because the medium of expression is text, which is inherently one-dimensional, algorithms are forced to be sequential. This sequentiality unnecessarily constrains the thinking of the programmer by forcing him or her to consider how to linearly organise every program, whether or not the algorithm requires it. The linearity of text has a similar detrimental effect on the programmer's conceptions of data, since even multidimensional structures such as graphs or arrays have to be represented in some linear fashion. These restriction were appropriate for machines with single main processors, but become an obstacle in new parallel architectures.

Textual programming, because of its natural language ancestry, has inherited a complex syntax. Unlike their natural counterparts, however, the syntax of programming languages is inflexible and unforgiving, forcing the programmer to deal with small syntactic details, rather than the important concepts of algorithms.

The first attempts to describe control in textual languages relied on the free use of **goto**s, which were soon discovered to produce unreadable and error-prone programs. As a result of negative experiences with these primitive controls, structured programming was introduced, enforcing a deeply nested organisation of programs. Unfortunately, the accompanying design methodology, based on stepwise refinement of pseudocode, can be applied only to a certain extent since early decisions about control structures can be invalidated by deeper design issues. For example, when a **while** loop is introduced, its control variables may be unknown since they originate in the body of the loop which has yet to be designed.

Textual programming languages are based on coding information in one-dimensional strings to be understood by computers. Of course, these strings should also be readily understood by humans and should therefore imitate natural languages, in which only a small number of the many combinations of symbols are meaningful. Consequently the information density of programs in such languages is very low [Aczel and Daroczy 1975].

Another well known and extensively discussed defect of textual programming languages is their use of variables [Backus 1978]. Variables originated as symbolic addresses, and have since been cast into various conflicting roles. They are used both as transmitters of local data within procedures, and as global data repositories, leading to the notion of variable scope, which adds to the confusion and unreadability of textual programs. A further problem arises from the fact that the name of a variable is used for two purposes, to identify the variable and to provide mnemonic information. These two uses are in conflict, since for mnemonic purposes names should be long, but to minimise typographical errors they should be short. Finally, the concept of variable is alien to languages based on ideograms, such as Chinese [Cheng 1988].

Textual languages are also deficient in expressing the concepts of object orientation [Cox 1986, Cox and Pietrzykowski 1989, Dahl et al. 1970, Goldberg and Robinson 1983]. For example the class hierarchy, a two dimensional graphical construct central to this programming paradigm, can be represented in text only by some kind of linear coding which detracts from the simplicity of this concept. Furthermore, referring to objects requires variables, creating a misconception that objects need names, and that the name of the variable is the name of the object. Objects, however, are anonymous by nature, their identification depending on the values of their attributes.

Describing data in textual languages has shortcomings too. Simple values such as numbers and strings are naturally represented by text and therefore cause no problems. However, structured data built from records and pointers can be represented only indirectly in text, by some linear coding. Most languages allow the simple components of structures to be viewed, while others provide codings for a limited range of structures, such as lists and terms in Lisp, Prolog and Smalltalk. Even in cases where such codings are available, however, they usually rely on mathematical formalisms such as functional expressions, and do not necessarily represent the underlying semantics. For example, a data structure which can be displayed as a directed acyclic graph, may be meant to represent the structure of some physical object, such as a mechanical device. Hence, even though a language provides a representation, it may be removed by many levels of abstraction from the intended semantics.

As mentioned above, the evolution of programming languages has been heavily influenced by the simple character-oriented input and output facilities of early hardware. This form of communication has remained essentially unchanged through the evolution from primitive punched card and tape devices to time-sharing via remote ASCII terminals. A fundamental change occurred with the advent of modern, single-user computers with high resolution graphics and pointing devices, leading to a revolution in the design of operating systems which now have interfaces relying on windows, icons and menus. This originated from research at Xerox PARC.

3.2.2 The Use of Pictoriality in Programming

Visuality has a long association with computers and programming. Before the advent of digital computers, analogue machines were widely used for a variety of tasks such as the solution of differential equations. These machines were programmed in a pictorial fashion by designing diagrams to specify connections between computing elements. Pictures have also played a key role in programming digital computers; for example, flowcharts are often used as a heuristic aid in designing algorithms, and data structure diagrams in planning the traversal and manipulation of record and pointer structures. The development of computers with powerful graphics has made possible the direct use of pictures in the computing process, and as a result pictorial programming has become an intensively researched area, for example [Chua et al. 1988, Cox and Pietrzykowski 1985, Cox and Pietrzykowski 1989, Cox and Pietrzykowski 1988a, Cox and Pietrzykowski 1988b, Glinert 1986, Glinert and Tanimoto 1984, GPL Manual 1981, Hirakawa et al. 1986, Ingalls et al. 1988, Matsumara and Tayama 1986, Matwin and Pietrzykowski 1985, Pong 1986, Smith 1987, Vose and Williams 1986].

It is important that the development of pictorial languages and programming environments should not be hampered by the traditional approaches outlined in section 3.2.1. We will therefore describe in general terms the characteristics that pictorial programming environments should have.

It is clear that the components of a programming language should be a natural extension of the environment provided by the host computer. Consequently, a pictorial language should employ all the usual interface devices such as windows, menus and icons. Similarly, in the programming environment provided by the implementation of the language, the user's actions should evoke a "predictable" response. For example, if a double click on an icon in the host operating system opens a window, this convention should be followed in the programming environment, so that double-clicking an icon representing a program element should open a window revealing the internal structure of that element.

A pictorial programming language should represent the underlying concepts in as natural a way as possible. For example, representing a class hierarchy should be accomplished by displaying it as a tree or graph. Also, devices necessary to accomplish certain goals in textual languages should not be propagated into pictorial ones: for example, linearly coded nested structures, keywords, punctuation, sequentiality, and data transmission by local variables.

In textual languages, program elements have no physical manifestation, but are referred to only by abstract identifying names. For example, the name of a procedure used in a call does not itself carry any features to identify the reference as a procedure. This information is usually declared somewhere else in the program, and determined by the context of this particular occurrence of the name. Even worse is the situation in some languages which use context only without declarations to determine the characteristics of the entity referred to by a name, FORTRAN for example. In pictorial languages, however, the icon for a program element can communicate these characteristics, while the name is used only to distinguish it from others of the same category.

Pictoriality can also play an important role in the representation of data. As mentioned above, most languages can directly display only simple data. Using pictures, however, complex data may be represented at any level of abstraction, from arrays of machine addresses to any picture that captures the semantics appropriate to the particular application. For example, an instance of a class "Window" could be represented as a window on the screen, or an instance of a class "bicycle" by a picture of a bicycle.

Graphics provide potential for a rich program development environment, consisting of graphical editors, an interpreter, and various debugging and diagnostic tools. An editor for a pictorial language should allow the user to construct programs using mouse clicks, menu selections and a minimum of keypresses. Actions which have no meaning in the host operating system should be uniformly interpreted in the editor. For example, a click in an empty part of a window, meaningless in the Macintosh operating system, could be used consistently for creating appropriate program elements. If a graph represents some part of a program, dragging nodes of this graph should preserve its topology by adjusting all edges. A program element of a particular category should be easily transformable into another category where appropriate, altering its pictorial representation and adjusting related parts of the program accordingly. An editor for a pictorial language should take advantage of cursor location to determine the interpretation of a mouse click. For instance, if a "rubber band" joins an icon to the cursor, a click on another icon may be establish a connection: however, if the click is in an empty part of the window, a new icon may be created and connected. This context sensitive interpretation of cursor clicks can obviously be used to ensure that only appropriate actions are perfomed, thereby preventing the construction of any syntactically incorrect program.

The structure of a pictorial language should be such that states of execution can be directly represented by different drawing modes for program elements. An execution device, either interpreter or compiled code, should therefore be able to use these different drawing modes to provide an animated display of execution. For example, pictures may display stacks of icons representing calls, while the progress of execution through the individual calls could also be shown. If an execution error occurs, its origin should be displayed so that the editor can be immediately used to rectify it, and the effect of editing on the state of execution should then be observable.

Finally, since a pictorial programming system must be implemented in an environment with a powerful graphical interface, it should provide the programmer with the tools to create applications taking full advantage of this interface.

3.3 PROGRAPH

In this section we describe the pictorial programming environment Prograph which was designed according to the above principles. We will describe how Prograph represents the main concepts of object oriented programming, classes, attributes and methods and how a method's representation defines the semantics of its dataflow, data driven execution. In particular, we indicate how parallelism, sequencing, iteration and conditional constructs are modelled in Prograph. A more complete description of the language features of Prograph is given in [Cox and Pietrzykowski 1988a]. The design of Prograph developed from research on the role of pictures in describing functional programs [Matwin and Pietrzykowski 1985]. In further research it was discovered that pictoriality could be used to replace the familiar nested control structures by multiplexes and Prolog-like case structures, and to naturally represent object-orientation with single inheritance [Cox and Pietrzykowski 1988a, Cox and Pietrzykowski 1988b].

3.3.1 Classes

A class in object-oriented programming provides a mechanism for defining a data type with attributes and methods which apply to objects of that type [Cox 1986]. Classes in Prograph are organised in hierarchies: the class structure of a Prograph program is displyed in the **Classes** window. This window contains a visual representation of the current forest of classes. Each class is represented by an icon and each parent-child class relationship is represented by a line from the parent's icon down to the child's.

There are two types of classes in Prograph; system classes and user classes. Prograph has a predefined hierarchy of system classes which provide user-interface features such as windows, menus, dialogs, buttons and lists for a Prograph application. An instance of a system class will have system attributes and an appropriate behavior when the Prograph application is running. Also, Prograph has primitive methods which apply to instances of particular system classes, such as methods to cut, copy and paste strings of text between a **text** instance and the Macintosh "clipboard". System classes are distinguished pictorially from user classes by a double bar at the bottom of the class icon.

The example we use throughout this chapter is a Prograph application which allows a user to browse a list of literature reviews such as those of the ACM Computing Reviews. The user can import reviews from a text file, insert, delete and modify review contents and examine individual reviews. The application also provides an index which supports access to reviews according to index values.

Figure 3.1 illustrates the full set of system classes and user classes **Index**, **Index Entry**, **Review**, **Book**, and **Nonbook** for this application. Note that the icon in the window's title bar indicates that this is a class window. This provides a visual indication of the window's contents and is a feature of each of the window types within the Prograph edit environment. A class's icon contains two smaller icons symbolising *attributes* and *methods*, the components of a class. Each class will inherit all attributes and methods from its ancestor classes and may have additional attributes and methods.

Attributes of a class are represented as named triangular icons in an *attribute window* for the class. A class may have *class attributes* which are invariant for all instances of the class and *instance attributes* which may have distinct values for individual instances. Figure 3.2 illustrates some of the attributes of user classes **Index**, **Index Entry**, and **Book**.

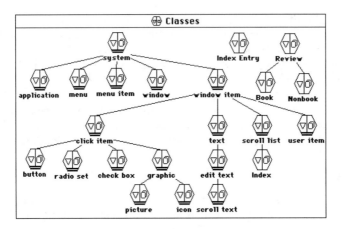

Figure 3.1

A horizontal line separates class from instance attributes. An attribute inherited from an ancestor is indicated by an arrowhead in the attribute's icon. As shown in Figure 3.2, class **Book** has no class attributes, instance attributes **Review #**, **Author**, and **Title** are inherited from class **Review**, while instance attributes **Publisher**, **Year**, and **ISBN** originate in this class. Class **Index** includes the system instance attributes **select list**, **value list**, and **click method** and the new attribute **entries**. Note that system attributes are indicated by a bar along the bottom sides of the attribute's icon. Each attribute has a default value

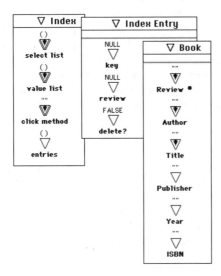

Figure 3.2

which is used to initialise a new instance of the class, and displayed above the attribute's icon. For example, the default value of each attribute of a **Book** instance is the empty string, "".

3.3.2 Methods

A Prograph method is either a *class* method or a *universal* method belonging to no class. Universal methods include built-in Prograph primitives. Class methods are represented as named icons in a methods window for the class and user-defined universal methods are represented by icons in the **Universal** window. A method consists of a sequence of *cases*, where each case is a dataflow structure, consisting of data inputs, data outputs, a set of operations and connections between them.

The definition of a case is illustrated graphically within a window for the case. Input into the case is indicated by *roots* on an input bar at the top of the case's window, and output by *terminals* on a bottom output bar. The input and output arities of a case are its numbers of roots and terminals respectively, and all cases of a method have the same input and output arities. An operation within a case is represented by an icon containing the name of the operation. Input and output data for an operation are defined by terminals and roots at the top and bottom of the operation's icon. Operations within the case are connected by *data links* which carry data from the roots of operations to terminals of other operations. An operation is analogous to a procedure call and terminals and roots for an operation act as parameters of a procedure. However, unlike many textual programming languages, data values are untyped, and a terminal or root of an operation indicates the action of copying a data value between the calling operation and the associated method. A root may be attached to several data links, but a terminal can be connected to at most one. The arity of an operation must be the same as that of the definition for the associated method.

The following table summarizes the different operations available in Prograph. Note that the type of each operation is indicated by the shape of its icon.

Operation	*Sample Call*	*Action*
Input		Copy value from terminal of calling operation
Output		Copy value to root of calling operation
Simple	**Quicksort**	Call user method Quicksort
Constant	256	Output constant 256 on root
Match	**NULL** ⨯	Next case if value on terminal is not NULL
Persistent	**Reviews**	Output value of persistent Reviews in root
Instance	**Index Entry**	Output new Index Entry instance on root
Get Attribute	**key**	Output value of attribute key of input instance on right root

Operation	Sample Call	Action
Set Attribute	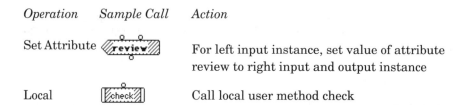	For left input instance, set value of attribute review to right input and output instance
Local		Call local user method check

The *input* operation of a method's case copies data values from the terminals of the calling operation to the corresponding roots of the input bar and the *output* operation copies data values from the terminals of the output bar to the roots of the operation.

A *simple* operation may be a call to a user-defined method, a Prograph primitive, or a method from the Macintosh toolbox. A call to a Prograph primitive is indicated by a bar on the bottom of the operation's icon and a call to Macintosh toolbox routine by bars on the top and bottom of the icon.

The *constant* operation is labelled by a constant which is produced as the value of its ouput. The constant's type must be one of the built-in Prograph types such as Boolean, integer, list and string.

Prograph has a mechanism for the permanent storage of data in objects called *persistents*. A persistent may contain data of any type and is retained during and between executions of Prograph methods. In our sample application, the list of reviews, **Reviews**, is a persistent. The value of a persistent is accessed within a method through the *persistent* operation which is represented by an oval icon labelled by the name of the persistent. If the persistent operation has a terminal, then, during execution, the value on the terminal will be assigned to the corresponding persistent. Similarly, if it has a root, the value of the persistent will appear on this root during execution.

A new instance of a class is generated by the *instance* operation which is labelled by the name of the class and outputs the new instance. Normally, the attribute values of the new instance will be the default values specified in the attributes window for the class.

Attribute values of a class instance are accessed through the *get attribute* and *set attribute* operations. Each of these operations inputs a class instance and is labelled by the name of an attribute. The get attribute operation outputs the instance and the value of the named attribute for the instance. The second input of the set attribute operation is a data value and the operation outputs a copy of the instance with the named attribute set to the given value.

Finally, a *local* operation is a call to an inner, locally defined method which cannot be called by other operations.

Figure 3.3a depicts methods of class **Index** and the details of method **Index/Sort**, a method for sorting attribute **entries** of a instance of class **Index**. Note that prefixing the name of a method with the name of a class indicates that the method belongs to class. Here, **Index/Sort** is a method of class **Index**.

Execution of a Prograph method begins with a call to the method and the passing of input data to the input roots. The first case in the method's case sequence then begins execution. Execution of a case follows the data driven, dataflow paradigm determined from the graphical representation of the case. That is, an operation with input is not called within an executing case until it receives all its input

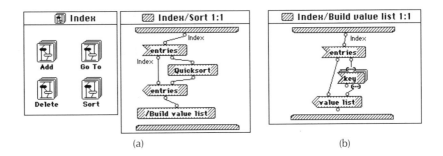

Figure 3.3

data, and otherwise, operations for which there are no data interdependencies are considered to logically execute in parallel. Output from a case is available only when the case's execution terminates. Normally, a case does not terminate until all operations within the case have executed.

Method **Index/Sort** of Figure 3.3a sorts a list of index entries and displays the sorted values. In the execution of case 1 of **Index/Sort**, the first operation is input, which copies the data value from the terminal of the calling operation. The expected input data is an instance of class **Index**. The next operation is a get attribute which inputs the **Index** instance and outputs it together with the value of the named attribute, **entries**, which in our sample application is a list of **Index entry** instances. The value of **entries** is then passed to method **Quicksort** which outputs the elements of **entries** sorted on attribute **key**. This output is passed to the set attribute operation which updates the value of **entries**. Next the class instance is passed to **/Build value list**, shown in Figure 3.3b, which constructs the new display list of entries. Finally, the case and therefore the method **Index/Sort**, terminates with no output.

Data values in Prograph are untyped. When case 1 of **Index/Sort** is defined, it is unnecessary to specify that the input is an instance of class **Index**. Indeed, in order for the execution of this method to successfully terminate, it is necessary only that the get attribute, set attribute, **Quicksort** and **/Build value list** operations succeed. The get attribute and set attribute operations will succeed on input of an instance of any class which has an attribute named **entries**. This is an example of late binding in Prograph.

Simple polymorphism in Prograph is illustrated by the selection of a method called by an operation. If there is no prefix on an operation's name, the method called is a universal one. Thus the operation **Quicksort** refers to a universal method. If the name is prefixed by /, then the operation is polymorphic, calling a method applicable to the class of the instance arriving on the leftmost input terminal. This class can be determined only at run-time. In Figure 3.3a, operation **/Build value list** is a call to method **Build value list** of class **Index**, provided that at run-time the leftmost input is indeed an instance of class **Index**. For the sake of completeness, we note that if an operation's name is prefixed by //, then the called method is in the same class as the method containing the calling operation.

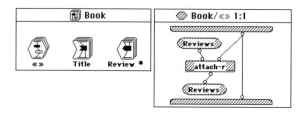

Figure 3.4

A *comment* may be attached to any icon or program element and serves only to provide additional information for the viewer. Thus the the comment "Index" attached to the input root for the first case of method **Index/Sort** in Figure 3a reinforces the interpretation that the input to **Index/Sort** *should* be an instance of class **Index**.

An *initialisation* method for a class *overshadows* the standard instance generation for the class in that the initialisation method is automatically called whenever a new instance of the class is generated. In our example, whenever a new **Book** instance is created by the instance operation, the initialisation method **Book/«»** is called and adds the new book to the persistent list **Reviews**. This is shown in Figure 3.4.

Similarly, there may be *extraction* and *assignment* class methods which overshadow the standard get attribute and set attribute respectively. Inputs for such overshadowing methods are copied from the terminals of the associated operation, the method executes, and then the method's outputs are copied to the roots of the operation. Figure 3.4 also illustrates that there is an extraction method for attribute **Review** and an assignment method for attribute **Review #**. Note that the icon shapes for initialisation, extraction, and assignment class methods indicate the functions of these methods.

The value of any data is shown within a *value window* by the primitive **display**. In Figure 3.5, execution of the **display** operation opens the value window on the

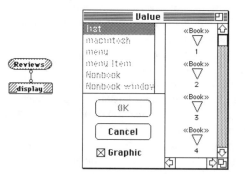

Figure 3.5

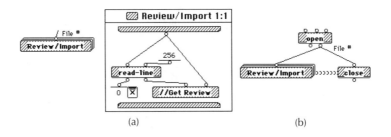

(a)   (b)

Figure 3.6

right for a view of the persistent **Reviews**, an instance of built-in class list. In this example, the user can toggle between textual and graphic representations of **Reviews** by clicking on the "Graphic" checkbox of the value window.

3.3.3 Multiplexes and controls

Iteration and parallelism are common programming paradigms and Prograph provides a rich set of iteration and parallelism mechanisms through *multiplexes*. Again, multiplexes in Prograph are represented pictorially.

Lists, one of the fundamental data types in Prograph, can be processed using several different multiplexes. Method **Index/Build value list**, shown in Figure 3.3b, illustrates how multiplexing provides a mechanism for parallel processing of lists. After being called with input of an instance of class **Index**, such as in method **Index/Sort**, case 1 of the method gets the value of attribute **entries**. The value of attribute **entries**, a list of instances of class **Index Entry**, is passed to the get attribute multiplex which has a list annotation, **(∙∙)**, on its input terminal and an output root. This indicates that the multiplex expects a list as input, applies the operation to each element of the list, and assembles the results into a list on the list root. The list elements may be processed in parallel. In our application, the output should be a list of **key** values, which is then set as the **value list** of the input **Index** instance.

Another multiplex associated with list processing is the *partition multiplex*, which applies a Boolean operation to each element of an input list. The left output is the list of elements for which the Boolean operation produces TRUE and the right is the list of elements which produce FALSE. The partition multiplex is used in case 2 of method **Quicksort**, shown in Figure 3.7a.

We next describe a technique for terminating the execution of a multiplex. When an operation executes, it may succeed, fail or generate an error. Normally an operation succeeds after the associated method is called, but failure can be generated within the method. For example, a match operation will succeed or fail. When a *terminate-on-failure control* is associated with a match operation, failure of the match terminates the multiplex which calls the method containing the match operation. Figure 3.6a illustrates a *repeat multiplex*. When executed, case 1 of method **File/Import** inputs a system file number and repeatedly reads review data from the file and adds reviews to the database through calls to **Review/Get**

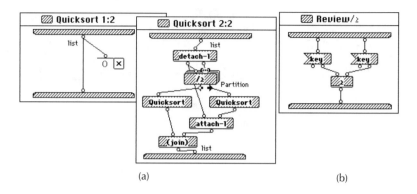

(a)   (b)

Figure 3.7

Review. Primitive **read-line** outputs an error number of zero if and only if the file read is successful. In particular, if end-of-file is TRUE before the call to **read-line**, then the error number output by **read-line** is non-zero, the match operation fails and the terminate-on-failure control, indicated by the symbol ⊠ on the match operation, ends the execution of the multiplex. This is an example of a *while not end-of-file do* loop in Prograph.

As we mentioned previously, a method consists of a sequence of cases and a call to a method initiates the execution of its first case. Controls can be used to halt execution of the current case of a method and begin execution of the method's next case. To illustrate this, we next describe a Prograph implementation of the well-known recursive quicksort algorithm to sort a list of index entries by key value. The method **Quicksort** is shown in Figure 3.7a and contains two cases.

The first case of **Quicksort** handles the input of an empty list and the second case handles a nonempty list. Case 1 matches its input with the empty list, (). If the match succeeds, then case 1 outputs the empty list to the root of the call. If the match fails, then the *next-on-failure* control, indicated by the symbol ⊠ on the operation, dictates that case 2 is to begin execution. Case 2 of **Quicksort** calls the system primitive **detach-l**, which inputs a list and outputs the left (first) element of the list and a list of the remaining elements. The left element is used as the "pivot" element for the quicksort algorithm. The next operation in case 2 is a partition multiplex which partitions the rest of the list into two sublists. The partition is determined by the Boolean output of the call to method ≥ belonging to the class of the left input of the operation. In our sample application, the left input of /≥ should be an instance of class **Review**, so ≥ should be a method of class **Review**, as shown in Figure 3.7b. The two sublists are then sorted by recursive calls to **Quicksort**. Finally, the sorted lists and pivot element are joined together to give the complete sorted list which is then output by method **Quicksort**.

Generally, operations between which there are no input/output dependencies are considered to execute in parallel. Thus, for example, there is parallelism in the two recursive calls to **Quicksort** within case 2 of method **Quicksort**. When it is necessary to specify that one operation must execute before another the user can

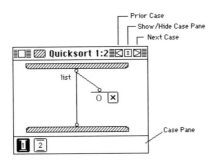

Figure 3.8

sequence operations with the *synchro* mechanism which is indicated pictorially by a succession of rounded arrowheads from the operation which must execute first to the second operation. Figure 3.6b illustrates sequencing of the importing of review data from an input file, followed by the closing of the file.

3.4 ENVIRONMENT

The Prograph environment has three main components, the *editor*, *interpreter*, and *application builder*. The editor is used for program design and construction, the interpreter executes a program and provides debugging facilities, and the application builder simplifies the task of constructing a graphical user interface for a program.

3.4.1 Editor

The editor is the key component of the Prograph programming environment and serves the user in several tasks and contexts. The editor is used to define any data attached to Prograph elements. Each major component of a program is displayed and edited within an appropriate *edit window*. There are edit windows for classes, attributes, persistents, methods, cases and instances.

The user interacts with the editor through mouse and keyboard actions which are uniformly interpreted by the editor according to the context of the action As mentioned in section 3.2, the behavior of the editor is consistent with other Macintosh applications. For example, the different cases of a method can be accessed by clicking on boxes on the right side of the title bar of a window for one of the method's cases, or from the *Cases Pane*, as shown in Figure 3.8. Clicking on the "Show Case Pane" box toggles between showing and hiding the Case Pane. Clicking on the "Prior Case" or "Next Case" box opens a window for the prior or next case in the method's sequence of cases. Manipulation of cases in the Case Pane is consistent with the general mouse operations of the Prograph environment. For example, a new case between the current cases 1 and 2 of **Quicksort**'s case sequence is added by clicking in the background of the Case Pane between the icons for cases 1 and 2.

The editor provides mechanisms to help prevent the creation of syntactic and logical errors. For example, the user is not permitted to make incorrect connections, such as a root to a root. One area that is open to misconstruction is the relationship between the numbers of terminals and roots of an operation and the numbers of input bar roots and output bar terminals of the cases of the associated method. In order to assist the programmer with arities, the editor has features to ensure that newly created or modified methods, cases and operations have arities which match their corresponding Prograph components.

3.4.2 Interpreter

The interpreter contains many features which facilitate the edit-execute cycle of program development and debugging. Debugging involves detecting and correcting syntax and logical errors. When an error in an executing program is detected by the interpreter, it immediately localises the error, provides access to the editor for modification of the program's components, including active data values, and may intelligently suggest a correction of the error. The programmer can use other debugging facilities of the interpreter to eliminate logical program errors.

A program execution will be suspended when the interpreter detects an error. For example, a case may call a primitive operation with input that is outside the acceptable range for the primitive. If such an error occurs, the interpreter suspends execution at the operation call, opens an *execution window* for the case, and presents an error message.

An execution window for a case illustrates the current execution state of the case and is based on its edit window. Operations which have already executed are shown normally, the suspended operation call is flashing, operations which have not yet executed are dimmed, and the background is dotted to distinguish this window from the case's edit window. Note that there may be several occurrences of a case on the execution stack, each with an associated execution window. Figure 3.9a shows an execution window for case 1 of method **Book/«»**, with execution suspended at the call to primitive **attach-r**.

In order to assist the determination and correction of logical errors, the programmer can control when the interpreter will suspend a running program. For example, the programmer can set breakpoints on operations so that the interpreter will suspend execution of the case just before calling an operation with a breakpoint. When a case is suspended because an operation breakpoint is reached by the interpreter, the system opens an execution window in which the operation with the breakpoint is highlighted.

The Prograph interpreter provides a powerful tool for the top down development of a program, automatic run-time creation of methods. During top down refinement of a program, operations may be included for which there are no corresponding method definition. When attempting to execute such an operation, the interpreter generates a message indicating that the corresponding method does not exist and asking if it should be created. Given a positive response, the interpreter creates the required new method with arity is the same as that of the calling operation, and begins to execute it in stepwise manner, opening an execution window on its first case.

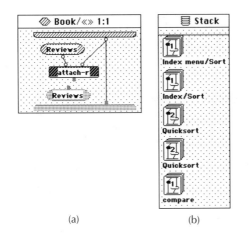

(a)   (b)

Figure 3.9

The user can open an edit window for a suspended case by double clicking in the background of an execution window for the case. If the user double clicks on an executed root or terminal of an execution window, the interpreter opens a value window for the data value in which the user can edit the data. For example, double clicking on the left terminal of operation **attach-r** of Figure 3.9a opens the value window similar to that shown in Figure 3.5.

The user can make a menu selection to open a *stack window* which illustrates the current stack of active calls, each represented by a method icon. As the interpreter adds calls, the stack in this window grows from top to bottom and the window contents scroll to ensure that the stack top is always visible. An execute window for any case in the stack window can be opened by double clicking on the case's icon. Figure 3.9b illustrates the stack window during a sort of the index entries.

While a program is suspended, the programmer has access to all its components and can make changes which effect its execution state. If this occurs, the interpreter performs an execution rollback to accommodate these changes, setting the point of suspension to the latest state which is not affected by the changes. The programmer can resume a suspended execution by pressing the Return key.

The programmer may also trace execution through dynamic views of program execution. In one such view, an execution window of a case is used to highlight the operation icons and segments of the case during execution. If the stack window is open during program execution, the window is updated dynamically as the stack of calls to user methods changes.

3.4.3 Application Builder

Myers defines a *User Interface Management System (UIMS)* as "a tool that helps a programmer create and manage all aspects of user interfaces" [Myers 1988]. Myers surveys many UIMS's and describes Peridot, a graphical UIMS which generates Interlisp-D code. This dichotomy of application development, generating

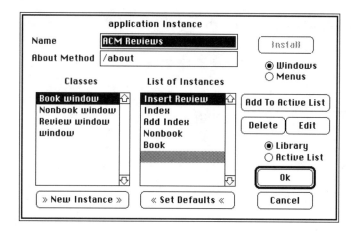

Figure 3.10

and integrating code in a textual language with a graphical UIMS, is typical of most other UIMS's. For example, Smalltalk-80 [Goldberg and Robinson 1983], is a textual language, edited and executed on a graphics workstation. The Interface Builder of the NeXT Computer [Thompson 1989], is a graphical system for generating Objective-C code which manages the graphical interface of an application written in Objective-C. HyperCard is a tool for developing certain types of applications with pictorial interfaces, programmed with the textual language HyperTalk [Goodman 1987]. In each case, the programmer works with two types of environment; one for the task of writing and editing programs in a textual language, and the other for constructing and testing the user interface. Prograph's *application builder* is a seamless UIMS. Using graphical editors, the programmer constructs menu, window, and window item objects which form the graphical interface of an application written in a visual, object-oriented programming language. In this section we discuss the editing of the graphical interface components of an application and the behavior of a running application.

Prograph's system classes define the objects for building an interface based on menus, windows, and events. A system class has *system attributes* which include static properties of instances and properties for the run-time, event-driven behavior of class instances. For example, static attributes of a **Window** instance include the name of the window and the list of **window item** instances for the window. Run-time attributes include the names of methods to call when, at run-time, particular events occur. For example, system attribute **key method** of a **Window** instance is the the name of a method to call if a keyboard event occurs while the window is the front window of the running application.

The application builder has editors for the different system classes. Figure 3.10 illustrates the *application editor*, with which the programmer can, among other things, name the application, add windows and menus to the application, and specify a method to call when the user selects the "About..." menu command while the running application is running.

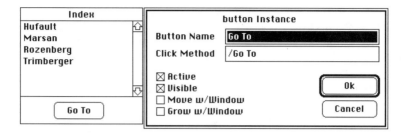

Figure 3.11

Each application window can be edited via the *window editor* with which the user specifies a window's size, type, and run-time behavior. The user can add items such as buttons, lists and text to a window and determine the static and run-time behavior of these items. Figure 3.11 illustrates the edit window for a window titled "Index" and the dialog that opens when the programmer double-clicks the "Go To" button. Here, the programmer has specified that a method **Go To** is to be called when, at run-time, the user clicks the "Go To" button.

The *menu editor* for a menu is a dialog which depicts the menu as it will appear when the user pulls it down. The programmer can add and delete menu items, specify their appearance, and give the names of a methods to call at run-time when the user selects menu items.

The user starts execution of the application by an appropriate menu command. The interpreter then switches context, displays the application's active menus and windows, and enters an event-handling loop for the application. The interpreter receives and processes all events generated by the operating system. While the application is running, the user can give menu commands to suspend execution and then access program components through the editors.

A graphical UIMS is an excellent prototyping tool. In the case of Prograph, the application builder is more than a prototyper. The application builder provides instant access to the user interface of a program during all phases of application development, design, implementation, testing and maintenance, and is therefore an integral part of software development in Prograph. This style of interactive execution and editing is discussed in [Ingalls et al. 1988].

3.5 CONCLUSIONS AND FUTURE DEVELOPMENTS

In the above we have explored the use of pictoriality in developing an integrated programming environment not influenced by traditional programming language design. It is important, however, to identify appropriate roles for text in the programming environment, since pictures clearly have drawbacks in certain situations. A prime example of the superiority of text is in expressing well-known and compact concepts which are inherently textual, such as algebraic formulae. Text is also useful for naming program elements which are pictorial, to distinguish individuals of the same kind: for example in Prograph, textual names are used to identify methods of the same class. Finally, comments obviously require text, since the information they convey is informal and explanatory. However, when the formal structure of the programming language is pictorial, comments do not become confused with the logical elements as in textual programming languages. In general, pictures provide a better representation of most complex structures, such as algorithms, since they correspond more closely with the mental model of these structures. Expressing such things in text introduces an unnecessary layer of abstraction which must be removed by parsing the text to mentally construct a picture.

The Prograph language can be extended to include some useful mechanisms which are not well expressed in text. Multiple inheritance, in which classes can inherit methods and attributes from more than one parent can clearly be added by allowing the graph that specifies the class hierarchy to be a directed acyclic graph rather than a tree. A well-known problem of multiple inheritance arises when a class has several parents to which distinct methods of the same name apply. Pictorial devices can be used in resolving such conflicts. First, classes with conflicts can be visually distinguished from those without. Second, a window can be opened on to a class with a conflict, displaying a grid with one row for each ambiguous method name, and one column for each parent class. The user can then resolve the conflict for each of the listed methods by selecting the appropriate square in the grid. In contrast, in textual languages, conflicts are resolved either by some defaults, which are not necessarily appropriate in every application, or by complex textual specifications.

In section 3.2 we discussed the use of pictures for representing data in whatever form is appropriate to the application. Prograph currently supports such representations for system classes, for example, representing an instance of class **Window** as a window. Future extensions [Cox and Pietrzykowski 1989] will allow any representation for instances of classes to be programmed by the user.

Another planned extension [Cox and Pietrzykowski 1989] is to allow methods to be attached directly to instances rather than just to classes. This will reduce the necessity for creating many special classes simply to capture slight differences in behaviour.

REFERENCES

[Aczel and Daroczy 1975] J. Aczel and B. Daroczy, *On Measures of Information and their Characterizations*, Academic Press, 1975.

[Backus 1978] J. Backus, "Can programming be liberated from the von Neumann style?" *Communications of ACM*, Vol 21, 1978, pp. 613–641.

[Cheng 1988] H-D. Cheng, private communication, 1988.

[Chua et al. 1988] T.S. Chua, K.P. Tan, and P.T. Lee, *EXT-DFD: A Visual Language for Extended DFD*, TRA1/88, Dept. of Information Systems and Computer Science, National University of Singapore, 1988.

[Cox 1986] B. Cox, *Object-oriented Programming, an Evolutionary Approach*, Addison-Wesley, Reading, 1986.

[Cox and Pietrzykowski 1985] P.T. Cox and T. Pietrzykowski, "Solving graph problems using LOGRAPH," in *Proc. of Symposium on the Role of Language in Problem Solving I*, (B. Hamill, D. Weintraub, and R. Jernigan, Eds.), North-Holland, 1985, pp. 221–233.

[Cox and Pietrzykowski 1988a] P.T. Cox and T. Pietrzykowski, "Using a pictorial representation to combine dataflow and object-orientation in a language-independent programming mechanism," in *Proc. Int. Computer Science Conference*, Hong Kong, 1988, pp. 695–704.

[Cox and Pietrzykowski 1988b] P.T. Cox and T. Pietrzykowski, *Prograph: A Visual, Dataflow, Object-Oriented Software Engineering Environment*, Technical report, School of Computer Science, Technical University of Nova Scotia, 1988.

[Cox and Pietrzykowski 1989] P.T. Cox and T. Pietrzykowski, *Prograph: A Pictorial View of Object-Oriented Programming*, Technical report 8902, School of Computer Science, Technical University of Nova Scotia, 1989.

[Dahl et al. 1970] O.J. Dahl, B. Mihrhang, and K. Nygaard, *Simula67 Common Base Language*, Norwegian Computing Centre, S-22, 1970.

[Glinert] E.P. Glinert, "Towards 'Second Generation' Interactive Graphical Programming Environments," in *Proc. IEEE Workshop on Visual Languages*, 1986, pp. 61–70.

[Glinert and Tanimoto 1984] E.P. Glinert and S.L. Tanimoto, "PICT: An interactive graphical programming environment," *IEEE Computer*, 1984, Vol. 17, No. 11, pp. 7–28.

[Goldberg and Robinson 1983] Adele Goldberg and Dave Robinson, *Smalltalk-80: The Language and Its Implementation*, Addison-Welsey, Reading, 1983.

[Goodman 1987] D. Goodman, *The Complete HyperCard Handbook*, Bantam, New York, 1987.

[GPL Manual 1981] *GPL Programming Manual*, Research report, Computer Science Department, University of Utah, 1981.

[Hirakawa et al. 1986] M. Hirakawa, I. Yoshimoto, M. Tanaka, T. Ichakawa, and S. Iwata, "HI-VISUAL iconic programming," in *Proc. IEEE Workshop on Visual Languages*, 1986, pp. 34–43.

[Ingalls et al. 1988] D. Ingalls et al., "Fabrik: a visual programming environment," *Proc. OOPSLA'88*, 1988, pp. 76–190.

[Matsumara and Tayama 1986] K. Matsumara and S. Tayama, "Visual man–machine interface for program design and production," in *Proc. IEEE Workshop on Visual Languages*, 1986, pp. 71–80.

[Matwin and Pietrzykowski 1985] S. Matwin and T. Pietrzykowski, "PROGRAPH: A preliminary report," *Comput. Lang.*, 1985, Vol. 10, No. 2, pp. 91–126.

[Myers 1988] Brad A. Myers, *Creating User Interfaces by Demonstration*, Academic Press, Boston, 1988.

[Pong 1986] M-C. Pong, "A graphical language for concurrent programming," in *Proc. IEEE Workshop on Visual Languages*, 1986, pp. 26–33.

[Smith 1987] D.N. Smith, *InterCONS: Interface CONstruction Set*, RC18108 (#58439), IBM T.J. Watson Res. Centre, 1987.

[Thompson 1989] T. Thompson, "The next step," *Byte*, March 1989, pp. 265–269.

[Vose and Williams 1986] G.M. Vose and G. Williams, "LabVIEW: Laboratory visual instrument engineering workbench," *Byte*, September 1986, pp. 84–92.

CHAPTER 4 ❏ ❏ ❏ ❏

The Design of a Completely Visual OOP Language

WAYNE CITRIN, MICHAEL DOHERTY, AND
BENJAMIN ZORN

CONTENTS

67

A problem with textual object-oriented languages is that some mechanisms, particularly those concerned with polymorphism and the dynamic dispatch of messages, while making certain constructs easier to write, often make the resulting programs difficult to read and understand. This problem is known as the *yo-yo problem*, because the programmer's search for the sequence of methods invoked in responding to a message involves repeatedly searching up and down in the inheritance hierarchy. In this chapter, the authors describe a completely visual approach that exposes these mechanisms by explicitly representing the dynamic behavior of object-oriented programs. The approach is illustrated through the visual object-oriented programming language VIPR.

4.1 INTRODUCTION

Object-oriented programming requires an understanding of a number of complex concepts, which can be difficult even for experienced programmers of procedural languages such as C and Pascal. In this chapter, we will describe a visual object-oriented language that has many of the object-oriented features of a language like C++, but whose semantics can be explained using simple graphical rules. We intentionally chose to provide semantics similar to C++ for two reasons. First, C++ provides the most important features of the object-oriented paradigm very efficiently, and thus VIPR programs will execute efficiently. Second, many programmers are familiar with the semantics of C++, and thus will have an easier time understanding VIPR. In our representation, aspects of programs normally not visible to programmers of textual languages, such as where the return from a procedure will go, may be made explicit. While our language allows every aspect of program execution to be explicit and visual, we provide for a programming environment to hide as much detail as the user desires.

Object-oriented languages, such as Smalltalk [Goldberg and Robson 1983] and C++ [Stroustrup 1991] facilitate programming by providing powerful features such as inheritance, polymorphism, and dynamic dispatch. Such features can greatly reduce the amount of code needed to solve a specific problem and also facilitate code reuse. However, debugging, and modifying object-oriented programs can be more difficult than doing the same things to procedural programs. Furthermore, learning how to program in an object-oriented paradigm can be very difficult. Features such as polymorphism and dynamic method look-up can reduce the readability of object-oriented programs and require the programmer to understand more complex semantics than procedural programs.

Existing solutions to some of these problems are based on sophisticated programming environments that help reduce and resolve ambiguities that arise. Some of these tools, such as browsers, are based on simple visualizations of some part of the program (e.g., the structure of the class hierarchy). In this chapter, we will argue that a completely visual object-oriented programming language, VIPR (visual imperative programming), has significant advantages over textual object-oriented languages.

The design of VIPR was inspired by Kahn's Pictorial Janus [Kahn and Saraswat 1990]. In VIPR, programs are represented as nested circles and language features such as continuations and dynamic dispatch, which exist implicitly in the textual representation, can be made explicit. Our language can be characterized succinctly as viewing a program flowchart from the point of view of a bead moving along the flow lines. Furthermore, although our language is two dimensional, its visual properties suggest that it is a projection of a three-dimensional representation. In this chapter, we will briefly discuss the basic language features of VIPR, and then specifically describe how VIPR supports object-oriented programming with objects, classes, inheritance, polymorphism, and dynamic dispatch.

VIPR provides the following advantages over existing visual and textual programming languages. First, the semantics of programs written in the language may be understood in terms of a small number of graphical rewrite rules, enhancing learnability and understandability. In particular, programmers do not have to be familiar with or understand textual programming languages to write programs in VIPR. Second, because VIPR is completely visual, all aspects of the static and dynamic execution of programs in VIPR are understandable with the same visual metaphor. Thus, our framework integrates existing environment frameworks for visual debugging, browsing, and visual execution environments. Third, our language makes explicit aspects of program execution that are normally hidden from programmers. For example, the semantics of program continuations, dynamic dispatch, and class inheritance are all explicitly represented in VIPR. While making these features explicit may increase a programmer's ability to understand how they work, for an experienced programmer such information is unnecessary. Thus, we will also describe how an environment for VIPR can be constructed that eliminates unwanted details in displaying the program. VIPR has significant advantages for large-scale programming because its semantics are based on topological information, and as such, programming environments have freedom to translate and scale parts of programs as desired to expose or hide details as necessary.

VIPR supports object-oriented programming in the following ways. VIPR defines objects and classes by aggregating definitions of data and procedures visually. Class interfaces are defined by "hiding" all the private methods and data from clients using the classes. Only when method code defined inside a class is executed are the private parts of a class exposed. Inheritance is implemented by defining subclasses spatially inside the superclass. Polymorphism is provided by allowing the kind of object a variable denotes to change dynamically. Thus, during the visual execution of a program, the current type of a variable changes based on the object to which it points. Dynamic dispatch is encoded visually, that is, a dynamically dispatched method contains branches to all the appropriate implementations of the method, and the correct branch is selected dynamically based on the type of the object being called. We will present sample VIPR programs illustrating all of these concepts.

We have considered several two-dimensional program representations that can be obtained by viewing a flowchart in three dimensions and projecting it back onto two dimensions. Changing the projection used and the point of view of the viewer can give such a program representation interesting visual properties. We feel that the representation we have chosen has certain advantages over other choices. In particular, only a small number of simple principles are required to understand VIPR programs and we have been able to formally define them. Nevertheless, we feel that further research in this area is called for and that our research investigates only one of several possible interesting representation choices.

This chapter has the following sections. Section 4.2 discusses why a completely visual object-oriented programming language is useful. Section 4.3 describes related work and Section 4.4 presents a overview of the basic features of VIPR. Section 4.5 describes specifically how VIPR supports the features required for object-oriented programming and Section 4.6 summarizes our thoughts.

4.2 MOTIVATION

In this section, we will discuss some of the problems encountered in using object-oriented languages and then describe why a completely visual object-oriented language appropriately addresses these problems.

4.2.1 Problems with the Object-Oriented Paradigm

Object-oriented programming provides significant advantages over procedural programming, including software reuse, increased reliability, and reduction in code size. On the other hand, writing, debugging, and modifying object-oriented programs can be more difficult than doing the same things to procedural programs for a number of reasons. Furthermore, learning the semantics of object-oriented languages presents challenges to procedural programmers. Here, we will outline some of the problems programmers encounter.

Object-oriented programming provides polymorphic variables. In particular, a variable denoting a superclass can at a later time be used to denote an object of any subclass. As such, when a method associated with that variable is called, the specific method will depend on the current object denoted, which will change dynamically. Thus, programmers looking at the static program text cannot know what specific methods will be called at runtime. This situation may require care in programming because all possible runtime behaviors need to be considered to ensure that a program will execute correctly. This problem has led some researchers to wonder aloud whether using polymorphism is the modern equivalent of programming with **goto**s [Ponder and Bush 1992].

Object-oriented programming requires the programmer to understand a complex execution model of method invocation. Unlike simple call/return semantics, method invocation semantics may involve dynamic method look-up, which is a concept generally unfamiliar to procedural programmers. The specific method that will be invoked when a message is sent depends on one's understanding both of the execution model and the structure of the class hierarchy. Our experience teaching these concepts leads us to believe that many programmers have difficulty understanding them. We are aware of companies that are now expending considerable effort to retrain procedural programmers (e.g., of COBOL) to write object-oriented programs in C++.

Object-oriented programming requires the programmer to factor the problem being solved in ways that are different from procedural programming. Specifically, programmers need to determine what classes are needed, how these classes relate to existing classes, and what data and operations these classes support. While object-oriented design methods exist, there is still relatively limited experience with them as compared to more traditional methods.

Object-oriented programming often involves the creation of highly interconnected heap data structures. Programmers encounter problems operating on (e.g., traversing, inserting into, etc.) these structures and also have difficulty correctly deallocating objects that are not longer in use. While this problem is not unique to object-oriented programming, such programs will probably benefit more from language support for visual debugging of heap structures..

4.2.2 Weaknesses of Existing Solutions

Historically, sophisticated programming environments have been employed to reduce the difficulty of writing, understanding, and modifying object-oriented programs. Such environments may include class browsers to see the high-level organization of the class hierarchy, data structure visualization support, and domain-specific execution visualizations. In this way, all aspects of a program, including the static text, the data structures, and the dynamic control flow, can be visualized to a limited extent. We address each of these tools in turn and discuss their individual weaknesses.

Class browsers   These tools provide a static view of a program's class hierarchy [e.g., Haarslev and Moeller 1990]. Browsers are not intended to be used to understand the dynamic behavior of a program, and the browsing metaphor does not extend to understanding other aspects of the static program structure. Thus, a programmer requires additional environment support beyond browsers to understand, modify, and debug object-oriented programs.

Data structure visualizers   These tools range widely in their complexity and include extensions to debuggers to display lists or trees [e.g., Myers 1983, Myers 1988]. As an example of a text-based data structure visualizer, almost every Lisp environment provides automatic code and data pretty-printing support. Common Lisp has such support built into its definition [Steele 1990].

The problem with this approach is that one can view only program data with such tools and not the program itself (except, to a limited extent, in Lisp, where the program and data have the same form). Also, since the tools are often wedded closely with the debugger, they tend to be ad hoc extensions of a mostly textual debugging paradigm.

Domain-specific execution visualizations   These tools include toolkits for building domain-specific visualizations of the execution of programs, including object-oriented programs. With such toolkits, programmers can visualize state-transition diagrams, oscilloscopes, logic circuits, or any of a number of simulation applications [e.g., Morley et al. 1991]. These toolkits are ad hoc because they do not provide a general framework for understanding the behavior of programs, but instead allow applications in particular domains to be visualized.

A weakness of all of these approaches is that they usually stand alone and are not designed to be coordinated with each other. What is missing is a standard visual framework for understanding the program, its data, and its dynamic execution through a single integrated tool. We seek to unify static and dynamic aspects of a program and its data with a visual metaphor, just as the form of the program and the data are unified in Lisp with a textual metaphor.

While environment support is very useful and necessary, we feel that a more appropriate approach to increasing the comprehensibility of object-oriented languages is to program and execute the languages using a completely visual metaphor. This approach allows all the tools described above to work together in a unified framework, which has distinct advantages. First, the programmer avoids having to translate back and forth between the different representations used to present the static and dynamic forms. Second, the programmer avoids the need to learn a number of different ad hoc program representations. Finally, the semantics of a completely visual language are described entirely by a small number of graphical rewrite rules, and as such are relatively easy to learn.

4.3 RELATED WORK

In this section we will describe other work in completely visual programming languages and in visual object-oriented programming languages.

4.3.1 Completely Visual Languages

Although much visual language work has concentrated on visual models of basically textual languages, in which the semantics of the visual language derive from the semantics of the underlying textual language (and not from the graphical properties of the visual representation), a few visual languages have been designed whose semantics derive entirely or predominantly from graphical rules. The most significant such language is Pictorial Janus [Kahn and Saraswat 1990], which was originally designed to model the execution of the constraint logic programming language Janus, but whose execution semantics may be derived from graphical rules applied to the visual representation. Kahn described such languages as "completely visual."

Pictorial Janus is unique in that a snapshot of the dynamically executing program contains a complete copy of the static program being executed. Kahn's definition of completely visual languages included this requirement, but if we relax the definition to allow languages where the state and the program are separate, another class of languages may be considered completely visual: the graphical transformation languages. In these languages, a program consists of a set of before/after pairs of diagrams. State consists of a set of graphical entities and their relationships. If the *before* part of a before/after pair matches part of the state, the state is transformed to conform to the *after* part of the pair. BITPICT [Furnas

1981] is one of the simplest of such languages, in that its before/after pairs are simple pixel patterns. ChemTrains [Bell and Lewis 1993] and Vampire [McIntyre and Glinert 1992] allow more complex visual entities and relations, and also permit variables in the transformation rules.

Completely visual languages of both types have the advantage that the user does not need to understand two different (albeit related) sets of semantics, the semantics of the visual model and that of the underlying textual model, but can understand and write programs with knowledge of only the visual semantics.

4.3.2 Visual Object-Oriented Languages

A number of visual object-oriented environments have been proposed, although none of them have been completely visual. In fact, most of them simply visualize objects, but set aside the problem of how methods should be visualized.

Rogers proposed an object-oriented visual language in which classes and methods are defined in terms of relations between objects [Rogers 1988]. This language employs visual representations of methods, but the relational approach taken in this system does not appear to be applicable to the visual modeling of an imperative language.

More commonly, visual object-oriented environments use visual representations to define the relationships between classes, and to create new classes by assembling prototypes of previously defined classes. ObjectWorld and Rehearsal World are typical systems of this type. Penz's ObjectWorld models an imperative object-oriented language [Penz 1991], however, only the objects are represented visually. The methods by which they interact with each other are defined in Smalltalk. These methods are displayed in pop-up windows, which may be hidden while the program executes. Finzer and Gould's Rehearsal World is a similar Smalltalk-based visual environment in which the objects, but not the methods, are visualized [Finzer and Gould 1984]. In Rehearsal World, however, methods may be defined by demonstration as well as textually, but the representations of methods maintained by the system are textual Smalltalk.

Demonstrational systems are a natural application for visual object-orientation. Borning's ThingLab is probably the most famous such system [Borning 1981]. ThingLab employs a constraint model rather than an imperative model, however, and while the constraints may be represented graphically [Borning 1986], the methods for resolving the constraints are displayed textually.

A number of other visual languages provide object-oriented features. Prograph [Cox et al. 1989, Cox and Pietrzykowski 1988], for example, provides a class system where the hierarchy is presented graphically. Inheritance, instance variables, dynamic dispatch, and polymorphism are all provided in Prograph, although dynamic dispatch and polymorphism are not shown graphically. Forms/3 [Burnett 1991, Burnett 1993], although not explicitly an object-oriented language, offers data abstraction and polymorphism. Class inheritance is not provided.

4.4   AN INTRODUCTION TO VIPR

VIPR is a programming language and not a program representation. This distinction is important to understand, as graphical representations of textual languages are sometimes supported in CASE tools. The distinction between existing graphical representations and VIPR is that VIPR is intended to be an executable specification. That is, programs written in VIPR are intended to be executed, and we have defined graphical rewrite rules that define the semantics of that execution [Citrin et al. 1993b]. Unlike VIPR, program representations are not executable and are simply intended to make some aspect of a textual language more understandable.

One reason that VIPR may be confused with program representation methods is because we intentionally have defined VIPR to have semantics similar to familiar textual languages, such as C++. As such, we will describe the semantics of VIPR constructs by defining them in terms of their C++ equivalent. This use of C++ is solely for purposes of readability; as we have mentioned, one of the most significant features of VIPR is that its semantics may be defined exclusively in terms of graphical transformation rules, with no reference at all to any textual language.

4.4.1   Control Constructs

Although the control constructs of VIPR are interesting in themselves [Citrin et al. 1993a], a detailed discussion is outside the scope of this chapter and we will provide only sufficient information to appreciate the unusual aspects of a completely visual programming language and to understand the subsequent discussion of objects and how they are handled in the language.

The design of VIPR is closely related to Kahn's Pictorial Janus. While Pictorial Janus visually models constraint logic programming, and therefore makes allowances for nondeterminism, VIPR is intended to model conventional imperative constructs (with the addition of objects and class inheritance). It is modeled after C++, and is statically scoped and typed.

To force sequentiality and determinism in our model, we have modified the Pictorial Janus model to require the participation of a *state* object in every graphical transformation (each of which corresponds to a computation step), and we then provide a single state object to participate in the first step.

A program in VIPR is represented as a set of nested rings (see Figure 4.1). A computation step is represented by the combination (merging) of two such nested rings, which may combine only when a state object is present and attached to the outermost of the merging rings. A ring contains an optional textual condition, which may reference a state, and which must be true for the ring to participate in a merging. (If no condition is present, the default condition is true.) If there are two or more rings nested inside a ring with an attached state object, the conditions of all these rings are evaluated, and one of the true rings will be evaluated. (If more than one ring has a true condition, the result is undefined.) Figure 4.2 illustrates what an if-statement looks like in VIPR.

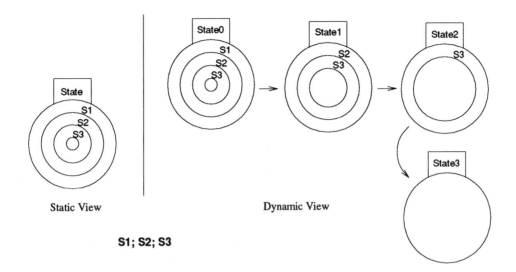

Figure 4.1   Static and dynamic VIPR representations of sequential statements S1, S2, and S3

The result of merging two rings is to execute the action, generally defined textually, associated with the innermost of the two rings being merged. These actions are usually assignments or I/O statements. We can therefore view execution as a

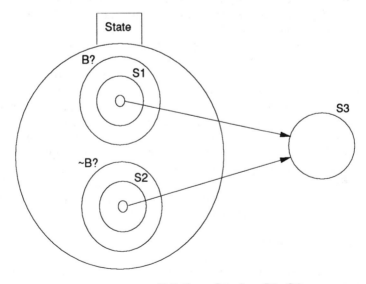

Figure 4.2   Static VIPR representation of an if statement

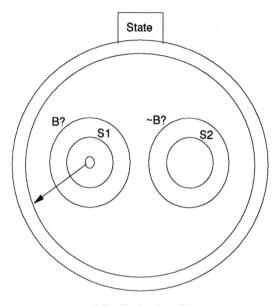

while B do S1; S2

Figure 4.3   Static VIPR representation of a while statement

series of rings merging outward from the center and progressively altering the program state by combining with the outermost ring. Alternatively, we can visualize the nested rings as a pipe receding into the distance, and execution as traveling down the pipe, choosing branches based on conditions written on the inside of the pipe at branch points, and carrying the state with us so that we can modify it based on actions written on the inside of the pipe as we pass.

Some simple examples provided in Figures 4.1–3 illustrate the flavor of control constructs in VIPR. For each construct, we present the equivalent textual language construct, although the semantics of VIPR constructs can be understood without any reference to, or even knowledge of, textual languages. The boldface text present at the bottom of the figures is not present in VIPR programs—we present it only to clarify which construct is being illustrated. Figure 4.1 illustrates sequential constructs, Figure 4.2 illustrates conditionals, and Figure 4.3 illustrates iteration. In Figures 4.2 and 4.3, note the arrows connecting one ring to another. These arrows represent substitution and indicate that the construct at the destination end of the arrow may replace the ring at the source end.

4.4.2 Procedures and Functions

Procedures and functions are sets of nested rings outside the main procedure's rings (Figure 4.4), and therefore outside of the normal linear course of execution.

A procedure call is represented by a ring possessing an arrow pointing to the procedure being called. Since the arrow represents substitution, a copy of the

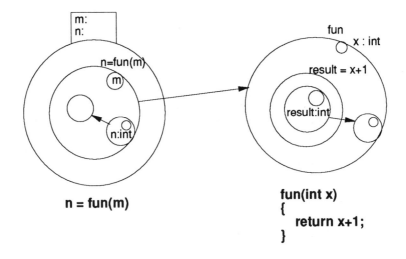

Figure 4.4   Static VIPR representation of a function definition and call

procedure may then be substituted for the procedure. Nodes attached to the procedure call represent arguments, and corresponding nodes attached to the outermost ring of the procedure represent parameters. Each procedure must have at
least one parameter, representing the continuation, or return address. A procedure call must have a corresponding argument containing an arrow pointing to
the statement to be executed after the procedure call returns. A procedure return
statement is a ring with an arrow pointing to the continuation parameter. It indicates that return may be performed by substituting the continuation value for the
return statement ring.

Procedure calls can be viewed as graphical substitution. An arrow represents
the substitution of a copy of the thing pointed to for the thing from which the
arrow originates. Alternatively, procedures may be visualized as pipe segments
which are spliced into the mainline pipe in place of the procedure call segments.

Parameter passing and function return values are also handled graphically. A
return continuation is simply a specialized form of parameter, and generalized
parameters may also be represented as small circles within the rings representing
procedures and procedure calls. Parameters are matched either positionally, with
respect to their position in terms of the return continuation which is always
present, or by name, when optional parameter names can be provided. At call
time, when a copy of the procedure body is substituted for the call, the argument
rings and the parameter rings merge, and whatever values corresponded to the
arguments now correspond to the parameters. All arguments are passed by value,
although pointers (represented by arrows) may be explicitly passed to simulate a
call by reference.

Return values are passed back through the return continuation. The statement
following the procedure call (that is, inside the call ring) possesses a small ring
representing the return value. Correspondingly, there are small rings associated

with the function's return continuation parameter and the ring representing the return statement. All of these larger rings are linked by arrow chains representing substitution (that is, the return continuation parameter gets substituted for the return statement, and the statement to be executed after the call gets substituted for the return continuation parameter), and in the course of these substitutions the return value gets passed back to the caller as the corresponding small rings are merged. Note also in the example that the argument (x) and the return value (result) are both typed as integers. Such type annotations are included to provide more static information about the behavior of functions and procedures. The fact that VIPR is statically typed is a preference of the designers—we feel that static type indications will generally lead to more robust programs.

4.5 OBJECT-ORIENTED PROGRAMMING IN VIPR

In this section, we will describe how VIPR supports all the mechanisms commonly found in object-oriented languages. We will illustrate these ideas with complete, simple examples (i.e., point and shape classes) that are commonly used to describe object-oriented features. At the end of the section, we will discuss what we expect a programming environment for VIPR to include and we will indicate why we believe that VIPR will scale to solving larger, more complex problems.

4.5.1 Objects and Classes

Many object-oriented languages provide classes, which are a means of describing a collection of objects with common characteristics, and objects, which represent instances of the classes. Objects usually contain data and operations that manipulate that data (*instance variables* and *methods* are the terms commonly used). Furthermore, classes also provide a means of encapsulation and information hiding (e.g., private instance variables and methods in C++ classes). VIPR describes classes by aggregating data and methods physically and enclosing them. In this section, by example, we will illustrate how VIPR supports all of these features.

First consider the C++ definition of a very simple point class, presented in Figure 4.5. This example illustrates many of the issues related to objects and classes as outlined above. Figure 4.6 shows the same class defined in VIPR. As the figure shows, the VIPR definition groups methods and instance variables by enclosing them with a dotted line. In essence, a VIPR class is a grouping of individual methods, each of which looks like a strand of fiber being viewed head-on. Thus, VIPR's classes look like fiber bundles with some data associated with them. Note that in VIPR, as opposed to C++, all objects are heap-allocated and thus all variables denote references to objects.

VIPR also supports information hiding and the separation of the class interface from its implementation. In VIPR, instance variables or methods that are private

```
class point {
    int x, y;
public:
    void moveTo(int newx, int newy)
       { x = newx; y = newy; }

    int xDistance(point* p)
       {
          // Statement 3
          return p->x - x;
       }
};
```

Figure 4.5   C++ point class

to a class are indicated by enclosing them with double boxes or circles (e.g., the variables x and y in the point class are private).

To see how these private values and implementation details are hidden from the users of a class, we must see how objects and classes in VIPR are declared, created, and used. Consider the C++ code fragment in Figure 4.7, which allocates two point objects, moves them, and computes the distance between their x-coordinates. The following figures show the visual execution of the VIPR version of this program. In particular, they show the state of the program at statements 1, 2, 3, and 4 as indicated by the C++ comments in the text. Note that statement 3 is inside the **xDistance** method in Figure 4.5.

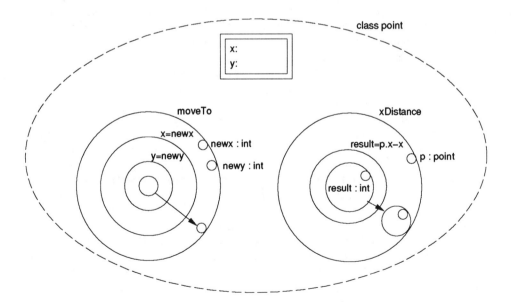

Figure 4.6   VIPR point class

```
main()
{
    point *p1, *p2;
    int d;
                            // Statement 1
    p1 = new point;
    p2 = new point;
    p1->moveTo(3,4);
    p2->moveTo(0,0);
                            // Statement 2
    d = p1->xDistance(p2);
                            // Statement 3
}
```

Figure 4.7   C++ program using the point class

Figure 4.8 shows the VIPR program before execution has begun (i.e., at state-ment 1). The variables **p1** and **p2**, declared to be of type point, have not been given values yet. As such, they currently denote pointers to small instances of the VIPR point class that are shaded, indicating that the instances are not actual objects (we call such instances pseudo-instances). Also note that only the public parts of the point class definition are visible to users of the class. Only when methods of the class are entered are the private portions of the class definition made visible. The figure also indicates what the statements in the main program look like in VIPR. Because the program is entirely sequential, the main program is denoted by a set of nested rings, as mentioned. Each ring has an associated action, such as assignment (e.g., **p1 = new point**) or a method call (e.g., **p1.moveTo(3, 4)**). In the figure, we see the arguments to the methods being passed by matching argument indicators, and we also see a return value being returned from the **xDistance** method. Later figures illustrate how this program looks when it is being executed.

Figures 4.9, 4.10, and 4.11 show the VIPR program just before the call to **p1.xDistance**, just inside the **xDistance** method, and just after the return from the **xDistance** method, respectively.

Figure 4.9 shows the VIPR program after the variables **p1** and **p2** have been given values (i.e., at statement 2). Now the pseudo-instances of the point class have been replaced by actual instances. The two calls to **moveTo** have also been executed, and so the instances have been given specific values for **x** and **y** (although the values are not currently visible). In Figure 4.9, we now see the call to **xDistance** being set up, with the object **p2** as the parameter to the method. The call also clearly shows that the method returns a value (indicated by the parameter being passed back to the continuation parameter).

In Figure 4.10, we have now entered **p1**'s **xDistance** method, which has been expanded to provide more detail. Because we have entered **xDistance**, the scope has changed. Thus, the private instance variables **x** and **y** are now part of the environment, as well as self, the name of the object whose method is currently exe-cuting, as well as all the parameters to the current method (in this case, the point **p**). Furthermore, the names **p1**, **p2**, and **d**, which are local to the main procedure,

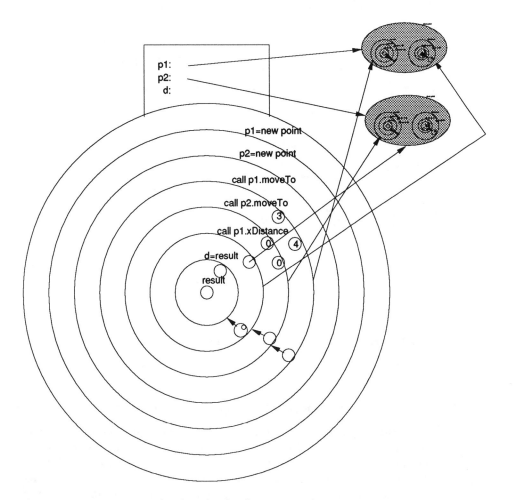

Figure 4.8 VIPR program using the point class (at statement 1)

are no longer available. We also see that the text **p.x** in the method now has specific meaning because the parameter **p** is now bound to a specific point object. Note that result is the name given to the return value of the method, indicated by the small circle attached with the innermost ring, that is matched with the continuation parameter when the method returns.

In Figure 4.11, we see the program after **p1.xDistance** has returned. The return continuation of **xDistance** provides a place and a name for the return value (in this case –3), and the final operation the program performs is to assign that value to the variable **d**. Note that because we have returned to main, the scope has changed back to the original scope.

This example has served to illustrate how VIPR supports objects, classes, and all the semantics related to creating, defining, and manipulating objects.

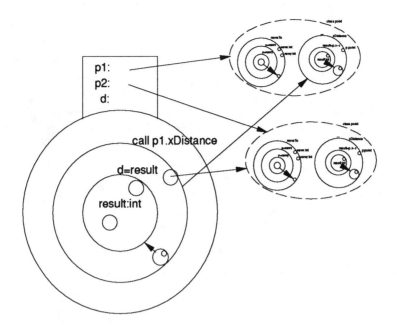

Figure 4.9   VIPR program using the point class (at statement 2)

4.5.2 Inheritance, Polymorphism, and Dynamic Dispatch

To show how VIPR supports inheritance, polymorphism, and dynamic dispatch, we will extend the example provided in the previous section to include these features. Specifically, we will consider subclasses of the point class that implement objects of different shapes. The C++ definition of these subclasses is shown in Figure 4.12. Note that the method **point::area** is defined to be **= 0**, indicating that subclasses of point are required to define this method appropriately. The VIPR definition of these classes is shown in Figure 4.13. Shape is a class with two subclasses, square and circle, each of which have private instance variables. VIPR represents this relationship by including the definition of the shape class inside the point class. Spatial inclusion is used to represent subclass relations because it allows the semantics of inheritance to be spatially suggested. Specifically, the implication that superclasses "include" subclasses spatially suggests the subtype principle.

Using spatial inclusion has some costs. In particular, adding new subclasses requires modifying the superclass (by defining the subclass inside it). Fortunately, VIPR's semantics allow automatic translation and scaling, and so the user would not be responsible for reorganizing the contents of a class when defining a new subclass. We also note that VIPR supports only single inheritance. Thus the spatial inclusion metaphor is appropriate for VIPR. If we had chosen multiple inheritance semantics, using inclusion would be problematic. We leave a visual representation of multiple inheritance semantics in VIPR for future work.

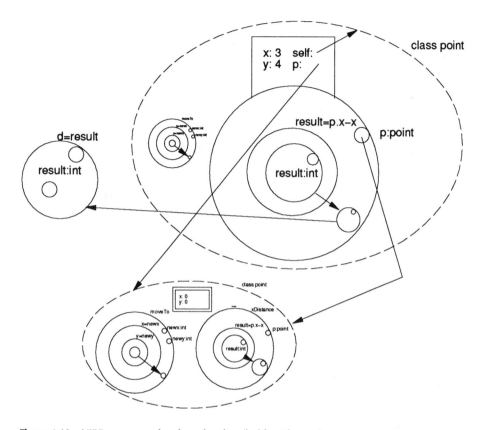

Figure 4.10   VIPR program using the point class (inside xDistance)

The **area** method is a dynamically dispatched method defined in shape that is redefined both in square and circle. Calls to **area** may be calls to either **square::area** or **circle::area**, depending on the type of the object invoking the method. This relationship is indicated by showing the area method with type conditions indicating that either the square or circle method may actually be invoked at runtime. Thus, the behavior of dynamically dispatched methods is explicit and very clear from the visual representation. Note that this representation does not denote or imply a specific implementation (i.e., using vtables as C++ does). Instead, it represents the underlying semantics of dynamic dispatch explicitly.

To understand how a VIPR program uses polymorphism and dynamic dispatch, we include a sample program that sums the areas of objects in a polymorphic array of shapes. Figure 4.14 shows the C++ version of this program, while Figure 4.15 shows the static representation of the VIPR equivalent. The program initializes a loop index **i**, and the elements of the polymorphic **shapes** array. It then loops over the elements of the array, summing the areas of all the shapes in it. The VIPR code illustrates the use of a conditional to test the loop index, and the looping embodied by the arrow jumping out of the loop body. Because the array

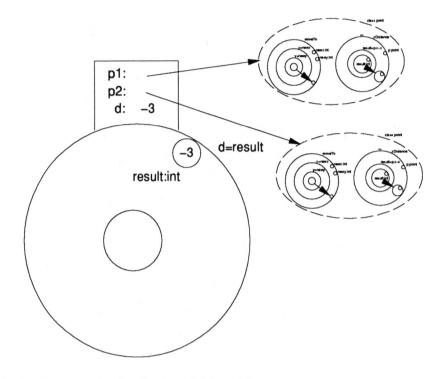

Figure 4.11   VIPR program using the point class (at statement 4)

```
class shape : public point {
public:
      virtual double area() = 0;
};

class square : public shape {
      int side;
public:
      double area() { return side * side ; }
};

class circle : public shape {
      double rad;
public:
      double area() { return 3.14 * rad * rad ; }
};
```

Figure 4.12   C++ shape, square, and circle classes

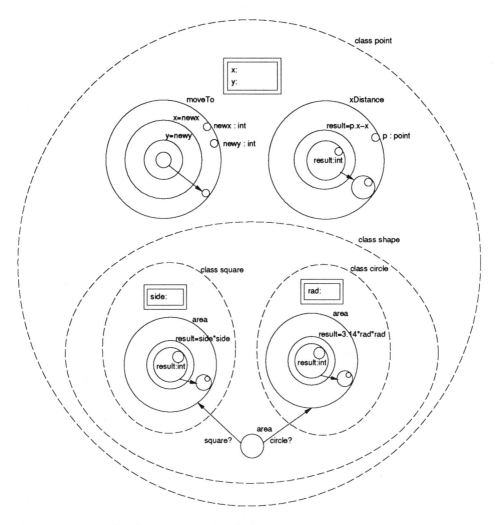

Figure 4.13   VIPR point, shape, square, and circle classes

shapes and variable **s** have not been initialized, we see that they currently indicate a pseudo-instance of the shape class, with all possible subclasses available.

Figures 4.16, 4.17, and 4.18 show the dynamic execution of this program at
statement 1 (indicated in the C++ text), inside the area method of the square
instance, and at statement 1 again (with **i = 1**), respectively. These snapshots illustrate how polymorphic variables can point to objects of different types, and how
dynamically dispatched methods in these objects are actually dispatched.

Note that in Figure 4.16, the array **shapes** has been initialized, and each element points to a different shape subclass. Because the specific subclass of each
array element is now known, we see that the thumbnail diagram of each instance

```
main()
    int i = 0;
    double sum;
    shape *shapes[2], *s;

    shapes[0] = new square;
    shapes[1] = new circle;

    while (i < 2) {
        s = shapes[i];
                        // Statement 1
        sum += s->area();
        i += 1;
    }
    cout << "Total Area = " << sum << "\n";
}
```

Figure 4.14   C++ program using polymorphic objects with dynamic dispach

has been refined to show only the methods and instance variables associated with the particular subclass. Also, we see that dynamically the area method for each array element has been resolved and so dynamic dispatch is no longer necessary. Again, while the underlying implementation may not behave in this way (i.e., it may not resolve the dynamic dispatch by eliminating the indirection), the semantics of assigning a specific object type to the array elements are explicitly shown. Figure 4.16 also shows the variable *s* pointing to the first object in the array. Thus, when the **s->area** method is called in the next statement, the **square::area** method will be invoked. Finally, Figure 4.16 shows that the body of the **while** loop has been replicated in the innermost ring of the loop, indicating another unfolding of the loop has occurred.

In Figure 4.17, we have just entered the **square::area** method. As with the **xDistance** method in the previous example, this figure illustrates the change of environment that occurs when a method is invoked. Similarly, the **square::area** method returns a value via a return continuation.

In Figure 4.18, we are again at statement 1, but now **i** has the value 1. In this case, the variable **s** denotes a circle object and the **circle::area** method is about to be invoked. As in the previous diagram, the next iteration of the loop has been unfolded by applying the arrow substitution rule (i.e., the destination of an arrow can be used to replace the contents of the source ring of the arrow).

4.5.3 Scalability and Environment Support for VIPR

The examples we have used to illustrate the object-oriented features of VIPR are quite small; the visual complexity of these examples must immediately raise some concern about the scalability of programs written in VIPR. To address concerns of scalability, we feel that VIPR will naturally be used in a programming environment specifically designed to support the creation of large VIPR programs. Furthermore, we feel that properties of VIPR's representation allow VIPR programs

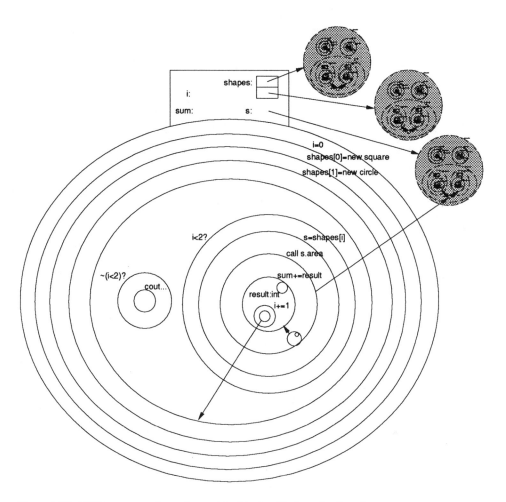

Figure 4.15   VIPR program using polymorphic objects with dynamic dispach

to be easily manipulated by such an environment. Specifically, because VIPR's semantics are based entirely on topological relationships (e.g., containment and connectedness), VIPR programs can be dramatically transformed without modifying their meaning. Specifically, parts of the program can be greatly expanded while other parts are shrunk down. Procedures, functions, and objects can be translated and scaled arbitrarily as long as the connections between them are maintained. The previous examples in this section illustrate such scaling to some extent—the part of the program that is currently executing should be enlarged to make it easier to see. Likewise, instances of objects that are not currently being used remain at thumbnail sketch size until they are needed.

We also anticipate that the environment will smoothly animate transitions between computation steps (i.e., growing and shrinking elements as necessary) in order to make the visualization of execution easier to follow. Investigators have

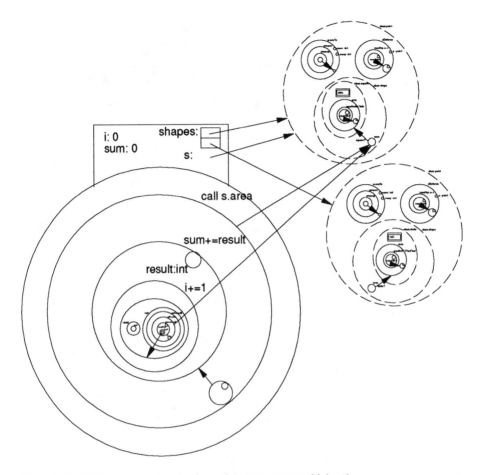

Figure 4.16   VIPR program using the shape class (statement 1 with i = 0)

noted the importance of smooth transitions and animation in dynamic visualizations [Robertson et al. 1991] and Kahn incorporated it into his Pictorial Janus system [Kahn 1992].

Another problematic aspect of the VIPR language is the use of arrows. Arrows represent connections between things, and too many arrows make a program confusing. We anticipate that a support environment will allow connections indicated by arrows to also be indicated using textual names. We do not dislike the use of text in programs, and we believe that text should be included in VIPR programs any place where it simplifies the representation. Note that the use of textual variable names throughout the examples is an instance of such a use of text. Each variable name in fact represents an arrow to the storage associated with that variable. While the VIPR program has meaning without the variable names, it is clearly more readable, at least to an experienced programmer, if variable names

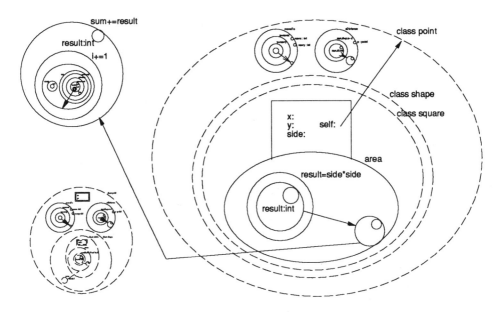

Figure 4.17   VIPR program using the shape class (inside square area method)

are used. Likewise, the semantics of expressions can be specified completely visually in VIPR (because expressions are just a composition of functions), but for the most part expressions such as **a + b** are easier to understand in their textual form.

We also expect that a VIPR environment will leave out certain connections most of the time, unless the programmer explicitly requests them. For example, if there were 10 **area** methods in our example, the lines connecting the dynamically dispatched method to each of the implementation methods could be elided. The connections between function and procedure calls and the function being called could also be elided in the same way.

Another kind of support the environment can provide is related to viewing class hierarchies. For example, suppose a programmer only wants to see the instance variables and methods related to the class **square** in Figure 4.15. In this case, all instance variables and methods related to "non-square" classes could be eliminated from view. In general, we expect the environment to support a number of different views of the program, and that these views will be based on the visual framework provided by VIPR.

Finally, environmental support in VIPR will provide techniques such as graying-out pseudo-instances to provide clues about the status and accessibility of objects and object methods. We will count on the environment to support the separation of program interfaces from implementations by physically hiding information that is unavailable, as we have indicated in the examples. Likewise, while VIPR makes explicit many aspects of programs that are implicit in textual languages (i.e., continuations, environments, etc), we will allow the environment to hide this information from programmers if they choose not to see it. Thus, expert

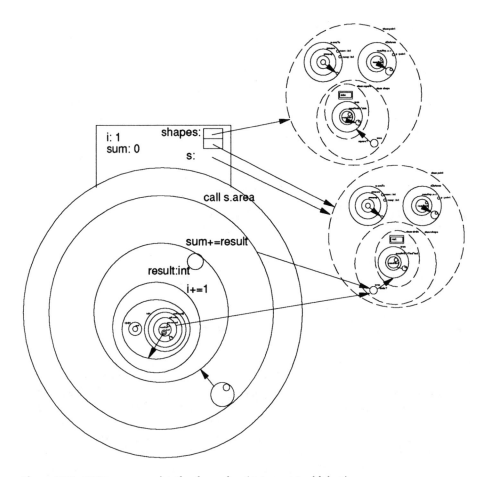

Figure 4.18   VIPR program using the shape class (statement 1 with i =1)

programmers who will not benefit from the explicit representation of this information will not suffer from its presence either.

We believe that all these techniques will improve the scalability of VIPR to practical programming tasks.

4.6 SUMMARY

Object-oriented programming languages provide powerful features such as objects, classes, inheritance, polymorphism, and dynamic dispatch to make solving large, complex programming problems easier. These same features, however, make the languages more difficult to learn, and make programs more difficult to understand, modify, and debug. To address these problems, we have described VIPR, a completely visual object-oriented programming language. Succinctly, the VIPR visual metaphor is that of viewing a program flow-chart from the point-of-view of a bead flowing along the control lines.

VIPR offers the following advantages over textual object-oriented languages. First, the semantics of VIPR programs can be completely understood in terms of easy-to-understand graphical rewrite rules such as merging of adjacent rings and substitution by following arrows. Second, VIPR provides a unifying framework for visualizing static and dynamic program execution upon which a support environment can be designed based on the metaphor provided. Because VIPR semantics are topological, transformations of programs involving scaling and translation will not change the programs' semantics. Third, our language can, but does not have to, make visible aspects of program execution that are normally hidden from the programmer. The explicit representation of concepts such as dynamic dispatch, continuation passing, and environments will allow programmers unfamiliar with these concepts to more easily understand program semantics. Finally, we have discussed how a language environment for VIPR can reduce the visual complexity of VIPR programs and hide information that the programmer does not desire to see.

ACKNOWLEDGEMENTS

We would like to thank the anonymous reviewers for their insightful comments. We would also like to thank Clayton Lewis for his helpful suggestions.

REFERENCES

[Bell and Lewis 1993] B. Bell and C. Lewis, "ChemTrains: A language for creating behaving pictures," in *Proceedings of the 1993 IEEE Symposium on Visual Languages*, Bergen, Norway, 1993, pp. 188–195.

[Borning 1981] A. Borning, "Programming language aspects of ThingLab," *ACM Transactions on Programming Languages and Systems*, 1981, Vol. 3, No. 4, pp. 353–387.

[Borning 1986] A. Borning, "Defining constraints graphically," in *Proceedings of CHI'86—Human Factors in Computing*, ACM Press, New York, 1986, pp. 137–143.

[Burnett 1991] M. Burnett, "Abstraction in the Demand-Driven, Temporal-Assignment, Visual Language Model," PhD thesis, University of Kansas, 1991.

[Burnett 1993] M. Burnett, "Types and type inference in a visual programming language," in *Proc. 1993 IEEE Symposium on Visual Languages*, IEEE Computer Society Press, Bergen, Norway, 1993.

[Citrin et al. 1993a] Wayne Citrin, Michael Doherty, and Benjamin Zorn, "Control constructs in a completely visual imperative programming language," Technical report CU-CS-673-93, Department of Computer Science, University of Colorado, Boulder, September 1993.

[Citrin et al. 1993b] Wayne Citrin, Michael Doherty, and Benjamin Zorn, "Formal semantics of control constructs in a completely visual imperative language," Technical report CU-CS-673-93, Department of Computer Science, University of Colorado, Boulder, September 1993. In preparation.

[Cox et al. 1989] P.T. Cox, F.R. Giles, and T. Pietrzykowski, "Prograph: a step towards liberating programming from textual conditioning," in *Proc. 1989 IEEE Workshop on Visual Languages*, IEEE Computer Society Press, Rome, 1989.

[Cox and Pietrzykowski 1988] P. T. Cox and T. Pietrzykowski, "Using a pictorial representation to combine dataflow and object-orientation in a language independent programming paradigm," in *Proc. Intl. Computer Science Conference*, Hong Kong, 1988.

[Finzer and Gould 1984] W. Finzer and L. Gould, "Programming by rehearsal." *Byte*, June 1984, pp. 187–210.

[Furnas 1981] G. W. Furnas, "New graphical reasoning models for understanding graphical interfaces," in *Proceedings of CHI'91*, ACM Press, pp. 71–78, Anaheim, CA, April 1981.

[Goldberg and Robson 1983] Adele Goldberg and David Robson, "Smalltalk-80: the Language and Its Implementation," series in *Computer Science*, Addison-Wesley, Palo Alto, 1983.

[Haarslev and Moeller 1990] V Haarslev and R. Moeller, "A framework for visualizing object-oriented systems," in *Proceedings of ECOOP/OOPSLA'90*, October 1990, pp. 237–244.

[Kahn 1992] K. M. Kahn, "Towards Visual concurrent constraint programming," Technical report SSL-91-092, Xerox PARC, Palo Alto, 1992.

[Kahn and Saraswat 1990] K. M. Kahn and V. A. Saraswat, "Complete Visualizations of concurrent programs and their executions," in *Proceedings of the 1990 IEEE Workshop on Visual Languages*, Skokie, IL, October 1990, pp. 7–15.

[McIntyre and Glinert 1992] D. W. McIntyre and E. P. Glinert, "Visual tools for creating iconic programming environments," in *Proceedings of the 1992 IEEE Workshop on Visual Languages*, IEEE Computer Society, Seattle, September 1992, pp. 162–168.

[Morley et al. 1991] Ross P. Morley, Pieter S. van der Meulen, and Peter Baltus, "Getting a GRASP on interactive simulation," in *Proceedings of the SCS Multiconference on Object-Oriented Simulation*, Raimund K. Ege, editor, Anaheim, January 1991, pp. 151–157.

[Myers 1983] B. A. Myers, "Incense: A system for displaying data structures," in *Computer Graphics: SIGGRAPH '83 Conference Proceedings*, July 1983, pp. 115–125.

[Myers et al.] B. A. Myers, R. Chandhok, and A. Sareen, "Automatic data visualization for novice pascal programmers," in *Proceedings of the 1988 IEEE Workshop on Visual Languages*, IEEE Computer Society, Pittsburgh, October 1988, pp. 192–198.

[Penz 1991] F. Penz, "Visual programming in the ObjectWorld," *Journal of Visual Languages and Computing*, March 1991, Vol. 2, p. 1741.

[Ponder and Bush 1992] Carl Ponder and Bill Bush, "Polymorphism considered harmful," *SIGPLAN Notices*, June 1992, Vol. 27, No. 6, pp. 76–79.

[Robertson et al. 1991] George G. Robertson, Jock D. Mackinlay, and Stuart K. Card, "Cone trees: Animated 3D Visualizations of hierarchical information," in *Proceedings of the Conference on Human Factors in Computing Systems (CHI'91)*, 1991, pp. 189–194.

[Rogers 1988] G. Rogers, "Visual programming with objects and relations," in *Proceedings of the 1988 IEEE Workshop on Visual Languages*, IEEE Computer Society, Pittsburgh, October 1988, pp. 29–36.

[Steele 1990] Guy L. Steele, Jr, *Common Lisp: The Language*, Digital Press, Burlington, MA, 2nd edition, 1990.

[Stroustrup 1991] Bjarne Stroustrup, *The C++ Programming Language*, Addison-Wesley, Reading, 2nd edition, 1991.

CHAPTER 5 ❏ ❏ ❏ ❏

Interface Issues in Visual Shell Programming

FRANCESMARY MODUGNO

CONTENTS

95

Although the combination of visual representations and direct manipulation are among the main features that make visual object-oriented programming languages attractive, devising the representations and interaction protocols so that they contain enough precision to be suitable for programming is not an easy task, and developing approaches to address this problem is an active area of research. In this chapter, the issues involved in this task are explored in the context of a visual object-based language for shell programming.

5.1 INTRODUCTION

A visual shell is a direct manipulation interface to a file system. Examples include the Macintosh Finder and the Xerox Star. While visual shells have made computers easier to use, they have some well-recognized limitations. There is no easy way to write quick "pipeline" programs directly in the interface, or to access the functionality of complex data manipulating utilities such as the UNIX utilities *awk* and *sed*. In addition, current visual shells are difficult or impossible to program, even for expert programmers. The ability to automate tasks is almost completely lost.

This chapter introduces Pursuit, a visual shell design that combines visual program specification, visual language representation, and object-oriented techniques, to address some of the problems of visual shells, and discusses some of the issues relevant to making Pursuit's approach viable. First, Pursuit extends the concept of a concrete, directly manipulable object to all interface objects, so that the output of any utility can be selected as input (i.e., piped) to other utilities. Second, Pursuit incorporates a Programming by Demonstration (PBD) system into the interface. This enables nonprogrammers to construct programs by manipulating representations of file system objects, such as files and folders, directly in the interface. Finally, Pursuit introduces an object-specific, state-based visual representation language for programs. Programs are static, editable representations of objects and behaviors that reflect the interface.

Although both the extended object model and the PBD specification technique are not original to Pursuit, this work is unique in its attempt to combine and extend these technologies in the visual shell domain. One objective of this chapter is to examine the many technical issues raised by combining these technologies. While some of these issues are addressed in this or other works, several remain unsolved and require deeper investigation. Furthermore, this chapter emphasizes providing power to the *end user*, not the application programmer or system maintainer. Its focus is on the user interface, not on the underlying operating system. Finally, the object-specific, state-based visual programming language is an innovation of Pursuit.

5.2 TODAY'S VISUAL SHELL

The concept of a direct manipulation interface, in which objects on the screen can be manipulated using the mouse and keyboard, was introduced in 1981 on the Xerox Star, and popularized by the Apple Macintosh. The success of direct manipulation interfaces is often attributed to the constantly visible, concrete, familiar representation of data objects. For example, a file is not just a string of text denoting a name. Instead, it is a manipulable object in the interface which resembles the real world analogue that it represents. Unlike textual interfaces, users need not guess whether what they see is a string representing a file name or just a line of text. Instead, objects in the interface can be easily identified by looking at them, just as objects in the real world can be identified by their appearance.

In addition to concrete representation, visual shells give the illusion of concrete manipulation of objects. For example, to move a file, the user drags it to its destination. Unlike textual interfaces, users do not need to remember command names and syntax. Hence, the analogy between an object's appearance and behavior in the physical world, and its representation and corresponding behavior in the interface enables users to transfer some knowledge from their real world experience to their computer task.

However, while visual shells have existed for over ten years, current systems fall short of exploiting the full power of the direct manipulation paradigm. For example, only files and folders on the desktop can be manipulated because only they are viewed as "objects." All other information, such as dates and sizes, is viewed as text that cannot be manipulated in the traditional direct manipulation way.

Similarly, many utilities output only text strings in a dialog box. This text is neither selectable nor manipulable. Thus, users must often do extra processing to complete a task. For example, the Macintosh *Find File* utility (prior to System 7.0) outputs a dialog box containing a list of file names. Our experience has shown that users think of these strings as representing the actual files, not just as a list of strings. Assume that a user wishes to copy those files. To do so, the user must open the appropriate folders, locate the corresponding files and then execute the *duplicate* command. Not only is this extra work, but it can also introduce errors, since the user may miss a file or open the wrong folder.

Finally, visual shells are limited in their programmability. Programming, if it exists at all, is most often achieved by using a standard textual language. Although some systems contain a macro recorder to make a transcript of user actions that can be generalized, users must edit, and therefore understand, a representation of the program in a textual programming language to generalize the transcript. This limits programming to those with the appropriate skills. In addition, these textual languages do not take advantage of the unique visual aspects of the interface. The conceptual simplification gained by the visual interface is lost when programming it. This makes visual shells more complex: users interact with the system visually, but program it in a textual language. Hence, users need to develop two very different bodies of knowledge: one for interacting with the system, and one for programming it.

5.3 RELATED WORK

While commercial visual shells (e.g., NeXT, HP Vue, and Looking Glass) have provided a Macintosh-like desktop for UNIX, more advanced features, such as pipelines, utilities, and shell programming, are not accessible in the visual shell interface. Instead, they are available only through a conventional textual shell window, which requires users to be familiar with UNIX.

Some visual shells contain a macro recorder (e.g., QuicKeys2, MacroMaker and Tempo II for the Macintosh, and HP NewWave) that makes a transcript of user actions which can be replayed later. Although effective in automating simple, repetitive tasks, macro recorders are limited because they record exactly what the user has done—only the object that is pointed to can be a parameter. The transcript consists of a straight-line sequence of commands. Macro recorders cannot automatically generalize, so the program cannot be applied to other objects. SmallStar [Halbert 1984] is a macro recorder that produces an "English-like" transcript of user actions containing icons for objects such as files and folders. The transcript can be generalized via a menu of commands. Users must determine where to add control constructs and how to generalize data.

Some visual shells have invented a special graphical programming language [Henry and Hudson 1988], [Haeberli 1988], and [Borg 1990] to enable users to write programs. Most of these languages are based on the data-flow model, in which icons represent utilities and lines connecting them represent data paths. Most contain no way to depict abstractions or control structures. The types of programs users can write are quite limited. In addition, these languages require users to learn a special programming language whose syntax differs significantly from what they see in the interface, and writing programs differs from the way users ordinarily interact with the system, requiring significant extra learning time.

Dynamic Windows [Mckay et al. 1989], which had its origin in the Genera operating system [Weinreb et al. 1987], is a user interface management system that introduced the idea of an extended object model. Interface objects are associated with underlying semantic objects, which are arranged in an object type lattice. Applications are defined in terms of the methods on the objects in the type lattice. The main difference between this work and Pursuit is that Pursuit's focus is on usability and understandability by the end user, whereas Dynamic Windows and Genera focus on lower level issues from the perspective of application programmers and operating system builders. Furthermore, Pursuit is investigating the use of visual language techniques for programming, whereas Dynamic Windows has explored traditional textual language techniques.

5.4 THE PURSUIT VISUAL SHELL DESIGN

Pursuit is our attempt to address the limitations of visual shells by fully exploiting the direct manipulation paradigm. This is achieved by combining techniques (both old and new) from the visual programming and object-oriented worlds. Visual programming and object-oriented techniques try to present a clear, simple conceptualization of complex behaviors. This is exactly what is needed in the visual shell domain: a way to simply and concisely present the complex working and behaviors of the underlying file system so that the full power of the computer is more accessible to end users.

Pursuit realizes its goal using three techniques. First (Section 5.4.1), we extend the concept of a concrete, directly manipulable object to all interface objects. In Pursuit, all interface objects, and thus all utility outputs, can be directly manipulated. Therefore, users can create straight-line programs (pipelines) by directly manipulating the interface. Second (Section 5.4.2), we incorporate a PBD system into the interface. PBD is a technique for specifying abstract programs concretely. This extends the direct manipulation paradigm to include a consistent method for program specification. Finally (Section 5.4.3), we present an editable, state-based visual language to explicitly represent program code. The visual language is designed to reflect the objects in the interface. This provides a way for users to create abstract programs.

5.4.1 The Pursuit Interface Model

In Pursuit, interface elements are real objects. Any object in the interface, such as a file, folder, login-id, network address, or date, can be manipulated in the traditional direct manipulation way. Utilities are specified by first selecting the input objects, and then either directly manipulating them using drag and drop, or by selecting a menu item. The meaning of an action or menu selection is defined by the methods of the object to which it is applied. For example, selecting a file and choosing the *sort* routine causes the file's contents to be sorted, whereas selecting all the owner objects in a folder and choosing *sort* causes the files in the folder to be reordered based on the lexigraphical ordering of their owner objects' strings.

Because Pursuit elements are treated as actual objects, all utilities output manipulable objects. The objects can be Pursuit basic objects, or they can be new objects composed of other objects or defined by the utility. The output of any utility can be selected and used directly as input to another utility. This allows users to create dynamic programs directly in the interface, in much the same way that UNIX pipelines are constructed.

In programming, the concept of object classes or types can be difficult for noncomputer scientists to understand. This is especially true in the textual domain. For example, a variable's name often provides little indication of its type or class, which is usually defined at its declaration. On the other hand, a visual representation of an object, such as a file, often provides enough information to indicate its type. Most nonobvious objects, such as dates, sizes, and owners, can often be inferred from their visual representations or surrounding contextual information.

Like the real world, a visual shell has the advantage of providing easy recognition of objects just by looking at them. By extending the concept of an object to all interface elements in a visual shell, we extend and take advantage of the concreteness provided by the direct manipulation paradigm.

5.4.2 The Pursuit Specification Language

The second objective of Pursuit is to extend the direct manipulation paradigm to enable programs to be specified by manipulating data objects directly. Specifying a program is a way of defining its functionality. Traditionally, a program is specified in some static programming language. The language may be textual or visual. In this way, a program's functionality is declared completely before it is executed.

Alternatively, a program's functionality can be specified concurrently with its execution. Programming by Demonstration (PBD) [Cypher 1993] is an example of this approach. In a PBD system, users demonstrate the functionality of the desired program on a particular piece of data. From this, the system attempts to create a general procedure [Myers 1991]. This is the specification model contained in Pursuit. Because Pursuit programs are specified by executing real actions on real data, the Pursuit specification language is identical to the interface language. This is particularly appealing in the visual domain because it allows users to specify programs in the same way that they invoke operations—through direct manipulation. Thus, by adding a PBD system into the interface, we have extended the direct manipulation paradigm in a way that enables users to specify a program in a familiar way.

5.4.3 The Pursuit Representation Language

PBD systems have several limitations: They can infer incorrectly. Most contain no static representation of the inferred program. Feedback is often obscure or missing. And few PBD systems provide editing facilities. This makes it difficult for users to know if the system has inferred correctly, to correct any errors, and to revise or change a program. Many of these problems can be overcome by providing users with a good representation of the program to review and edit. Such a representation must be conceptually simple, and must provide a good visualization of data objects and program functionality.

Pursuit addresses the limitations of PBD systems by presenting the evolving program in an editable, state-based *visual* language *while it is being constructed.* The Pursuit visual language [Modugno and Myers 1994] is based on the comic strip metaphor [Kurlander and Feiner 1988]. Familiar icons are used to represent data objects and changes in the data objects represent operations. Two panels are used to represent an operation: The prologue shows the data objects before the operation, and the epilogue shows the data objects after the operation. The operation is implicitly represented by the changes in the explicit representation of the data objects (see Figure 5.1). An operation's representation, therefore, looks very much like the changes the user sees in the real user interface when executing the operation. A program is a sequence of operations concatenated together along with

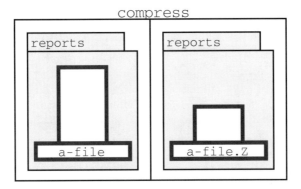

Figure 5.1   The *compress* operation. The file icon represents the file *a-file* located in the *reports* folder. The change in the file icon's height and in its name between the panels imply the *compress* operation. These differences are similar to the change in appearance of the real file icon users see in the actual user interface when the compress operation is executed: The file's icon is replaced with a shorter one and *.Z* is added to its name.

representations of control constructs and variables. Examples of Pursuit programs are shown in Figures 5.2 and 5.3.

Whereas all existing visual (and textual) programming languages explicitly represent program operations and usually require users to imagine the data in their head, the Pursuit visual language is unique in that it depicts the data objects of a program and describes operations in terms of these objects. By emphasizing the data, Pursuit's visual language taps into the object nature of the interface. Rather than thinking about a variable, its value, and how to operate on it, users relate a program object and its behavior (in terms of its visible state changes), to the associated object and its behavior in the interface. In essence, programs are symbolic representations of changes to data objects over time. They become concrete representations of behavior rather than abstract specifications of functions.

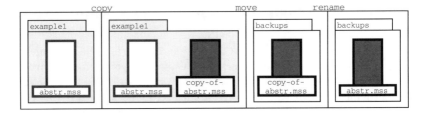

Figure 5.2   A Pursuit program that copies the file *abstr.mss* in the *example1* folder (panels 1 and 2), moves the copy to the *backups* folder (panels 2 and 3), and deletes the *copy-of-* prefix from its name (panels 3 and 4).

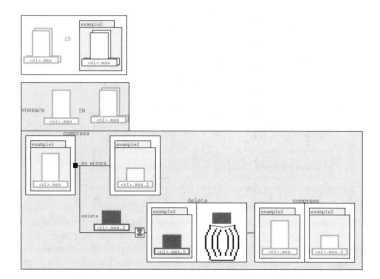

Figure 5.3   **The Pursuit program that compresses each *.mss* file in the *example2* folder. If the compress fails because of the existence of a file with the output file name, the program deletes that old output file, and reexecutes the compress operation. To produce this program, the user must demonstrate its actions on two actual file objects: one in which the compress operation executes successfully, and one in which the output file object already exists in the *example2* folder. This is depicted graphically by the visual branch and predicates after the prologue for the compress operation. The panel in the upper left corner is a declaration. It defines the set of files over which the loop executes to be all the *.mss* files in the *example2* folder.**

It is important to note that the Pursuit visual language is not an object-oriented language. Rather, it is a visual language that focuses on the object nature of the interface, and incorporates some object-oriented techniques within its design (further described below). Hence, it is classified as an object-based language [Wegner 1989].

5.5 BENEFITS OF PURSUIT'S APPROACH

The goal of Pursuit is to provide an interface that enables users to easily access the power of the underlying system. By combining techniques from the visual programming and object-oriented worlds, we hope to achieve an interface that provides this power. We have identified three potential ways that this goal may be reached: visual pipes, utility functionality, and programmability.

5.5.1 Visual Pipes

Programming can loosely be defined as a finite sequence of operations on data

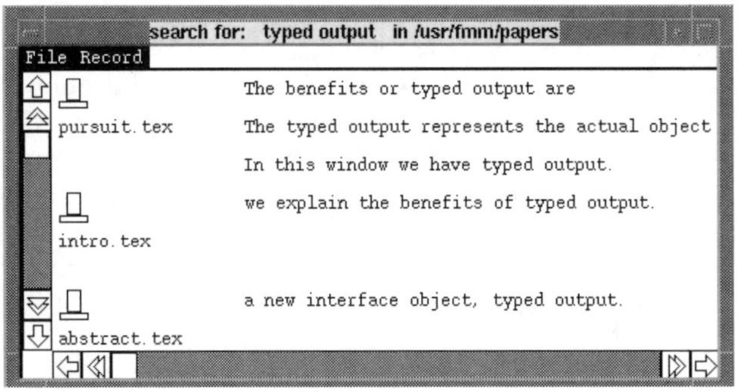

Figure 5.4   The output of the *search* utility, containing both file and string objects. The file objects are references to the files they represent. The strings are the places in those files where the searched-for string was found. Users can perform operations on the referenced files and have the operations affect the actual files. They can also perform operations on the string objects. In particular, double clicking on the string object with value *The benefits of typed output are* opens the *Pursuit.tex* file, scrolled to the position in the file containing that string.

objects. We can therefore consider programming to encompass any series of user-initiated actions regardless of whether an artifact is created to later reexecute. In the UNIX world, for example, writing a command sequence or pipeline can be considered a form of programming. The existence of pipes is one reason for the success of UNIX among expert users [Hanson et al. 1984]. Visual shells contain a similar form of this type of programming; however, it is limited only to file and folder data objects. In addition, it is inhibited by the need for users to continually stop, examine each utility's output, and associate that output with subsequent data objects. Little support exists for the piping mechanism.

Pursuit expands the concept of pipes in the visual shell domain. Because all utilities output objects and not just text, users can select all or part of the output of one utility and use it as input to other utilities directly. This enables them to construct visual pipelines in the interface. This power arises from the Pursuit interface model, which implicitly provides a symmetry of input and output forms for all utilities. Existing visual shells cannot support complete pipelining because they lack this symmetry. Usually, programs take as input iconic representations of objects (such as files), which can be directly manipulated, but often output streams of text (such as dialog boxes), which cannot be directly manipulated. Thus, they cannot use the same mechanism for pipes as for normal command invocation.

Visual pipes are illustrated in the following example. Assume a user wishes to delete from the current directory all files containing the string *typed output*. The user begins by invoking the Pursuit search utility and giving it the string *typed output*. The utility creates a window containing a collection of file and string objects, as shown in Figure 5.4. The files in the window are references to the actual files they represent. To remove the actual files, the user clicks on the icons in the *search* output window, and drags them to the trash—the same sequence of actions the user would use on the actual files to remove them. The user does not need to know any special languages or special flags to utilities. Instead, this power is accessed using a simple sequence of clicking, dragging, and dropping actions.

An equivalent UNIX shell command sequence is *rm 'grep "typed output" * |* *awk -F: '/print 1' | sort -u'*. It is similar in form to a shell script taken from a random sampling of shell scripts written by members of the Carnegie Mellon University School of Computer Science. This particular sequence requires users to know four utility names, two flags, and one special programming language, in addition to the correct way to format the command and how the output of each utility is structured.

5.5.2 Utility Functionality

One problem with most visual shells is that to achieve greater power, more and more utilities are introduced into the system. This requires users to learn new and different commands, arguments, and languages, increasing the complexity of the system.

The Pursuit interface model allows users to express some complex utility functionality in a simple way—by applying interaction techniques to interface objects. Since users are familiar with the objects, the interaction techniques, and the corresponding behaviors, this power is provided without requiring them to learn anything new. In addition, this power is provided directly, rather than by explicitly invoking utilities. For example, in the *search* example of the previous section, the user implicitly accessed the column selection functionality incorporated in the UNIX utility *awk* by interacting with the output file objects directly.

5.5.3 Programmability

In addition to visual pipes, Pursuit handles more traditional programming. By incorporating a PBD system along with an editable, graphical representation in the interface, users can write, edit, save, and reexecute programs with little programming skill. Figures 5.2 and 5.3 are examples of Pursuit programs.

The Pursuit visual language provides many useful features. First, it focuses on representing data objects. Both the class of an object and its observable behaviors are visually depicted. Each class of objects in the interface has a unique representation in the visual language. Users can identify an object's class just by looking at its icon. From an object's icon and the changes reflected in it, users can deduce an object's behavior.

In addition, all visual references to an object are instances of the prototype in the object's declaration. In Figure 5.3 the prototype of the set of files object with name value *<n1>.tex* is declared (in the upper left hand panel) to be the set of all file objects in the *example2* folder whose name object has value *<n1>.tex*. An instance of this set object serves as the loop set object of the *foreach* loop. Similarly, the single file object with name value *<n1>.tex* is defined as the loop iteration object. Instances of this object, along with their associated behaviors (state changes), appear in the panels for the *compress* operations. By editing an object's prototype, such as changing its name or location, all instances of the object become immediately updated.

5.6 ISSUES RAISED BY PURSUIT'S APPROACH

In order to determine the viability of this approach to a visual shell, we implemented a small prototype of Pursuit using the Garnet toolkit [Myers et al. 1990]. The examples discussed throughout this chapter illustrate some of the important technical issues uncovered by the prototype. In this section, we will discuss these issues, and where possible suggest how a real implementation might address them. However, many of these issues require further investigation.

5.6.1 Providing Mechanisms For User Communication

While applications can predefine the meaning of an action on a given object, the user may wish the meaning to be something different, or may actually believe it to be something different. For example, in the search example in Section 5.5.1, the user dragged the file references to the trash and the *original* files were deleted. However, what if the user only wants to delete those references, and leave the original files unchanged? How could the user communicate this to the system? Furthermore, assume that instead the user drags the references to another window. That action could move the original files, create copies of them, or create links to them. All three are reasonable outcomes, yet a utility should do only one. Which one should be the default, and how can the user override this default behavior? These questions can best be answered through user studies. For example, we could present several scenarios to the user. Each scenario would contain a different default behavior for an action on utility output. We could then ask the user which action seems "right." The most common right behavior could be the default. We could then investigate other ways to allow the user to specify different behaviors, such as through the use of modes.

5.6.2 Automatically Coercing Types

Sometimes a user may want to use an object as input to a utility, although the object may not match the utility's input type. For example, the user may wish to input to the mail utility an object other than an e-mail address that is a valid mail address, such as as a file owner object. How can one do this type conversion automatically? The object-oriented solution is to send the object a message requesting its value in the required type. Only objects that respond to the value request message could be valid arguments to the utility, and as new object types are introduced into the system, new methods would have to be added to existing objects so that they could respond to requests for values of the new type.

Another approach, found in Dynamic Windows [Mckay et al. 1989], is to require all coercions to be defined explicitly by the application programmer. That is, each utility must provide a *translator* from any object type to the utility's input type. A limitation of this approach is the growing number of translators needed as new objects and utilities are introduced. It also makes extending the system more complex.

Alternatively, the shell can do this "translation" automatically by requiring each object to have a method that returns its value as a string. When a conversion must be made from one type to another, the shell can get the string value of the first object and then locate in the system the object of the second type having the returned string value. Unfortunately, there is no guarantee that this approach will return an object or that it will return only one object. Nor is it certain if it is general enough to handle all coercions from one type to another.

Another issue that must be explored is how the user will perceive this automatic type coercion. Do users need to be aware of the type conversion or should it be invisible to them? Is the "magic" of automatic type conversion confusing to the nonprogramming user?

Finally, further research must be done to determine how (if at all) type coercion should be represented in the visual language.

5.6.3 Providing An Extensible Application Language

One of the most difficult yet very necessary properties of an interface is extensibility. In addition to allowing for the introduction of new utilities, we must make provisions for the introduction of new object classes and new interaction techniques, both of which must work successfully with the existing system. There are many issues that must be addressed in order for the system to be extensible. For example, suppose a new interaction technique is introduced into the system. There must be a way to define the meaning of this action on existing system objects. Similarly, if a new object is introduced into the system, care must be taken to insure that the meanings of all interaction techniques on this object are defined.

The Pursuit visual language must also be extensible to represent new utilities. To address this problem, we have developed a declarative language for specifying the visual representation of utilities that operate over file and folder objects. An interesting question is how to extend this language to cover polymorphic utilities and utilities that operate over objects other than files or folders.

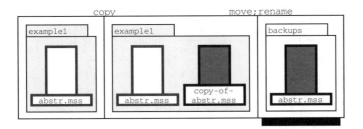

Figure 5.5   A more concise representation of the program in Figure 5.2. The third panel
contains multiple operations, as indicated by its shadow. Clicking on the
shadow reveals the panels for the individual operations, producing the representation in Figure 5.2.

5.6.4 Making the System Scalable

Like all visual languages, Pursuit's representations can grow large rather quickly
(for example, see Figure 5.3). In order to allow users to write more complex programs, some techniques for making programs compact must be employed. One
approach, found in Chimera [Kurlander and Feiner 1988], is to incorporate more
than one operation into a single panel. In Chimera, all operations specify how they
can be visually combined with other operations. Unfortunately, this approach is
limited because it is not easily extensible. Whenever a new application is added to
the system, all other applications must be updated to indicate how they can be
visually combined with the new operation.

Pursuit takes an alternative approach. Rather than having each utility determine when it can be combined with other utilities, all Pursuit utilities must
declare which data objects they affect and how they alter them. Pursuit uses heuristics that combine knowledge of the domain with this declarative knowledge
about operations to make programs more concise. For example, Pursuit determines when it can combine the prologue of an operation with the epilogue of the
previous operation. In Figure 5.2, the second panel serves as both the epilogue for
the *copy* operation and the prologue for the *move* operation. Pursuit also uses
these heuristics to determine when several operations can be represented in a single panel. The shadow beneath the third panel of Figure 5.5 indicates that it contains both the *move* and *rename* operations. By clicking on it, users can see the
individual panels for the two operations, resulting in the program of Figure 5.2.

Another way to address this problem is to allow users to select a set of panels to
collapse into a single panel. The problem here, however, is how to visually represent a user-defined composite panel in a way that is consistent with the visual language. Unlike panels that are collapsed automatically, the user may select a set of
incompatable panels to collapse together. For example, the panels may contain
two operations that change the same property of an object, such as a file name. It
would be difficult to determine which of these changes the composite panel would
reflect. Furthermore, if the set of operations contained within the panels manipulate multiple, unrelated objects, it would be difficult to represent clearly the different operations and the objects they affect.

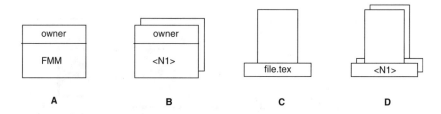

Figure 5.6   Examples of how different objects are represented in the Pursuit visual language: A) A single owner object whose value is *FMM*. B) A set of owner objects whose value is the abstract object *<N1>*. C) A single file object whose name is *file.tex*. D) A set of files whose name object is *<N1>*. Notice that while the visual objects used to represent files closely resembles their representation in the interface, other interface objects do not have as evocative a representation. The "best" representation of such objects remains an open question.

Another space-saving technique that can be incorporated into the visual language is to automatically collapse loops into a single miniature panel that could be expanded to allow users to examine its contents. While this approach is promising, it raises questions about how to handle nested loops and conditionals, as well as questions about program layout.

5.6.5 Representing Conceptually Abstract Objects

Although the Pursuit visual language has an easily identifiable representation of files and folders, no such representation exists for other interface objects. Currently, all other objects are represented as rectangles containing their names and classes (see Figure 5.6). However, these representations bear little resemblance to their interface counterparts. Further research is needed to determine if there is a good graphical representation for objects such as owners, dates, and sizes, in both the interface and the visual language. Furthermore, when choosing representations, care must be taken to maintain the goal of having the visual representation of programs mirror the changes in objects in the interface.

A related question is how to represent user-created objects (e.g., programs). Since users may make programs into icons, which can then be manipulated, these icons can be used in future programs (like subroutines or functions). How can we represent them in the visual language? One way is to have an abstract program object in the visual language. When one program is incorporated into another, the visual representation of the latter program can contain an abstract program object labeled with the former program's name. However, this approach strays from the goal of mirroring the interface object's representation. An alternative is to have users create their own icons for user-defined programs, and use these icons in programs. This is similar to the approach used by Forms/3 [Burnett and Ambler 1994] for allowing users to define the appearance of user-defined types. However, users may find it difficult or even annoying to have to design meaningful icons for every demonstrated program. Alternatively, the system can automatically try to generate an iconic representation using the changes in representations of a program's objects. This can be especially difficult for programs that manipulate a large number of unrelated objects.

5.7 SUMMARY

This chapter has introduced a new approach to a visual shell design. The approach incorporates some techniques of visual specification, visual representation, and object-oriented programming into the interface to provide users with much of the desired but absent power of visual shells.

In graphical domains users often view interface elements as more than just shapes or strings of text. By making all interface elements "real," they become objects that users can manipulate. This extends to users the ability to write programs and to access some common functionality of utilities directly in the interface without requiring that they know any special commands or languages.

The Pursuit PBD system provides a consistent form for the specification and representation of programs in the visual shell domain. This gives users the ability to write abstract programs with minimal programming skills. Because the visual language explicitly represents data and implicitly represents operations as changes to data objects, it reflects the objects and changes users see in the interface when operations are executed.

When manipulating objects in the interface, operations are centered around objects whose structure and behavior reflect the underlying structure and behavior of the system. Similarly, when constructing and viewing a program, computation is centered around objects whose structure and behavior reflect the structure and behavior of the interface. This provides a more uniform model—that of objects and behavior—for users to learn in order to understand, navigate, and program in Pursuit.

While the extended object model and PBD techniques presented here are not original to Pursuit, the way in which they are combined and extended, as well as the visual language, are original. Furthermore, Pursuit's approach has raised several technical issues that lie in both the object-oriented and visual language domains, such as how to provide mechanisms for determining user intent, how to convert objects from one type to another, how to make the system extensible and scalable, and how to integrate the representation of abstract objects into the visual language. While we have discussed some existing approaches to solving these problems and suggested some new ones, many require further investigation.

ACKNOWLEDGEMENTS

The author thanks Brad A. Myers for his continued support of this work. This research is funded by NSF grant IRI-9802089, and by grants from the Hertz Foundation and AAUW.

REFERENCES

[Borg 1990] K. Borg, "IShell: A visual UNIX shell," *Proceedings of CHI '90*, Seattle, Washington, April 1990, pp. 201–207.

[Burnett and Ambler 1994] M. Burnett and A. Ambler, "Interactive visual data abstraction in a declarative visual language," *Journal of Visual Languages and Computing*, Vol. 5, No. 1, March 1994.

[Cypher 1993] A. Cypher, *Watch What I Do: Programming by Demonstration*, The MIT Press, Cambridge, MA, 1993.

[Haeberli 1988] P.E. Haeberli, "ConMan: A visual programming language for interactive graphics," *Computer Graphics*, Vol. 22, No. 4, August 1988, pp. 103–111.

[Halbert 1984] D. Halbert, *Programming by Example*, PhD thesis, Computer Science Division, University of California, Berkeley, CA, 1984.

[Hanson et al. 1984] S. Hanson, R. Kraut, and J. Farber, "Interface design and multivariate analysis of UNIX command use," *ACM Transactions on Office Information Systems*, Vol. 2, No. 1, March 1984, pp. 42–57.

[Henry and Hudson 1988] T. Henry and S. Hudson, "Squish: A graphical shell for UNIX," *Proceedings of Graphics Interface '88*, pp. 43–49.

[Kurlander and Feiner 1988] D. Kurlander and S. Feiner, "Editable graphical histories," *Proceedings of the IEEE Workshop on Visual Languages*, Pittsburgh, PA, October 1988, pp. 127–134.

[Mckay et al. 1989] S. McKay, W. York, and M. McMahon, "A presentation manger based on application semantics," *Proceedings of the ACM SIGGRAPH Symposium on User Interface Software and Technology*, Williamsburg, Va, November 1989, pp. 141–148.

[Modugno and Myers 1994] F. Modugno and B. Myers, "Visual programming in a visual domain," Carnegie Mellon University Technical Report CMU-CS-94-109, January 1994.

[Myers et al. 1990] B. Myers, D. Giuse, R. Dannenberg, B. Vander Zanden, D. Kosbie, E. Pervin, A. Mickish, and P. Marchal, "Garnet: Comprehensive support for graphical, highly-interactive user interfaces," *IEEE Computer*, Vol. 23., No. 11, November 1990, pp. 71–85.

[Myers 1991] B. Myers, "Demonstrational interfaces: A step beyond direct manipulation," *IEEE Computer*, Vol. 25, No. 8, August 1992, pp. 61–73.

[Wegner 1989] P. Wegner, "Learning the language," *Byte Magazine*, Vol. 14, No. 3, March 1989, pp. 245–250.

[Weinreb et al. 1987] D. Weinreb, J. Walker, D. Moon and M. McMahon, "The Symbolics Genera programming environment," *IEEE Software*, Vol. 4, No. 6, November 1987, pp. 36–45.

CHAPTER 6   ❏ ❏ ❏ ❏

User-Interface Construction with Constraints†

JOHN H. MALONEY, ALAN BORNING, AND
BJORN N. FREEMAN-BENSON

CONTENTS

† Reprinted by permission of the publisher. Previously published as "Constraint technology for user-interface construction in ThingLab II," in *Proceedings OOPSLA'89, ACM SIGPLAN Notices*, Vol. 24, No. 10, 1989, pp. 381–388.

ThingLab was one of the earliest object-oriented visual programming languages. Like many of the later visual object-oriented programming languages, ThingLab integrates visual object-oriented technology with a second paradigm. In ThingLab, the second paradigm is constraint programming.

After its initial development by Alan Borning in 1979, ThingLab became an ongoing research project. Eventually a successor to the original system was born, ThingLab II. ThingLab II is a visual object-oriented constraint programming system designed specifically for interactive user interface construction. This chapter explores how constraint technology can be used for this purpose in a responsive visual object-oriented programming language, in a manner that achieves good interactive performance both at run time and during program construction.

6.1 INTRODUCTION

ThingLab II is an object-oriented, interactive constraint programming system implemented in Smalltalk-80. It is, as its name suggests, a direct descendent of ThingLab [Borning 79] but the emphasis is different. The original ThingLab developed and applied constraint programming techniques to interactive physics simulations, whereas ThingLab II applies constraint programming to user-interface construction. In keeping with its purpose, ThingLab II offers good performance, an object encapsulation mechanism, and a clean interface between constraints and the imperative parts of Smalltalk-80. In this chapter, we focus mainly on the techniques used to attain good interactive performance in ThingLab II.

6.1.1 What is Constraint Programming?

Pure constraint programming languages have no notion of assignment, procedures, or control flow. Instead, the programmer describes a set objects and a set of relationships, or *constraints*, that should hold between them. As the user (or a program) interacts with the objects, it is up to the *constraint satisfier* to decide when and how to enforce the constraints.

ThingLab II uses a dataflow implementation of constraints. Each constraint has a set of procedures that can be invoked to satisfy the constraint. Each procedure, or *method*, uses some of the constraint's variables to compute values for the remaining variables. (There is no relationship between constraint methods and Smalltalk methods). For example, one might wish to constrain the variable A to equal the sum of variables B and C. This constraint would have the three methods:

$$A \leftarrow B + C \qquad B \leftarrow A - C \qquad C \leftarrow A - B$$

The task of the ThingLab II constraint satisfier, then, is to decide which constraints should be satisfied, which method should be used to satisfy each constraint, and in what order the methods should be invoked to satisfy the constraints.

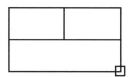

Figure 6.1

6.1.2 Using Constraints to Build User Interfaces

Constraint programming offers solutions to a number of problems in constructing user interfaces. First, constraints can be used to map between application objects and graphical objects on the display screen. In a simple piano-roll music editor, for example, a constraint might relate the vertical position of a note bar to the pitch field of a note object in the underlying score. Dragging the note bar up and down with the mouse would change the pitch of the underlying note object. Similarly, if a user-invoked command transposed the entire score up one octave, constraints would ensure that all note bars were moved accordingly.

Second, constraints can maintain consistency among multiple views of data. Suppose that a user interface presents two views of a number: a slider and a text field. Constraints can be used to keep the number consistent with both its views. If the application program changes the number or if either view of the number is edited, both the number text and the slider position will be updated accordingly. Other mechanisms have been developed to handle this problem, such as the Model-View-Controller change/update mechanism [MVC]. However, in MVC, programmers must insert explicit notification messages into their code to inform the system of changes that should trigger view updates. Constraints may prove to be a more convenient and reliable mechanism.

6.1.3 Two Examples

One example of the application of constraints to user interfaces is window layout. Figure 6.1 shows the skeleton of a widow with three panes. The window is divided in half vertically, and the top half is divided into equal left and right halves. Constraints are used to maintain the proportions of these sub-divisions as the window is resized.

Figure 6.2 shows several views of musical scores related by constraints. Two of the views are piano-roll score representations, related by a constraint that keeps the right-hand score four semitones higher in pitch than the left-hand score. The other two views, connected to the right-hand score object, report interesting statistics about the score and indicate when the score contains too many notes [Shaffer 81]. The statistical views are not editable, since we chose not to provide methods to generate scores from a set of statistics. However, when either piano-roll view is edited all four views are updated.

Both of these examples have been implemented in ThingLab II.

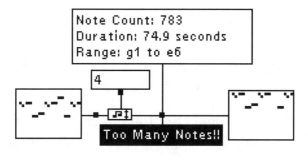

Figure 6.2

6.2 OBJECTS IN THINGLAB

In ThingLab II, as in Smalltalk, objects consist of state and behavior. In ThingLab II, however, the behavior of objects, or *Things*, is generally specified with constraints rather than methods. A new Thing is created by declaring a set of previously created objects to be the new Thing's *components*; the components are then interconnected with constraints. The system comes with a library of primitive Things that may be used as building blocks. Primitive Things are an exception to the rule that all behavior is specified with constraints: a primitive Thing has a small set of Smalltalk methods that define how it is displayed and how it responds to mouse and keyboard input events.

6.2.1 The Constraint Interpreter

The constraint interpreter mediates between the user and a Thing; it is the equivalent of the read-eval-print loop of the classic Lisp interpreter. The constraint interpreter adds and removes constraints in response to user actions, calls the constraint satisfier to satisfy the constraints, and graphically displays the state of the Thing being manipulated.

Built into the interpreter is a user-controlled clock. One of the primitive Things is a *history variable* that stores not only its current state but a number of previous states as well. The programmer may write constraints that refer to past states of a history variable (although past states are read-only, to ensure that time moves forwards). When the clock is running, the interpreter repeatedly advances all history variables, resatisfies all affected constraints, and displays the results. This allows us to create simple animations with constraints, as in Animus [Duisberg 86].

6.2.2 Thing Implementation

All Things are subclasses of class Thing, which manages the structure of the constraint graph and the state information used by the constraint satisfier. The components of a particular Thing are kept in a set of named instance variables, one per component. Components may be Things or ordinary Smalltalk objects. For example, a LineThing has two instance variables, *p1* and *p2*, each containing a PointThing. A PointThing has two instance variables, *x* and *y*, each containing an ordinary Smalltalk object (usually a Number). To make a new Thing, the system creates a new subclass of class Thing. Instance variables and access methods for each component are added to this class as the new Thing is constructed.

Each Thing has a list of constraints that it owns. For example, a HorizontalLine owns a constraint equating the *y* parts of its two endpoints. New instances of a Thing are created by copying the state and structure of a prototype instance, including the constraints owned by that prototype.

ThingLab II provides a graphical construction-kit user interface similar to that of Fabrik [Ingalls et al. 88]. During Thing construction, the users adds components to the new Thing by dragging them into the Thing from a "parts bin."

6.3   ADDRESSING THE NEED FOR RESPONSIVENESS

A user interface must be responsive. Two measures of responsiveness are latency and feedback bandwidth.

Latency is the time taken by the user interface to respond when the user first initiates an action. A typical user interaction is resizing a window by dragging its lower right corner. In ThingLab II this is implemented by attaching a mouse constraint to the corner point, generating a plan for constraint satisfaction, and executing that plan repeatedly as the user drags the window corner. The latency of the window resize operation is the time between the initial mouse press and the first visible motion of the window corner.

Feedback bandwidth is the rate at which information is presented to the user during an interaction after the initial latency time. In one cycle of an interaction such as window resizing, ThingLab II accepts data from the input devices, satisfies the relevant constraints, and updates the display. Feedback bandwidth is measured by the number of these cycles that are completed in a second.

ThingLab II addresses the need for responsiveness—both low latency and high feedback bandwidth—in two ways: by making judicious tradeoffs between compilation and interpretation, and by using an incremental algorithm for constraint satisfaction.

Compilation is an issue because of the desire to maximize the performance of constraint satisfaction. The ThingLab II constraint satisfier generates a *plan* for satisfying a given set of constraints. This plan is executed once during each cycle of the feedback loop. In the original ThingLab system, plans were compiled into Smalltalk methods to maximize feedback bandwidth. Unfortunately, the cost of compilation increased the latency of the system to tens—or even hundreds—of seconds. This problem was mitigated by caching compiled plans for later use. However, cached plans become useless if their assumptions are invalidated through the addition or removal of constraints, and adding and removing constraints is a frequent occurrence during the iterative refinement of a user interface. If

ThingLab II relied upon caching compiled plans, the user would frequently experience cache misses and the ensuing wait while a new plan was compiled. The average latency would go up and, worse, the system's responsiveness would be erratic. To avoid this problem, ThingLab II executes plans interpretively rather than compiling them into Smalltalk methods. By so doing, the overhead of interpretation during plan execution (and hence lower feedback bandwidth) is exchanged for decreased latency and a more consistent "feel."

As the complexity of a user interface grows, there comes a point when the number of constraints overwhelms the capacity of the system to provide timely responses. To forestall this problem, it is possible to compile parts of the interface using ThingLab II's module compiler. The module compiler takes three arguments: a set of variables, a set of constraints, and a list of those variables that will be visible outside the compiled module. Using these arguments, the compiler does three things. First, it combines each connected set of internal constraints into a single constraint among external variables, and compiles an optimized satisfaction method for that constraint. Second, it prunes away all unneeded internal constraints and variables. Finally, it compiles procedures to speed up subsequent processing of the module by the constraint satisfier. Naturally the compilation process takes time but the programmer can apply the process only when a component has been well tested, is not likely to change, and is expected to get frequent use. The module compiler is described in detail in a companion paper [Freeman-Benson 89].

6.4 INCREMENTAL CONSTRAINT SATISFACTION

In this section we briefly sketch the theory of constraint hierarchies and what it means to find "the best" solution to a given hierarchy. We then describe two algorithms for finding such solutions efficiently.

6.4.1 Constraint Hierarchy Theory

A constraint program consists of a a set of constraints C and a set of variables V. The programmer is often willing to relax some constraints (i.e., allow them to be unsatisfied) to permit the satisfaction of others. Based on the programmer's ranking, the set of constraints C is divided into partitions C_0, ..., C_n such that all constraints in C_i are preferred over those in C_{i+1}. The constraints in set C_0 are *required* to be satisfied. Constraints in C_1 through C_n are merely *preferred*. A set of constraints partitioned by preference level is called a *constraint hierarchy*.

A *solution* to a given constraint hierarchy is a mapping from variables to values. A solution that satisfies all the required constraints in the hierarchy is called *admissible*. A given constraint hierarchy may have a large number of admissible solutions. Some of these solutions will also satisfy some of the preferred constraints. By considering the set of preferred constraints that each admissible solution satisfies, a best solution may be chosen from the set of all admissible solutions. Intuitively, a best solution is one for which no better solution exists according to a formal goodness metric called a *comparator*.

There may actually be several equally good "best" solutions. Such multiple solutions arise when either the constraints allow some degrees of freedom (the underconstrained case) or when there a conflict between constraints at the same level of preference, forcing the constraint solver to choose among them (the overconstrained case). Multiple solutions are discussed in [Freeman-Benson 88]. The theory of constraint hierarchies was originally described in [Borning et al. 87], which also presented four useful solution comparators. The theory has recently been refined and extended in the context of logic programming [Borning et al. 88].

One of the simplest solution comparators is called **locally-predicate-better**. This comparator finds "intuitively plausible" solutions to a constraint hierarchy for a reasonable computational cost. Its definition is:

Given
> a constraint hierarchy with n levels, $\{C_0, ..., C_n\}$
> two solutions to be compared, X and Y, both satisfying the required
> > constraints in C_0

Then X is **locally-predicate-better** than Y iff there exists some level $k \le n$
> such that:
> > for each constraint c in C_1 through C_{k-1}, X satisfies c iff Y satisfies
> > > c, and
> > in C_k, X satisfies all the constraints that Y does and at least one more.

6.4.2 A Simple Algorithm

This definition leads to a simple algorithm, known as the Blue algorithm, for finding a **locally-predicate-better** solution to the constraint hierarchy. Recall that each constraint in ThingLab II has a set of *methods*, any of which may be executed to cause the constraint to be satisfied. Each method uses some of the constraint's variables as inputs and computes the others as outputs. A method may only be executed when all of its inputs and none of its outputs have been determined by other constraints.

satisfy: C
> partition C into sets C_0 through C_n
> D ← ∅   "the set of determined variables"
> repeat
> > progress ← self satisfyNext
> until
> > progress = false
> if $C_0 \ne \emptyset$ then
> > error: 'failed to satisfy a required constraint'

satisfyNext
    for C_i in C_0 to C_n do
        for each constraint c in C_i do
            for each method m in c's methods do
                if all of m's inputs are in D and
                    none of m's outputs is in D
                then
                        m execute
                        C_i remove: c
                        D addAll: m's outputs
                        ↑true
  ↑false

C is the set of all constraints in the constraint hierarchy and D is the set of variables whose values have been determined. A constraint can be satisfied only if it has a method whose inputs have been determined and whose outputs have not. **satisfy** calls **satisfyNext** to satisfy some most-preferred, satisfiable constraint. Since D is initially empty, the process starts by satisfying a constraint whose method has no input variables, such as a mouse constraint. Satisfying one constraint may make other constraints eligible for satisfaction, so the process is repeated until no further progress can be made. Notice that **satisfyNext** always starts with the most preferred constraints; this guarantees that the algorithm will find a **locally-predicate-better** solution to the constraint hierarchy. If the algorithm terminates and C_0 is not empty, then some of the required constraints could not be satisfied and the user is so notified.

If there are multiple **locally-predicate-better** solutions, the algorithm will pick one arbitrarily. This is appropriate for user interface construction. However, in other applications, one might want to find all such solutions. A facility to do this, the multiple solution browser [Freeman-Benson 88], was available in an earlier version of ThingLab and a similar facility is available in the Hierarchical Constraint Logic Programming language [Borning et al. 88].

6.4.3 An Incremental Algorithm

In many interactive applications, the constraint hierarchy evolves gradually, a fact that can be exploited by an *incremental* constraint satisfier. The task of an incremental algorithm is to decide how to modify the current solution to resatisfy the constraint hierarchy after a constraint is added or removed.

Consider attaching a required plus constraint to three numbers with attached stay constraints. (A stay constraint constrains the value of its operand to remain unchanged.)

The plus constraint has three methods, shown in Figure 6.3 as possible data flows. The method chosen to satisfy the plus constraint will determine the value of one of the constraint's operands, revoking (i.e., making unsatisfied) the stay constraint on that operand. Method B or method C would satisfy the required plus constraint at the cost of revoking a weakly preferred stay constraint. It is easy to see that these are both **locally-predicate-better** solutions since the other solution, method A, would revoke a strongly preferred constraint.

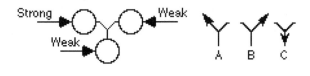

Figure 6.3

This example was chosen for clarity. It is more usual for each operand of a constraint to be connected to a network of other constraints and variables. The idea behind our incremental algorithm, known as the DeltaBlue algorithm, is to maintain sufficient information at each variable to allow the algorithm to predict the cost of adding a constraint by examining only the immediate operands of that constraint. This information is called the *walkabout strength* of the variable, defined as follows:

- If variable V is determined by method M of constraint C, the walkabout strength of V is the minimum of C's strength and the walkabout strengths of the inputs of M.

- If variable V is not determined by any constraint, the walkabout strength of V is *absoluteWeakest*.

The walkabout strength of a variable is the strength of the weakest constraint upstream of that variable in the current solution that could be revoked to allow the variable to be determined by another constraint. When DeltaBlue wishes to satisfy a constraint C, it attempts to find a method for C whose output variable has a walkabout strength weaker than C. If such a method cannot be found, C cannot be satisfied without revoking a constraint of the same strength or stronger. Revoking a constraint of the same strength as C would only lead to a different— not better—solution to the constraint hierarchy, so C is left unsatisfied in this case. Revoking a constraint stronger than C would lead to a worse solution (according to the **locally-predicate-better** comparator) so, again, C is left unsatisfied.

Let's see how DeltaBlue adds a constraint C to the hierarchy. DeltaBlue first chooses a potential method for C, one whose output has the weakest walkabout strength. (If several methods are tied for this honor, DeltaBlue chooses one arbitrarily.) Call the output variable of the chosen method O. If C is not stronger than the walkabout strength of O, DeltaBlue marks C unsatisfied and terminates. Otherwise, it computes a new walkabout strength for O and marks C as satisfied using the selected method.

In the latter case the work is not done, however, since in the old solution some other constraint, call it D, may have determined the value of O. Because C now determines O, D must be reconsidered. There are two possibilities. First, DeltaBlue may find another method to satisfy D, using the same criteria used to select a method for C. In this case, it marks D as satisfied using the new method, computes a new walkabout strength for the new method's output variable, and repeats the entire process on the constraint that previously determined D's new output variable. Alternatively, there may be no suitable method that can be used to satisfy D. In this case, D is marked as unsatisfied and the algorithm terminates.

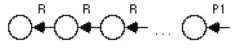

Figure 6.4

Thus, the effect of adding a constraint ripples through the constraint graph, guided by the walkabout strengths of the variables and stopping only when it reaches an unconstrained variable or a constraint that is too weak to be satisfied using any method. Only the constraints along one path through the constraint network are processed. If adding a constraint has only local effect (because, for example, a weak constraint is encountered before the propagation goes very far), the number of constraints processed can be much smaller than the total number of constraints in the hierarchy. At worst, the number of constraints processed to add a constraint will be equal to the number of constraints in the hierarchy. Removing a constraint is similar to adding one, except that a weaker walkabout strength is propagated, which may allow some currently unsatisfied constraint to become satisfied.

In this brief presentation of the DeltaBlue algorithm we have omitted certain details for the sake of clarity. For example, a list of ancestors is maintained at each variable to enable the algorithm to detect cycles. The interested reader is referred to [Freeman-Benson and Maloney 88] for the full story.

6.4.4 Analysis

It is enlightening to contrast the Blue and DeltaBlue algorithms. The worst case running time for Blue is proportional to the square of the total number of constraints, although improved bookkeeping can reduce this to nearly linear for typical hierarchies. To construct a given hierarchy from scratch, Blue does less work overall since DeltaBlue must recompute the walkabout strengths at every step. On the other hand, Blue must consider every constraint at least once every time it runs, whereas DeltaBlue need only consider the constraints effected by the last change. In short, Blue is appropriate for "batch" constraint solving, whereas DeltaBlue is good for interactive applications that make frequent, localized changes to the constraint hierarchy.

Neither algorithm is guaranteed to find a solution if there are cycles in the constraint graph, although cycles are detected and reported to the user. There are two ways to handle cycles in the constraint graph. The first way is to find a solution to the constraint hierarchy that does not have cycle its the dataflow graph, if such a solution exists. This would require backtracking to be added to the algorithm (either Blue or DeltaBlue), entailing a potentially exponential-time search. The second way is to apply a simultaneous equation solution technique, either numerical or symbolic, to each cycle. To keep the system simple and fast, we chose restrict

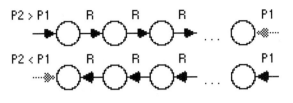

Figure 6.5

the domain of ThingLab II to constraint graphs without cycles. This is not too great a limitation since cycles are uncommon in a wide range of source-view style user interface applications. Cycles do arise in graphical layout, however, and in the future we plan to add one or more cycle-solvers to be called when needed by DeltaBlue.

6.5 PERFORMANCE

We measured the performance of the DeltaBlue algorithm implementation in ThingLab II in two situations. Both situations were based on a chain of Node objects and required "equals" constraints, as shown in Figure 6.4. A stay constraint of preference P_1 fixes the value of the rightmost Node object.

We measured the the time it took to satisfy the constraints incrementally when an input constraint with a preference of P_2 was added to the leftmost Node object. The two situations differed in the relative levels of preference of P_1 and P_2. In case one, P_2 was more preferred than P_1, causing the entire chain of equals constraints to be reversed and P_1 to be revoked. In case two, P_2 was less preferred than P_1, so the added constraint could not be satisfied and no other constraints were considered (see Figure 6.5).

The performance was measured for various chain lengths. In each case we measured the time taken to add the constraint, to construct a plan for recomputing all Node values from the input Node, to interpret that plan, and to remove the constraint again. The results of performing these tests under ParcPlace 2.3 Smalltalk on a Mac II are given in the following table. All times are in milliseconds. Poor clock resolution makes the times accurate only to within about 10 milliseconds.

	Case 1 ($P_2 > P_1$)			**Case 2 ($P_2 \leq P_1$)**		
	10 node	20 node	40 node	10 node	20 node	40 node
Add Constraint	230	498	1247	10	14	11
Make Plan	150	287	546	120	215	430
Execute Plan	11	13	45	0	0	0
Remove Constraint	373	1834	2259	0	3	3

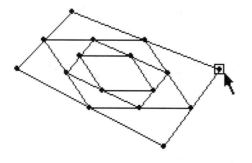

Figure 6.6

The results show that, indeed, it requires very little effort for DeltaBlue to add a constraint in case two, when the constraint added is too weak to overpower the other constraints. Even in this case, constructing the plan requires traversing the entire chain of constraints. However since all the values are ultimately determined from an object that is fixed by a stay constraint, the plan takes no time to execute.

In a user interface, the time to add a constraint and construct a plan would appear as latency, while the plan execution time would set the upper bound on feedback bandwidth. (Other things affect the feedback bandwidth, such as the cost of updating the display.) The time to remove the constraint would usually not be noticed, as it would occur in the dead time between interactions.

A second example is the "nested quadrilateral" example shown in Figure 6.6 [Borning et al. 87]. This example is structurally similar to resizing a window with scaling subpanes. The outer figure is an arbitrary quadrilateral. The corners of the inscribed figure are constrained to lie at the midpoints of the outer quadrilateral's sides. A theorem of geometry says that the inscribed figure will always be a parallelogram. The same construction technique was applied recursively to create the inner parallelograms. Including stay and mouse constraints, there are a total of fifty constraints in this example. We instrumented the constraint interpreter to measure the latency and feedback bandwidth when one of the corners of the outer quadrilateral was grabbed and dragged with the mouse. On our Mac II system, we measured:

ThingLab II Latency: 0.9 seconds
ThingLab II Feedback Bandwidth: 7.5 cycles/sec

These figures include the time taken to draw the figure, as well as the time to compute and execute a constraint satisfaction plan. The same example was implemented several years ago using the original ThingLab running under Tektronix Smalltalk on a Tektronix 4406 workstation, a system with performance comparable to our current Mac II system. The performance measurements for that system were:

Original ThingLab Latency: 7.4 seconds
Original ThingLab Feedback Bandwidth: not available

6.6 RELATED WORK

The notion of using constraints to specify the behavior of computer programs goes back to Ivan Sutherland's pioneering Sketchpad system [Sutherland 63] and has been explored by [Fikes 70, Borning 79, Steele 80, Gosling 83, Konopasek and Jayaraman 84, and Leler 86] among others. Recently, with the growing availability of low-cost graphical workstations, there has been a move to apply constraint technology to user interfaces. Brad Myers' Peridot system, for example, deduces constraints automatically as the user demonstrates the desired appearance and behavior of a user interface [Myers 87]. A system built by Epstein and LaLonde uses constraint hierarchies to control the layout of Smalltalk windows [Epstein and LaLonde 88]. Ege used constraints to build viewing filters that could be plugged together by the user to create custom user interfaces [Ege et al. 87].

Vander Zanden combined constraints and graphics with the attribute grammars developed for structured program editors to create *constraint grammars* [Vander Zanden 88]. His incremental constraint satisfier is similar to the one described here although it does not support different levels of constraint preference.

The goals of ThingLab II are similar to those of Szekely and Myers' Coral system, a user interface toolkit that uses a combination of constraints and active values to bind graphical objects to application data structures [Szekely and Myers 88]. In contrast to ThingLab II, Coral's constraints are uni-directional and Coral does not support the notion of constraint preferences. We hypothesize that the increased flexibility of multi-way constraints and the semantic expressiveness of constraint hierarchies make it easier to construct user interface components that are reusable and easy to understand. In this chapter, we demonstrated that ThingLab II's more powerful constraint system need not cost much in performance.

6.7 IMPLEMENTATION AND AVAILABILITY

The first version of ThingLab II was implemented in Smalltalk-80 by John Maloney and Bjorn Freeman-Benson over the four month period ending in February 1989. In addition to the constraint satisfier and the module compiler mentioned here, the system supports hierarchically composable, reusable objects called Things and a direct manipulation interface for assembling them. ThingLab II, including all source code, is available to other researchers. It requires a Smalltalk-80 system. Please contact the authors for further details.

Although the real test of ThingLab II—using it to produce full-scale user interfaces—lies ahead, our initial experiences with the system have been promising. In the applications we have tried latency is less than a second and the overhead for plan interpretation is much lower than expected.

ACKNOWLEDGEMENTS

This project was supported in part by the National Science Foundation under Grant Nos. IRI-8604923 and IRI-8803294, by a fellowship from Apple Computer for John Maloney, by a National Science Foundation Graduate Fellowship for Bjorn Freeman-Benson, and by a grant from the Washington Technology Center. Ed Grossman helped with the implementation.

REFERENCES

[Borning 79] Alan Borning, *ThingLab—A Constraint-Oriented Simulation Laboratory*, PhD thesis, Stanford University, published as Technical report SSL-79-3, Xerox Palo Alto Research Center, Palo Alto, July 1979.

[Borning et al. 87] Alan Borning, Robert Duisberg, Bjorn Freeman-Benson, Axel Kramer, and Michael Woolf, "Constraint hierarchies," in *OOPSLA'87 Conference Proceedings*, ACM, October 1987, pp. 48–60.

[Borning et al. 88] Alan Borning, Michael Maher, Amy Martindale, and Molly Wilson, "Constraint hierarchies and logic programming," in *Proceedings of the Sixth International Logic Programming Conference*, June 1989, pp. 149–164.

[Duisberg 86] Robert Duisberg, *Constraint-Based Animation: The Implementation of Temporal Constraints in the Animus System*, PhD thesis, University of Washington, published as Technical report 86-09-01, Department of Computer Science, University of Washington, Seattle, 1986.

[Ege et al. 87] Raimund K. Ege, David Maier, and Alan H. Borning, "The filter browser—defining interfaces graphically," in *Proceedings of the European Conference on Object-Oriented Programming*, Springer-Verlag, New York, June 1987.

[Epstein and LaLonde 88] Danny Epstein and Wilf LaLonde, "A Smalltalk window system based on constraints," in *OOPSLA '88 Conference Proceedings*, ACM, September 1988, pp. 83–94.

[Fikes 70] Richard Fikes, "REF-ARF: A system for solving problems stated as procedures," *Artificial Intelligence*, Spring 1970, pp. 27–120.

[Freeman-Benson 88] Bjorn Freeman-Benson, *Multiple Solutions from Constraint Hierarchies*, Technical report 88-04-02, Department of Computer Science, University of Washington, Seattle, April 1988.

[Freeman-Benson and Maloney 88] Bjorn Freeman-Benson and John Maloney, "The DeltaBlue algorithm: An incremental constraint hierarchy solver," in *Proceedings of the Eighth International Phoenix Conference on Computers and Communications*, Phoenix, March 1989. An expanded version is published as Technical report 88-11-09, Department of Computer Science, University of Washington, Seattle, November 1988.

[Freeman-Benson 89] Bjorn Freeman-Benson, "A module compiler for ThingLab II," in *OOPSLA '89 Conference Proceedings*, ACM, October 1989.

[Gosling 83] James Gosling, *Algebraic Constraints,* PhD thesis, Carnegie-Mellon University, published as Technical report CMU-CS-83-132, Computer Science Department, Carnegie-Mellon University, Pittsburgh, May 1983.

[Ingalls et al. 88] Dan Ingalls, Scott Wallace, Yu-Ying Chow, Frank Ludolph, and Ken Doyle, "Fabrik: A visual programming environment," in *OOPSLA '88 Conference Proceedings*, ACM, September 1988, pp. 176–190.

[Konopasek and Jayaraman 84] M. Konopasek and S. Jayaraman, *The TK!Solver Book*, Osborne/McGraw-Hill, 1984.

[Leler 86] Wm Leler, *Specification and Generation of Constraint Satisfaction Systems Using Augmented Term Rewriting*, PhD thesis, University of North Carolina at Chapel Hill, 1986. A revised version is published by Addison-Wesley, Reading, 1988.

[Myers 87] Brad Myers, *Creating User Interfaces by Demonstration,* PhD thesis, University of Toronto, May 1987. Published as Computer System Research Institute technical report CSRI-196 and also by Academic Press, 1988.

[Shaffer 81] Peter Shaffer, *Amadeus*, Penguin, 1981.

[Steele 80] Guy Steele, *The Definition and Implementation of a Computer Programming Language Based on Constraints*, PhD thesis, MIT, published as MIT-AI TR 595, August 1980.

[Sutherland 63] Ivan Sutherland, "Sketchpad: A man–machine graphical communication system," in *Proceedings of the Spring Joint Computer Conference*, pp. 329–345, IFIPS, 1963.

[Szekely and Myers 88] Pedro Szekely and Brad Myers, "A user-interface toolkit based on graphical objects and constraints," in *OOPSLA '88 Conference Proceedings*, ACM, September 1988, pp. 36–45.

[Vander Zanden 88] Bradley T. Vander Zanden, *An Incremental Planning Algorithm for Ordering Equations in a Multilinear System of Constraints*, PhD thesis, Cornell University, published as Technical report 88-910, Department of Computer Science, Cornell University, Ithaca, NY, April 1988.

CHAPTER 7   ❏ ❏ ❏ ❏

Design and Implementation with Vampire

DAVID W. MCINTYRE

CONTENTS

129

Many object-oriented visual programming languages are proving to be mark-edly different from their textual counterparts. For example, in other chapters in this book we have seen a visual language that combines constraints with object-oriented programming, a visual language that combines the dataflow paradigm with object-oriented programming, and a by-demonstration approach. These departures from tradition take designers into uncharted waters, and because of this, they require an experimental approach to their conceptual design. This chapter presents the approach used in the Vampire system for rapid prototyp-ing of new visual programming languages, which allows language designers to explore new concepts efficiently.

Vampire is itself a visual object-oriented programming language. It com-bines object-oriented programming with a rule-based approach in its incorpora-tion of graphical production rules to define the dynamic semantics of a new visual language. Once a new language is defined in this way, it can be used to create and execute programs.

7.1 INTRODUCTION

It is a great irony that the very people who promote visual program-ming languages as the wave of the future still have to create these languages and environments using "old-fashioned" textual programming languages, editors and compilers. Because visual programming tools stress user interaction, their pro-gramming can become very complex. Modification and debugging such a system can also be a difficult programming chore. Unfortunately, most toolkits that pro-vide help in creating user interfaces do not provide any support for noninterface graphics and the special needs of programming systems. Those toolkits that do provide noninterface graphics support commonly force the developer to program large amounts of code in Lisp or other high-level textual languages. Furthermore, they are frequently cumbersome and difficult to use.

In this chapter we will describe Vampire (Visual Metatools for Programming Iconic Environments), a system designed to solve these problems by providing a graphical environment specifically designed to aid in the creation of iconic pro-gramming languages. Vampire is a new model of programming which supports and formalizes concepts associated with the broad class of iconic languages, using a very minimum of text. Our model is based on the style of userinteraction, not on the application domain for which a particular environment may be intended, and therefore is capable of supporting systems used in a variety of domains. A more formal presentation of this model may be found in the literature [McIntyre 1992]. Vampire's support for object-oriented methodology is twofold: the language cre-ation process is object-oriented, and Vampire provides a vehicle for the creation of languages which themselves are object-oriented.

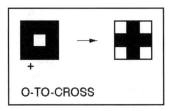

Figure 7.1   A BITPICT rule to convert a square to a cross

7.2 RELATED WORK

The Vampire system is closely related to several well-known rule-based graphical systems. Furnas' BITPICT system [Furnas 1990, 1991], a tool for exploring "graphical reasoning," was the inspiration for Vampire. BITPICT rules describe simple transformations on grids of pixels. When the configuration of pixels on the left side of the rule matches an area of the workspace, it is transformed into the configuration of pixels on the right side. Figure 7.1 shows a simple BITPICT rule which converts a square to a cross.

While this may seem quite simplistic, Furnas shows how such a system can be used to solve a number of problems which are otherwise difficult. One particularly vivid demonstration is the counting of a forest of tangled bifurcating trees. The trees are reduced to single pixels which fall to the bottom of the workspace. These single pixels are then transformed into a Roman numeric count of the trees. BITPICT has limitations, however; it is constrained to working with single pixels (there is no support for higher-level graphic entities such as lines or squares), and does not have support for variables in the rules. That is, the only matches possible are exact matches of the pixels in the left side of the rule. The BITPICT system allows geometric reflections and rotations of rules to be matched; Vampire does not allow these transformations.

Bell's ChemTrains system [Bell 1991, Bell and Lewis 1993] is very similar to Vampire, but has a different intent. ChemTrains is a graphical rule-based language intended to aid in the implementation of simulations by users with little or no programming experience. ChemTrains rules contain higher level graphical primitives, such as lines and boxes, and connections between them. Unlike Vampire, ChemTrains' graphical matching takes into account only topological aspects of the workspace diagram (such as containment and connectivity), and ignores geometrical aspects (such as relative position). ChemTrains does not support an association between elements in its rules and data structures or objects.

Although most of the examples shown by Bell are simple simulations, such as a population model of grasshoppers in a grassy field, ChemTrains shows a remarkable ability to model complex concepts (such as a Turing machine simulation and playing tic-tac-toe), although the solutions sometimes require a clever design. For example, Bell's Turing machine simulator uses several overlapping containment boxes to find the correct rule.

St. Denis demonstrates a system where graphical icon transformations and a textual production system language are combined to form a rapid prototyping system based on executing requirement specifications [St.-Denis 1990]. These textual and graphical production rules are kept distinct, as opposed to the Vampire system, where the textual and graphical components or the production rules are combined.

Also related to Vampire are the many visual language parsing systems [Helm et al. 1991, Golin 1991], which use textual productions to describe the structure of a visual language diagram. Vampire does not explicitly deal with parsing language diagrams; it instead deals with the semantics associated with combinations of icons in a program.

7.3 ATTRIBUTED GRAPHICAL RULES

Vampire's *attributed graphical rules* have much in common with the rules introduced in BITPICT and extended in ChemTrains. Like the rules in these systems, they contain on their left sides graphical elements which are matched against a runtime workspace. When an area of the runtime workspace matching this left side is found, it is transformed into the contents of the right side of the rule. Unlike both of the earlier systems, Vampire's attributed graphical rules can refer to values of attributes of these graphical elements, as well as to their purely graphical nature.

Each side of the rules contains two other components, a graphical component and a textual component. The textual area contains Smalltalk expressions which are used to evaluate and process nongraphical attributes of the graphical area. Figure 7.2 shows an empty attributed rule frame. The field between the two sides of the rule contains an integer which represents the rule priority, and which is used in the conflict resolution strategy during program execution.

7.3.1 Icons

An icon's position in a rule can be specified in one of three ways. Normal icons have fixed relative positions in the rules. Fuzzy icons have no fixed position, but can be constrained to follow certain geometric guidelines. Finally, icon positions can be specified through constraint points, which can be considered to be a fuzzy icon whose geometric positioning is restricted to locations which cover a specific point.

The type of an icon (normal, fuzzy, or constraint point) is determined solely by how it is added into the rule in a rule editor; however, their visual representations are distinct.

Normal Icons   The basic graphical building block of Vampire's rules is the normal icon, henceforth just called *icon*. Icons contain a set of graphical primitives which describe their appearance. Icons can be very simple (e.g., a small black square), or complicated (such as the well-known Emacs sink icon). A simple graphical editor is provided to build the icons' appearance.

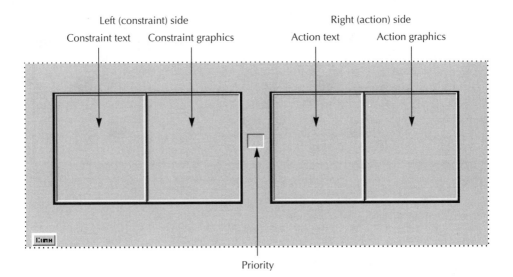

Figure 7.2   An empty attributed rule frame (viewed from the Vampire rule viewer)

Icons are placed into the two graphical areas of the rule via the rule editor. The position of an icon in a rule is significant; its relative position to other icons in that rule is used to determine matching. A set of icons in a rule match a set of icons in the programming workspace only if their relative geometric positions match exactly.

The difference in icon configuration between the two sides of the rule determines what actions are performed on the icons. For example, if an icon has a different position on the two sides, it will move to the right-side position if the left side of the rule matches. If an icon is present on the left side, but not on the right side, it will be deleted if the rule matches. Finally, if an icon is not present on the left side of a rule but is present on the right side of the rule, it will be created if the rule matches.

Drawn near each icon in the rule is a textual label, such as the *A* or *B* in Figure 7.3. This label is used to associate textual constraints and actions with the actual icons displayed in the graphical portions of the rule. These labels are assigned automatically by the rule editor.

Fuzzy Icons   Fuzzy icons differ from normal icons in that their relative geometric positioning within a rule is not taken into account during the matching process. In other words, a rule matches if the fuzzy icons specified on its left side merely exist somewhere in the runtime workspace. Their relative positions are insignificant; they are merely existential constraints on a particular icon. Fuzzy icons are visually differentiated from normal icons in rules by a set of three yellow wavy lines drawn over their top left corner.

Fuzzy icons on their own are sometimes useful, but more often we want to say "this rule matches if there is an icon of class x (or a subclass of x) *somewhere above and to the right* of this icon of class y." Vampire provides this type of matching

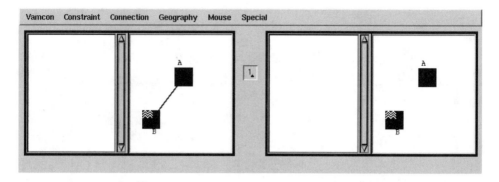

Figure 7.3   Rule containing a normal icon (A), a fuzzy icon (B), and a geometric constraint between them (in the manual rule editor)

through *geometric constraints*. Geometric constraints provide a positional imperative between a normal icon and a fuzzy icon. When a fuzzy icon is connected to a normal icon through a geometric constraint, its position becomes significant in that it must match the constraint. In other words, the rule matching process doesn't care exactly where the fuzzy icon is, as long as it matches the restrictions of the geometric constraint. Figure 7.3 shows an attributed graphical rule that contains one normal and one fuzzy icon. The thick line connecting their centers represents a geometric constraint. The nature of this constraint cannot be determined by simply looking at the rule; clicking on the constraint line will cause an informational window detailing the constraint conditions.

Constraint Points   Constraint points specify an exact position, relative to normal icons' positions, which an icon of a specific class must cover. The icon may be in any position in the workspace that covers the constraint point. Constraint points are a method of specifying the location of an icon that is more flexible than that for normal icons and yet more restrictive than fuzzy icons or fuzzy icons with geometric constraints. Figure 7.4 shows a rule with one normal icon and a

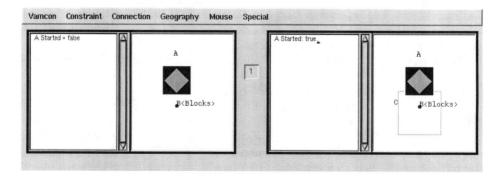

Figure 7.4   Rule containing a constraint point

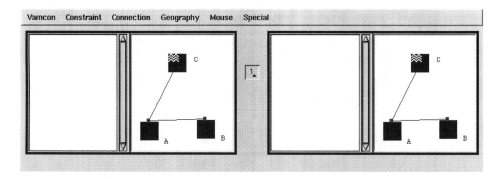

Figure 7.5   Rule containing a normal connection (between A and B) and a connection which includes a wildcard port (between A and C)

constraint point. This rule will match a runtime workspace only if an icon derived from class *Blocks* covers the constraint point. Note that the name of the constraint's class is displayed near the point.

A very useful aspect of constraint points is their ability to specify a NULL or empty class associated with their location, indicating that this point in the workspace must contain no icon. In this way, rules can maintain empty areas in the workspace.

7.3.2 Connections

Many iconic languages contain not only icons, but also some sort of "pipe" or connection between the icons through which data or control flows. These connections cannot be considered icons in themselves; rather they are topological relationships between the icons.

Icons in Vampire can contain *connection points*. These points determine where connections to an icon must terminate. An icon may have any number of connection points, which are added in the Vampire icon editor (discussed in Section 7.5). Icons (in both the left and right sides of rules) may have connections between their connection points. Connections on the left side of the rule must exist in the runtime workspace in order for the rule to match. Connections which are only on the right side of the rule are created if the rule matches. Connections within a rule must be either between two specific ports on two icons or between one specific port and one *wildcard port*. A wildcard port indicates that the icon's connection will match a connection to any port on the icon.

Figure 7.5 shows a rule that contains a connection between two specific ports (between icons A and B) and a connection to a normal or fuzzy icon's wildcard port (between icons A and C).

7.3.3 Mouse Clicks

Most iconic languages include some sort of user interaction in their behavior. Vampire rules support just a limited sort of interaction; mouse clicks within icons. A single mouse click (represented by a small computer-mouse glyph) can be placed

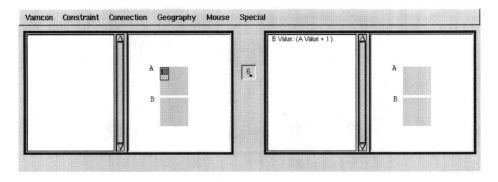

Figure 7.6   Rule containing a mouse click. This rule will not fire until all conditions on the left side of the rule are met and the user clicks on the leftmost icon in the rule.

inside an icon on the left side of a Vampire rule. This glyph indicates that the user must click the mouse on the specified icon in order for the rule to match. Figure 7.6 shows a rule containing a mouse click on the leftmost icon on the left side of the rule. This rule will not fire until the user clicks on that icon, even if all other conditions have been met.

7.3.4 Textual Constraints and Actions

Textual constraints and actions are used to test and specify the values of attributes of icons in a rule. For example, a textual constraint might assert that a certain icon's attribute must have a value greater than 12 in order for the rule to fire. A textual action might set that same icon's attribute to 0 when the rule fires.

Each attribute of an icon's class has two Smalltalk methods (a setter and a getter) associated with it. These methods are used to set and retrieve the values of these attributes. The getter method is simply the name of the attribute. The setter method is the name of the attribute followed by a colon.

The icons in the rules are identified by their labels, usually a single capital letter which is assigned automatically by the editor. These labels are used as objects in the Smalltalk code and are mapped to the icons in the workspace when a rule is matched to determine actions to be performed on them.

Textual Constraints   Smalltalk code to test the value of icon B's Value attribute looks like the following:

B Value > 8

This expression returns TRUE if the Value attribute of B is greater than 8. Such an expression can be used on the left side of a rule. Conjunctions are formed with the Smalltalk *and:* message, and disjunctions are formed with the *or:* message. Code to test that Value is either between 10 and 20 or greater than 30 looks like:

(B Value > 10 and: (B Value < 20)) or: (B Value > 30)

Note that parentheses may be necessary in some circumstances. All the Smalltalk code on the left side of a rule must take the form of a single expression (a series of predicates combined with Boolean operators) whose value is checked only after the rule's graphical constraints have actually been determined to match the runtime workspace instances.

Textual Actions Unlike the textual constraints, actions may take the form of one or more statements, separated by periods. An action which increments B's Value looks like:

B Value: (B Value + 1).

There are also three special actions which Vampire provides to assist in encapsulation. These three methods must be applied to the special object *runtime*, which is defined only in the right side of rules. The runtime object is bound to the actual runtime workspace mechanism just before program execution. The three special messages are:

runtime clear.
runtime storeToFile:
runtime loadFromFile:

The first message simply clears the current workspace. All icons and connections are deleted. The second message causes the current workspace configuration to be stored to a file. This includes all icons, their attribute values, and all connections. The third message reverses this process, loading a workspace configuration from a file. Typically, a workspace is cleared before a new configuration is loaded, and after a configuration has been stored.

7.3.5 Rule Editors

There are two editors used to create and change attributed graphical rules within a Vampire language definition: the manual rule editor and the demonstrational rule editor. Rules may be created in either editor; they may be changed only in the manual rule editor.

Manual Rule Editor The manual rule editor (shown in Figures 7.3–6) employs a direct manipulation interface to allow the user to create and edit rules. Both constraint and action sides of the rule are visible to the user at the same time, and changes can be made directly to all workspaces. This editor is intended for more advanced users of Vampire, because it allows complete flexibility in the rule editing process but provides little interactive assistance to the user.

Icons and fuzzy icons are added to the system through the *Icons* pull-down menu. Choices include positioning icons on the left side only, on the right side only, and on both the left and right sides (a special option exists to place the icon on both sides of the rule at the same position; otherwise, the icons are placed individually on the two sides). An icon chooser dialog box pops up with all available icons, and the selected icon is dragged and dropped into the appropriate workspace. Constraint points are added similarly. Connections are added through another

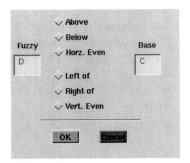

Figure 7.7   Geometric constraint dialog box

pull-down menu and by clicking on the appropriate ports, as are geometric constraints. All pull-down menu actions have keyboard shortcuts associated with them (e.g., the key combination *Alt-c* adds a connection; *Alt-r* removes a connection).

Geometric constraints are added by pulling down the *Geography* menu in the rule editor. The user is prompted to click first on a *base* or normal icon, and then on a fuzzy icon. Note that these geometric constraints can only be between one normal and one fuzzy icon or between two fuzzy icons (but there must be at least one normal icon in the rule in order to anchor the relative positioning).

Once the icons have been selected, the geometric constraint dialog box (Figure 7.7) appears. Constraints can be in either the vertical or horizontal direction or both. The appropriate selections are chosen and then the *OK* button is clicked. The new geometric constraint will appear in the rule as a solid line connecting the two constrained icons centers.

The textual workspaces are typical Smalltalk text editors, and allow any of the standard *yellow menu* actions such as cut, copy, paste, etc. The rule firing priority can be changed by typing a new value into its field.

Demonstrational Rule Editor   The demonstrational rule editor (Figure 7.8) is designed to provide a more naive user with the ability to create rules. It is also faster than the manual editor for simple rules. Only one side of the rule, constraint, or action, is displayed at a time, and no textual workspace is ever displayed, although textual constraints and actions can be specified through menu selections.

Figure 7.8   Demonstrational rule editor

For more complicated rules the user may either first use the demonstrational editor to specify geometric constraints and actions and then the manual editor to do the textual editing or may just use the manual editor exclusively.

Icons, connections, etc., are added to the single workspace to create the desired graphical constraint conditions. Constraints on nongeometric aspects of the icons (which would be entered in the textual workspace in the manual editor) are established through pop-up menus on the icons. The initial configuration is then accepted through a pull-down menu action.

The configuration of the workspace is then changed by the user to represent how the runtime workspace will appear after the rule is matched. Actions on nongeometric aspects of the icons are again entered through pop-up menus. The final configuration is then accepted through another pull-down menu action, and the rule is accepted.

During the rule acceptance process, the user is queried about intent. For instance, if there is a fuzzy icon above a normal icon, the user is asked if a geometric constraint between the two icons is necessary.

The demonstrational rule editor can create most of the rules necessary in many language systems. Any geometric relationship between icons can be entered easily; however, complicated textual attribute relationships must still be entered textually using the manual editor.

7.4 CLASS HIERARCHY AND EDITOR

Languages are specified through an object-oriented class hierarchy in Vampire. Classes within the hierarchy represent either elements of the language or abstract superclasses of elements of the language. Attributes (slots) contained in these classes determine the static and dynamic characteristics of the language being defined. The semantics of these attributes is different from the concept of class or instance variables in Smalltalk. Vampire's class attributes actually contain default values which are used to initialize the values of instances' attributes. Inherited attributes' default values can be overridden.

The behavior of these classes is specified through rule attributes. The positions of rule attributes within the class hierarchy are not taken into account when the runtime system is active; instead, all rules can be applied to icons of any class in the hierarchy. Rule attributes are included within the class hierarchy only as a design aid. When a rule attribute's value is overridden in a subclass, both versions of the rule can be applied to instances of all hierarchy classes. Although it is a clear violation of object-oriented principles, this methodology allows rules to coexist with the hierarchy without imposing unnecessary restrictions on their application.

Instances of Vampire classes have their attributes initialized with the default values; these values can then be changed within the runtime application. Classes which are to be instantiated and used in programs must contain attributes which represent their appearances (iconic attributes).

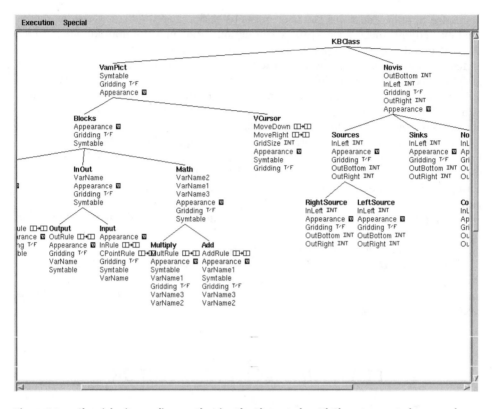

Figure 7.9   Class inheritance diagram showing the abstract class KbClass, two root classes, and several classes derived from the root classes (from the Vampire class editor)

Programming in Vampire is a matter of constructing the class hierarchy, defining the graphical and textual attributes of the classes which represent language semantics, and placing instances of these classes into a runtime workspace.

All language hierarchies defined in Vampire are derived from the Smalltalk KbClass class, which is predefined by Vampire. Typically, a *root class* is subclassed from KbClass and represents the base characteristics of all the elements in a language. From that root class the classes representing actual language elements are derived. It is this root class to which are added all the attributes that can be inherited throughout an entire language.

In Figure 7.9 we see that three languages have been developed in this hierarchy (two of whose names are displayed within the window); one characterized by Novis and the other by VamPict, their root classes.

The class editor (Figure 7.10) provides a graphical depiction of the language hierarchy tree being constructed. Much information about the structure of the hierarchy is presented in this window.

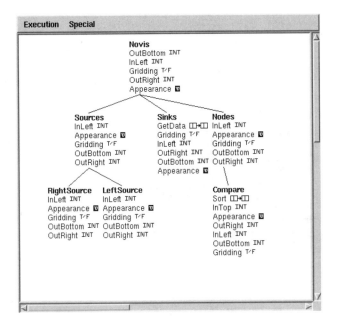

Figure 7.10   Class editor

Geometric Information   The base class of the language being developed is displayed at the top of the class editor window. Black lines between blocks of strings indicates subclassing. For example, in Figure 7.10, Sinks, Nodes, and Sources are all subclasses of the base class Novis.

Color Information   Text that appears in blue on-screen indicates class names. In Figure 7.10 the class names presented are Novis, Sinks, Nodes, Sources, Compare, LeftSource, and RightSource.

Text that appears in red on-screen indicates noninherited, or local, attributes. These are attributes which actually reside in the class under which they are depicted, and which are not inherited from a superclass. For example, in the class Novis, OutBottom and Gridding are local attributes.

Text that appears in green on-screen indicates inherited attributes. These are attributes whose values and names are inherited from a superclass, and which do not have a value special to the class under which they are depicted. For example, in the class Sinks, OutBottom and Gridding are inherited attributes; their values come from the class Novis.

Finally, text that appears in purple on-screen indicates shared attributes. Shared (or global) attributes are inherited by subclasses of the attributes' owner, just like normal attributes, but have only one value, which is shared among all the classes which contain it. When a shared attribute is edited, all classes that contain it reflect this same change. Shared attributes are analogous to class variables in many object-oriented languages. One common use for shared attributes in Vampire-defined languages is as a symbol table (as will be seen in Section 7.7.2). All icons within a program should refer to the same symbol table, and should not have their own individual copies.

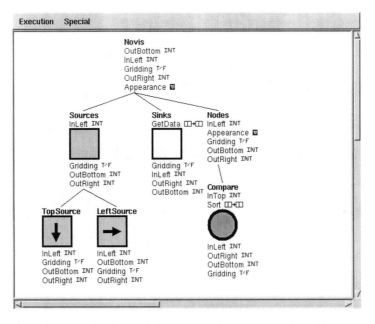

Figure 7.11   Class editor, viewing the same hierarchy as in Figure 7.10, but with the
icons graphically visualized

Attribute Type Glyphs   Attribute names in the class editor are followed by
a small icon or glyph that indicates the type of the value stored in the attribute. In
Figure 7.10, the attribute GetData of the class Sinks contains a rule, and the
glyph following the text *GetData* shows a tiny rule-like figure. Similarly, the
attribute Appearance is an icon, and the small glyph is a characterization of an
icon. Other attribute types have more textual glyphs; Boolean attributes are represented by a T/F glyph, and integer attributes are represented by *INT*. Iconic
attributes may also be visualized in the class editor, replacing their textual names
with their graphical name (see Figure 7.11).

Editing Classes   Classes are edited through a pop-up menu which appears
when a class name is selected by a mouse click. The choices include:

- **Add Subclass**   The user is prompted for the name of the new class to
  add to the hierarchy under the current class. This is the basic method for
  creating the hierarchy.

- **Remove Class**   Removes the current class. Entire subtrees can be
  deleted in this manner, but this is confirmed by the user before the actual
  deletion. This action cannot be undone.

- **Add Attribute**   The user is presented with the attribute type dialog box
  (Figure 7.12). The name of the new attribute is entered in the top section. If
  a standard attribute type is required, the second section of the dialog is
  used. If an arbitrary Smalltalk instance is to be used, the third section is
  used. Arbitrary instances can either be tied to a particular class, or can be
  completely polymorphic.

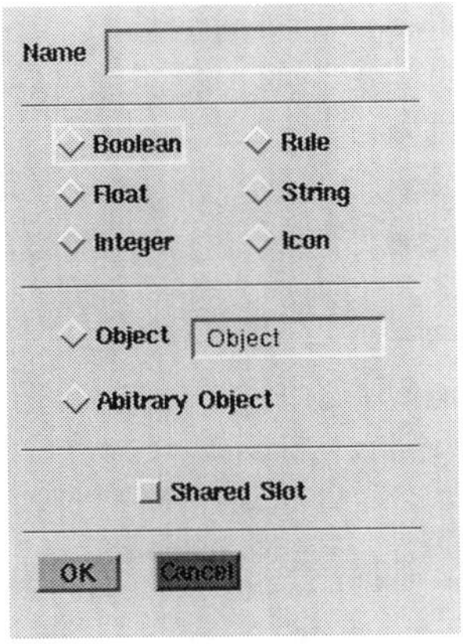

Figure 7.12 Attribute type dialog box

- **Inspect** A Smalltalk Inspector is instantiated on the current class. Values of the class can be viewed or altered (but this is not a standard way of programming in Vampire).

Editing Attributes Attributes are also edited through a pop-up menu which appears when an attribute name is selected by a mouse-click. The choices presented include:

- **Edit Attribute** This option causes an editor appropriate to the class of the value of the attribute to appear. For textual attributes such as integers and strings, the user is simply prompted for a new value. For graphically based attributes such as rules and icons, the special Vampire editor for that type appears. For arbitrary Smalltalk objects, the Smalltalk Inspector is invoked.

  When inherited attributes are edited in this manner, the original inherited value is overridden and replaced with the new value. When shared attributes are edited in this manner, the global copy of the attribute is changed, and all classes share in this new attribute value.

- **View Attribute** This option displays the value of the attribute in a window appropriate to its type.

- **Remove Attribute** This option removes the current attribute.

- **Inspect Attribute** This brings up a Smalltalk Inspector on the attribute instance.

7.5 ICON EDITOR

The Vampire icon editor is used to create the graphical images which represent the elements of the programming language (the icon attributes). The icon editor is a typical object-based graphical editor. Buttons exist to allow drawing of rectangles, circles, arrows, polygons, etc.

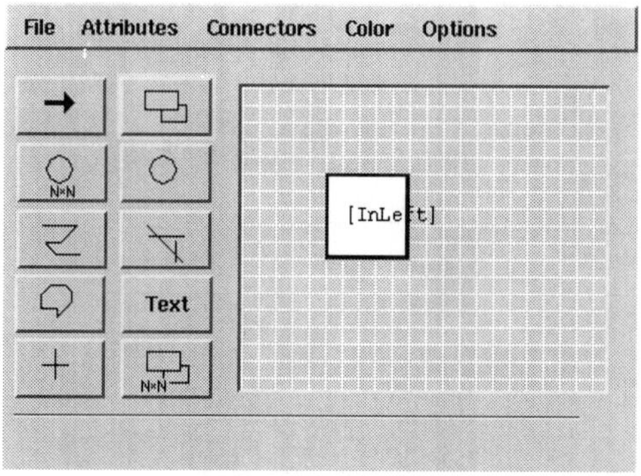

Figure 7.13   Icon editor. This icon has an attribute from its class (InLeft) visualized textually. When placed into the workspace, the value of this attribute will be displayed.

The icon editor includes several special features unique to Vampire:

- The color of any graphical object can be dependent on the value of another attribute from the same class to which the icon belongs.
- Connection ports can be added to the icon.
- Attributes from the class of the icon can be visualized textually (Figure 7.13).

7.6 THE RUNTIME WORKSPACE

The runtime workspace is where the language defined in a Vampire hierarchy can be used to create a program which can then be run! Icons are placed into the workspace, connections are made, attributes are edited, and the program is executed (Figure 7.14).

7.6.1 Creating a Program

Much as in the two rule editors, icons are placed into the runtime workspace through selections on pull-down menus The icon chooser pops up, and an icon of the appropriate class is dragged and dropped into the workspace. Icons can be moved and deleted through pop-up menus attached to each. Connections are also made through a pull-down menu selection, or through a keyboard shortcut. The user is prompted to click on two connection ports. Note that, unlike the rule editors, connections must be made only between two actual connection ports; wildcard connections, a concept used only to describe matching conditions within rules, are not allowed in the runtime workspace.

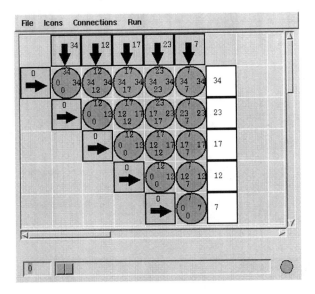

Figure 7.14   Runtime system, showing a program created with a language designed to simulate systolic algorithms

Each icon in the runtime workspace represents an instance of the class in which the icon attribute has resided. These instances each have a copy of all of their attributes (except of course for shared attributes, of which there is only one copy). These attribute values may be edited on an individual basis through each icon's pop-up menu.

Once a program has been created, it may be stored in a disk file through an option on the *File* pull-down menu. Similarly, previously stored files may be loaded for execution. Section 7.3.4 describes how similar actions can be added to the actions of rules.

7.6.2 Execution

The runtime system allows execution in two different styles: static and dynamic. In the static execution mode, rules are not matched and fired until the program is explicitly started through a selection on the *Run* pull-down menu. Static mode is indicated by a red circle in the lower right corner of the runtime window.

In the dynamic mode, any change to the workspace, the icons, or their attribute values begins an attempt to match and fire applicable rules. Execution is never explicitly started by the user. Dynamic mode (live mode) is indicated by a green circle in the lower right corner of the runtime window. If a language definition's rules include mouse click glyphs, the language requires the dynamic execution mode, since in the static mode the users' clicks would never be sent to the matching process.

Execution speed may be slowed by the scrollbar on the bottom of the runtime window. The value of this slider, which ranges from 0 to 2000, determines the number of milliseconds of delay between rounds of matching and firing. The default setting is 0, which should be suitable for most applications.

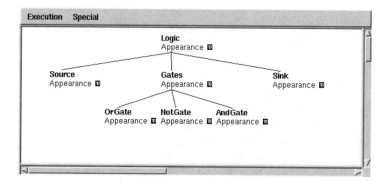

Figure 7.15   Class editor after the classes have been added, and the attribute Appearance has been added to Logic

7.7 EXAMPLES

We will present two sample language implementations. The first is a logic diagram language used to simulate simple electronic circuits. The second example will be an object-based controlflow language, similar in visual style to SunPict [Glinert and McIntyre 1989].

7.7.1 Logic Gate Language

The logic gate language requires sources of data values, sinks to show values, and various common logic gates such as AND, OR, and NOT. The language allows a user to place logic components into the runtime workspace, wire them together with connections, and simulate the circuit.

Adding the Classes   The necessary classes are broken down into three major subgroups: gates, sinks, and sources. The user starts the class editor, and when prompted for a base class name enters *Logic*. Three subclasses are added to Logic: (Gates, Sink, and Source), and three subclasses are added to Gates (And-Gate, OrGate and NotGate).

Adding the Appearance Attributes   All the classes have some sort of graphical appearance, so icon attributes are added to each class. An attribute named *Appearance* is added to the class Logic. When prompted with an attribute selection dialog box, the user selects the icon type. The hierarchy at this point is shown in Figure 7.15. Each of these icons will also show its current Boolean state, either TRUE or FALSE. This attribute, which will be visualized within the icon, must be added to the class before we can create the icon. The user adds an attribute named *State* of type Boolean, to the class Logic. Now the user edits the Appearance attribute, creating a small black rectangle.

Each classes' icon now needs some editing. Even the abstract superclasses like Logic require an appearance so that their instances can be placed into the rules as wildcards. In this logic language the Source icon is a black square and the Sink

Figure 7.16   Icons for the AndGate, OrGate, and NotGate classes. Note the connection
ports, shown in this figure as small shaded squares. The State attribute is not
visualized in this figure.

icon is a pink square, each with their State attribute value displayed in the middle. The user edits the Source icon (which inherits the black rectangle icon from Logic) and textually visualizes the State attribute in yellow. A port is added at the top of the icon for connection to other icons.

The Sink icon is then edited. The black rectangle inherited from Logic is replaced with a pink rectangle. The State attribute is textually visualized in black in the middle of the rectangle, and a connection port is added.

The icons for the three gate types are similar to the pictures used in schematic diagrams. Each has input and output ports.

First the AndGate is edited. The inherited black rectangle is again deleted and replaced with a crude sketch of a schematic AND. Two input ports and one output port are added to the edges of the figures. The State attribute is textually visualized in the center of the icon. This is repeated for the OrGate and the NotGate, resulting in the icons shown in Figure 7.16.

Once the icons have been drawn the class editor can graphically display all the icons in the hierarchy, as shown in Figure 7.17.

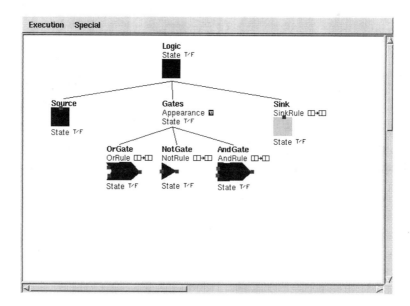

Figure 7.17   Class editor, with all logic gate icons defined and displayed graphically

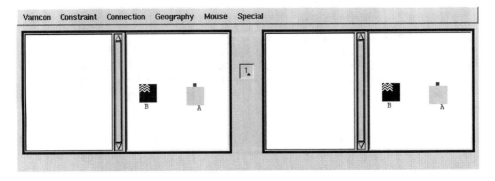

Figure 7.18   SinkRule after the icons have been added

Adding the Behavior of the Icons   The user must now determine the behavior of the icons. The rules used to do this mimic the behavior of the logic components in a Boolean logic circuit.

The simplest rule loads an incoming value into a sink icon. The user adds a rule attribute named *SinkRule* to the class Sink and edits it, starting the rule editor. Since this rule is about sinks, the users adds one to the center of the rule workspace by pulling down the *Icon* menu and choosing the *Add Icon LR+* selection. When the icon chooser appears with an instance of each icon in the hierarchy, the Sink icon is chosen. The user clicks the mouse in the graphical constraint portion of the rule to place the icon, and again to place the text label identifying the icon.

The other icon in the SinkRule must represent any icon to which the sink could possibly be attached. This can be represented by an icon of class Logic, since all the other classes are derived from Logic. The user again pulls down the *Icon* menu, but chooses *Add Fuzzy LR+* this time. The Logic icon is selected from the chooser and placed somewhere in the rule. Its textual label is placed nearby. The SinkRule is shown at this stage in Figure 7.18.

The abstract Logic icon must now be connected to the sink's port. Because the different classes derived from Logic have different port configurations (1 input and 1 output, 2 inputs and 1 output, etc.), the connection to the Logic icon must not be to any specific port. This can be done with a wildcard connection, one of the choices in the *Connection* menu.

Finally, the textual constraint and action must be added to the rule. Their meaning is simple: if the value of the logic icon is different than the one contained in the sink icon, copy the value over.

The following constraint ensures that the SinkRule fires only if it is presented with a value different than its current:

A State ~= B State

The following action copies the state of the icon labeled *B* (the abstract Logic icon) to the icon labeled *A* (the Sink icon):

A State: (B State).

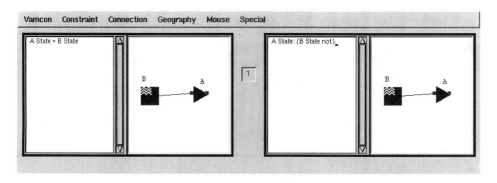

Figure 7.19   NotRule

The NotRule is very similar to the Sink rule, except for a slight difference in the textual constraint and action. The constraint

A State = B State

forces the rule to fire only if the icon supplying the input value has the same state as the NotGate. The action

A State: (B State not).

copies the negation of that state into the NotGate icon. The complete NotRule is shown in Figure 7.19.

The AndGate's rule is a little different because it contains two connections. Other than that, it is very similar to the NotRule and the SinkRule. This rule contains two fuzzy Logic icons and a single AndGate icon. Wildcard connections join the two abstract icons to the input ports of the AndGate icon. The constraint

A State ~= B State and: (C State)

fires the rule only when necessary, and the action

A State: (B State and: (C State)).

copies the conjunction of the input States to the State value of the AndGate icon. The complete AndRule is shown in Figure 7.20. The OrRule is exactly the same as the AndRule, with the substitution of *or:* for *and:* in the textual constraint and action.

Fanout of logic values from a single source to multiple gates is handled by these rules: any number of icons can request a value from the same source. However, multiple outputs can also be connected to a single input—current rule semantics do not provide a way to prevent this!

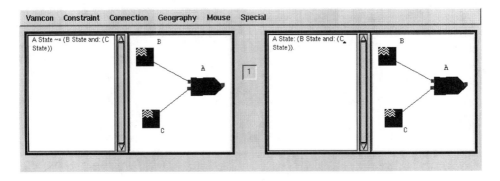

Figure 7.20   AndRule

Running the Application   At this point everything necessary to define the language has been completed. A "circuit" can now be composed from these icons.

The runtime application is started through a pull-down menu selection. As a sample application, the user places two Source icons, an AndGate icon and a Sink icon into the workspace using the *add* selection of the *Icons* menu, and connects them, via the *connect* selection of the *Connections* menu, as shown in Figure 7.21.

The value of any of the State attributes can be edited using a pull-down menu attached to each icon. Once any necessary changes have been made, the circuit can be run by pulling down the *Run* menu and selecting *execute*.   For a more

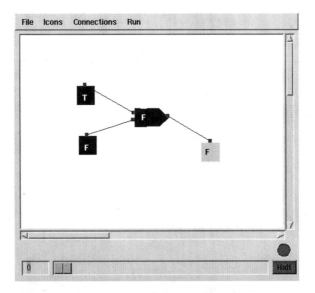

Figure 7.21   Simple logic diagram. Two sources feed values (one TRUE, one FALSE) to an AndGate, which sends the value FALSE to a sink.

dynamic demonstration the runtime application can be put into live mode by selecting *Live On* from the *Run* menu. When in this mode the circuit will instantly respond to any changes in the values within the circuit.

Although this sample circuit is quite simple, any circuit constructed from these iconic components can be simulated.

Extending the Language This logic-based dataflow language can easily become an object-flow language. The type of the State attribute could be changed into any type of arbitrary Smalltalk instance that responds to the *and:*, *or:*, and *not:* messages used by the constraints and actions in the rules.

7.7.2 Controlflow Example

This example will be a controlflow language similar in style to SunPict. It differs from the first example in that:

1 Icons are snapped to a grid in the workspace.

2 The programming style is controlflow, as opposed to dataflow.

In this visual programming language, an execution cursor will move over the icons in the program, indicating which is currently being executed. The icons will contain simple functions that input, output, and compute on integer variables. The controlflow language differs from the logic gate example in that data do not flow between icons; instead, the icons take turns executing sequentially.

Adding the Classes The base class for this language will be called *VamPict*. It will have two major subclasses, Blocks and VCursor (Smalltalk already includes a class named Cursor). Blocks will contain most of the functionality of the language; VCursor will provide the execution cursor which moves as the control flows through the program. The class Block will have the subclasses Control, Math, and InOut.

The classes Start and Stop will be derived from Control, and will delimit VamPict programs. From the InOut class, Input and Output will be derived, which provide the simplistic user interface, will be derived, and whatever mathematical functionality is required from Math. Figure 7.22 shows the VamPict class hierarchy after these classes have been constructed in the class editor.

Adding Attributes The VamPict language will use a symbol table to store variables' values within a program. Some classes, such as Input and Output, will have to store the name of the variable whose value they will affect. A string attribute named VarName, added to the class InOut, will hold this information. Most math icons will be able to affect up to three variable values, so three string attributes named VarName1, VarName2, and VarName3 will be added to Math.

As in the logic gate example, an icon attribute named *Appearance* will be added to the root class, in this case VamPict.

Each VamPict program's icons will all manipulate the same set of variables; the symbol table must therefore be shared amongst them. A shared Smalltalk object attribute of class Dictionary named *Symtable* is added to the root class. It can then be used as a *shared* or *global* attribute by all instances of all classes derived from the root.

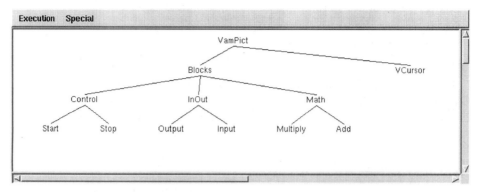

Figure 7.22   VamPict's hierarchy after all the classes have been added

Because the icons in a VamPict program will be positioned in a grid layout, the special attribute *Gridding* will be added to the VamPict class. This attribute indicates to the Vampire tools that icons may only be positioned at regular intervals. The default size of the interval is 50 pixels, but that may be overridden for any class with the GridSize attribute. Because the cursor will be larger than the rest of VamPict's icons, but must be able to move among the icons, a GridSize attribute will be added to Cursor and given a value of 10, which will allow it to be positioned between block icons.

Editing the Appearance Attributes   The VamPict icons are straightforward. The abstract superclass Blocks gets a simple white-bordered blue icon. Start is specialized by adding a green diamond, and Stop by adding a red octagonal stopsign.

The InOut icon is a white-bordered pink icon, with VarName displayed in yellow at its bottom. The Input and Output icons are distinguished by yellow arrows indicating flow into or out of the variable name.

The Math icon is a simple arrangement of the three variables names, with a textual = between the first and second names. Math's subclasses will specialize this icon by adding the operator symbols + or * between the second and third names.

Finally the VCursor icon becomes a simple 70-pixel unfilled orange square (10 pixels larger than the other icons on each side). This square will fit neatly around all the other icons.

Icon Behavior   VamPict will have two basic rules for the flow of its control: if there is an icon below the current icon, move the cursor down. If there is no icon below the current icon, but there is an icon to the right, move the cursor right. This can be specified using the two rules shown in Figures 7.23 and 7.24.

Note that the priority of the down rule is 2 and the priority of the right rule is 3. Through these priorities we can ensure that right motion will only happen if downward motion is not possible. There are four possible situations:

1   Only downward motion is possible. In this case, only the MoveDown rule will match the workspace, and it will fire after any priority 1 rules which match the workspace have been fired.

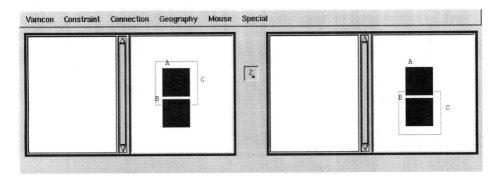

Figure 7.23 VamPict's downward motion rule

2 **Only right motion is possible**. In that case, only the MoveRight rule will match the workspace, and it will fire after any priority 1 and 2 rules which match the workspace have been fired.

3 **Both downward and right motion are possible**. In that case, both MoveDown and MoveRight rules will match. After any priority 1 rules which match have fired, MoveDown will be fired. This moves the execution cursor, and invalidates the mapping which was created by the MoveRight matching process. MoveRight is no longer a valid match, and the execution process continues.

4 **Neither downward nor right motion is possible**. In this case, no motion rules match or fire.

The icons used in both motion rules are Blocks, which will match any of the classes derived from them and hence any icon in the language.

While these two rules govern cursor motion once a cursor is in place, we need rules to both start and stop cursor motion. The rule which begins cursor motion is

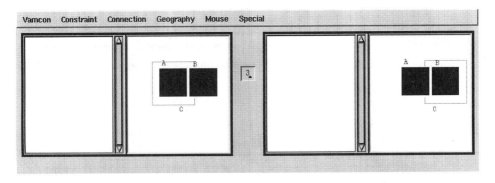

Figure 7.24 VamPict's rightward motion rule

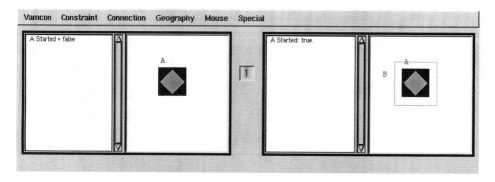

Figure 7.25   Start class' StartRule attribute

the StartRule rule attribute of the Start class. This rule causes a VCursor icon to appear around a Start icon. We add a Boolean attribute named *Started* to the Start class to limit the number of VCursors to one. The textual constraint on Started indicates that it must be FALSE for the rule to fire, and the textual action sets it to TRUE when the rule fires. Without this limiter, a new VCursor would appear at each runtime match/fire iteration. Figure 7.25 shows the StartRule.

The rule which ends cursor motion is the StopRule rule attribute of the Stop class. It is a very simple rule: if there is a VCursor icon around a Stop icon it is deleted. This rule is shown in Figure 7.26.

The InputRule is also quite simple, but uses the most complicated Smalltalk action of any shown so far in these examples. When the cursor is around an Input icon, the user is prompted for a value which is inserted into the symbol table at the proper variable name. The action is:

(A Symtable) at: (A VarName)
        put: ((DialogView request: 'Enter value for ',(A VarName)) asNumber).

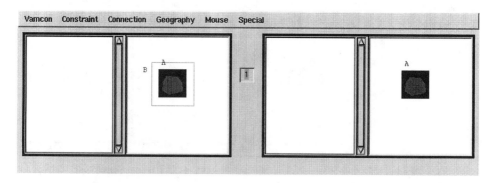

Figure 7.26   Stop class' StopRule attribute

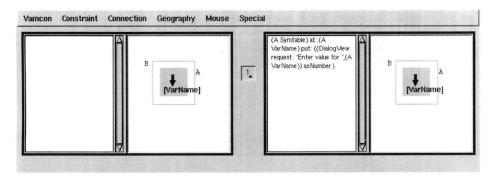

Figure 7.27   VamPict's InputRule, which uses a Smalltalk dialog box to prompt the user

This action takes advantage of Smalltalk's built-in dialogs to request the proper value from the user. The complete rule is shown in Figure 7.27.

The OutputRule is very similar, and is shown in Figure 7.28. The value is displayed in a standard Smalltalk pop-up dialog box.

The only other rules used in VamPict are those in each of the Math subclasses. They are all very similar, and have as their Smalltalk action

(A Symtable) at: (A VarName1) put:
    ((A Symtable) at: (A VarName2)) * ((A Symtable) at: (A VarName3)).

or a similar action with the * replaced by whatever the particular operation is for that class. The MultiplyRule is shown in Figure 7.29. The complete VamPict hierarchy is shown in Figure 7.30.

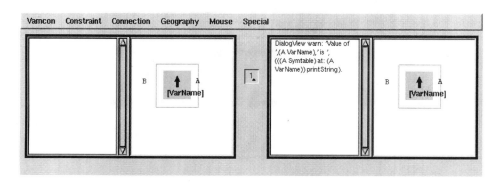

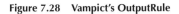
Figure 7.28   Vampict's OutputRule

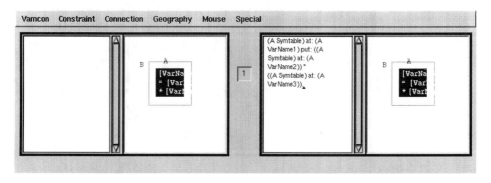

Figure 7.29   VamPict's MultiplyRule

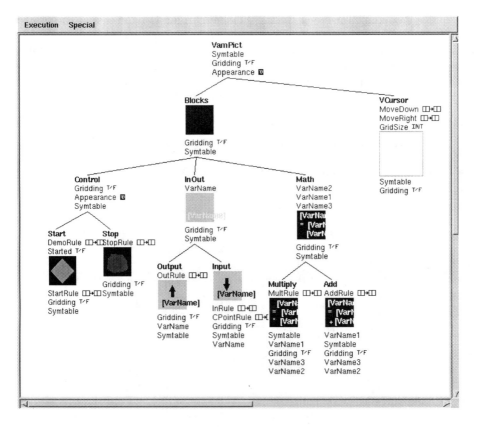

Figure 7.30   Complete VamPict hierarchy, after all attributes (including rules) have been added, with iconic attributes displayed graphically

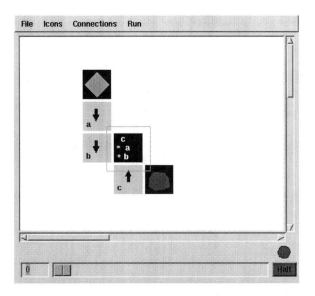

Figure 7.31   Sample VamPict program, which prompts the user for two values and displays their product in a dialog box, during execution (note execution cursor over multiply)

Running the Application   VamPict programs are constructed by placing strings of icons next to each other. In the example program in Figure 7.31, the user is prompted for two values whose product is returned.

Extending VamPict   Once the base VamPict language has been designed, it can be extended in many different ways. In this section, we will add subfunctions to the language definition. This extension will require the redefinition of the StopRule, and the addition of a new subclass of Block, the FCall.

As subprograms are called, information about the runtime stack must be stored in a global variable. We will therefore add a new shared variable to the VamPict class. *Stack* will be a Smalltalk object attribute of type OrderedCollection.

The FCall class will include a string attribute named *FName* which will store the name of the subprogram to load and execute. FCall will also contain a rule, *FCallRule*, which determines the runtime behavior of a function call. FCallRule has no textual constraints, but has a complicated action:

(A Symtable) at: #filename put: (runtime randomString).
runtime storeToFile: ((A Symtable) at: #filename).
(A Stack) addLast: (A Symtable).
A Symtable: Dictionary new. runtime clear.
runtime loadFromFile: (A FName).

We'll analyze this action line by line. The first line gets a random string from the runtime object, and inserts it into the symbol table at the variable name #filename. The second line stores the current runtime workspace contents into a file with this same name. The third line stores the current symbol table onto the stack. At this point all the necessary runtime information to return to this stack frame has been stored.

The fourth line sets up a new symbol table value for the new workspace about to be loaded. The fifth action clears the runtime workspace, which is then filled by the function indicated in the original FName attribute. Once this action has fired, the runtime workspace is reloaded with a new function, which then begins execution.

Corresponding changes must be made to the StopRule, in order to return from a subfunction call. The graphical portion of the rule remains the same, but the following textual action is added:

```
(A Stack size > 0) ifTrue: [
    A Symtable: A Stack removeLast.
    runtime clear.
    runtime loadFromFile: ((A Symtable) at: #filename).
].
```

This action first checks if there is are any frames on the stack; if there are none, nothing else is done. If there are, the symbol table is reloaded from the stack. The calling function's filename is restored from the symbol table, the runtime workspace is cleared, and the calling function is reloaded.

This example shows the flexibility available to language developers who use Vampire. Once a language has been designed, new features, including quite involved ones, are easily added to the language definition. The Smalltalk involved in this last extension is quite lengthy and complicated. However, the functionality added to the VamPict language is significant.

7.8 SUMMARY

This chapter has described Vampire, a new graphical means of rapidly implementing iconic visual programming languages. Vampire uses attributed graphical rules to describe the dynamic semantics of a visual programming language, and an object-oriented class hierarchy tree to describe its structure.

Vampire has several weaknesses (such as the lack of drag and drop and other advanced user interaction styles) which prevent it from representing all visual languages. Its inability to restrict legal syntax in a language prevents it from being able to produce a truly robust programming environment. It is, however, able to represent nearly every type of visual language presented in the visual programming literature. Section 7.7 highlights just two of these languages, which have very different appearances and semantics. Vampire is designed to be readily extensible, in the hopes that it will be able to readily adapt to new language paradigms and interactions as they are discovered.

We believe that systems such as Vampire will aid in the advancement of the field of visual programming by dramatically reducing the amount of programming necessary to test a new concept in iconic languages. Vampire provides heretofore unknown flexibility in the design and implementation of visual languages which we hope will promote the discovery of new and better languages!

REFERENCES

[Bell 1991] B. Bell, *Using Programming Walkthroughs to Design a Visual Language*, PhD thesis, University of Colorado, 1991.

[Bell and Lewis 1993] B. Bell and C. Lewis, "Chemtrains: A language for creating behaving pictures," in *Proceedings 1993 IEEE Symposium Visual Languages*, Bergen Norway, August 1993, pp. 188–195.

[Furnas 1990] G. W. Furnas, "Graphical reasoning for graphical interfaces," in *CHI '90 Technical Video Program—User Interface Technologies and Applications*, videotape, Seattle, 1990.

[Furnas 1991] G. W. Furnas, "New graphical reasoning models for understanding graphical interfaces.," in *Proceedings CHI '91*, New Orleans, April 1991, pp. 71–78.

[Glinert and McIntyre 1989] E. P. Glinert and D. W. McIntyre, "The user's view of SunPict, an extensible visual environment for intermediate-scale procedural programming," in *Fourth Israel Conference on Computer Systems and Software Engineering*, Israel, June 1989, pp. 49–58.

[Golin 1991] E. J. Golin, "Parsing visual languages with picture layout grammars," *J. Visual Languages and Computing*, Dec. 1991, Vol. 2, No. 4, pp. 371–394.

[Helm et al. 1991] R. Helm, K. Marriot, and M. Odersky, "Building visual language parsers," in *Proceedings CHI '91, New Orleans*, April 1991, pp. 105–112.

[McIntyre 1992] D. W. McIntyre, *A Visual Method for Generating Iconic Programming Environments*, PhD thesis, Rensselaer Polytechnic Institute, 1992.

[St.-Denis 1990] R. St.-Denis, "Specification by example using graphical animation and a production system," in *Proceedings 23rd Hawaii International Conference on Systems Science*, Hawaii, 1990, pp. 237–246.

CHAPTER 8 ❏ ❏ ❏ ❏

Seven Programming Language Issues

MARGARET M. BURNETT

CONTENTS

161

Visual object-oriented programming languages integrate object-oriented concepts with visual programming. The goal is to combine the strengths of those two approaches into a new, improved kind of language. Combining these strengths is challenging because incompatibilities—such as information hiding versus visibility—are difficult to resolve. This chapter enumerates and describes the importance of issues critical in the design of visual object-oriented programming languages. Ways to address some of these issues are illustrated with the language Forms/3.

8.1 INTRODUCTION

A strength of object-oriented programming (OOP) is its support for leveraging existing software. OOP classes can be used unchanged and easily can be extended for reuse in new applications. Visual programming can reduce the time and effort required to write and debug programs, and can increase the programmer's accessibility to information about the program's behavior. Designers of visual OOP systems—both languages and environments—aim to draw from the strengths of both of these approaches, but must avoid undermining the strengths of one in attempting to incorporate the other.

This chapter presents some of the issues that are specific to the design of visual OOP *languages*. Visual OOP languages are designed with different goals and with different parameters than are visual *environments* for textual OOP languages. The goal of visual environments is to add direct manipulation and visualization capabilities to the way in which programmers develop programs with a textual OOP language. The textual OOP language itself remains unchanged, although parts of it may be hidden or superseded by capabilities provided by the visual environment. In contrast, visual OOP languages are entirely new languages that combine the properties of OOP with the properties of visual programming. In creating a visual OOP language, the designer has the opportunity to devise a language that is designed specifically to mesh with the visual techniques he or she wishes to emphasize, and is not required to find ways to provide visual capabilities for a predefined language.

In the next section, we discuss characteristics of visual programming languages (VPLs). Next we introduce Forms/3 [Burnett 1991 and Burnett and Ambler 1994], a VPL that supports many of the central concepts of visual OOP, including data abstraction and data visibility, and that provides language support for interactivity. The rest of the chapter discusses issues in designing visual OOP languages, with sample solutions using Forms/3.

This work was partially supported by the National Science Foundation under Grants CCR-9215030/9396134 and CCR-9308649.

8.1.1 Characteristics of Visual Programming Languages

The goals of visual programming languages are to use graphics and other visual techniques to allow a programmer to express the desired logic of a program, to see or trace the changes in program state during execution, and to help the programmer understand how the program works. These goals cannot be realized solely by switching the user interface from using text tokens to using pictures. Rather, VPLs employ one or more of the following four characteristics to attain these goals:

- *Conceptual simplicity*   A VPL with this characteristic simplifies the programmer's view of the concepts of programming languages, emphasizing the logic directly pertinent to the application as versus programming mechanics. For example, most VPLs eliminate the need to consider event loops, storage allocation, and how scope rules dictate which object is referenced.

- *Concreteness*   A VPL may use concreteness to facilitate program creation, either in the form of the language elements or in how the elements are physically manipulated. For example, pointing directly at an element may be used instead of a name.

- *Explicitness*   A VPL with this characteristic shows relationships explicitly through diagrams and connections. Dataflow and constraint diagrams are typical examples.

- *Immediate visual feedback*   The extent to which this ability is provided in a VPL is called its degree of *liveness* [Tanimoto 1990]. A fully live VPL system automatically displays the effects of any program changes. There is no need to traverse through several levels of a data structure trying to access the object of interest, and there is no need to ask the system to update the information on the screen. The system automatically keeps all information on the screen up-to-date.

8.1.2 Overview of Forms/3

Forms/3 is a VPL for general-purpose programming. It supports user-defined abstractions that are programmed by direct manipulation of a mixture of graphics and text in a fully live environment, and it incorporates concrete examples and a minimum of concepts. Forms/3 has a strong orientation towards object-oriented technology because of its emphasis on data abstraction.[*]

Forms/3 incorporates a number of techniques originally devised for computer-based spreadsheets. In Forms/3, there are no variables; instead, *cells* hold objects. A programmer specifies a *formula* that computes the object that resides in the cell. Cells are organized into a group called a *form*. A Sample form is shown in Figure 8.1. One difference between Forms/3 and spreadsheets is that the programmer can add structure to a program by organizing the cells into forms. Other features of Forms/3 not found in spreadsheets are support for data abstraction,

---

[*] However, Forms/3 does not include inheritance or explicit message-passing.

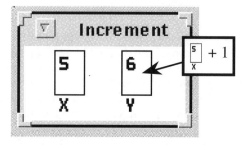

Figure 8.1 The user has created a new form with two cells and has named the form Increment. Each cell has a formula. Y's formula is X+1. The formula shown is superimposed on the actual screen snapshot.

procedural abstraction, polymorphic typing with type inference, and high-level events.

In Forms/3, data (values) and operations (formulas) are tightly intertwined. Every object resides in a cell and is defined declaratively in terms of a formula. Formulas may contain multiple cell references. An object can come into existence only through the formula defining it, and every formula results in an object. A way to think about a formula is as an operation that requests results from other objects (calculations and transformations) to achieve a new object. There is no explicit message-passing. Rather, an operation is expressed as a formula, and multiple operations are defined separately in multiple formulas, each of which results in a new object. The details of encapsulation, data privacy, and enforcement of appropriate use of an object type with multiple operations will be discussed in later sections.

The Forms/3 programmer enters a program by creating a new form (selecting from a menu of language manipulation options), naming it, instantiating cells copied from a palette on the form, and defining formulas. The programmer entered the formulas for the cells in Figure 8.1 by selecting cell X and typing 5 and then the return key; and selecting cell Y, clicking on X, and typing +1 and the return key. Just as in spreadsheet programming, when entering the formula for Y, the programmer could have typed the cell name X instead of clicking on it. However, names are not required for cells, since all references can be performed by direct manipulation.

The presence of text in Forms/3 formulas is a feature of Forms/3. Forms/3 does not aim to eliminate text entirely. Its objective is to use visual techniques, such as direct manipulation and continuous visual feedback, with a flexible mixture of text and graphics, to enhance the concreteness of programming. For example, direct manipulation is part of the language dynamics, and its purpose is to remove a level of indirection from the process of referencing cells. However, sometimes text is more convenient, and for this reason it is also possible for the programmer to name cells and to refer to them by these textual names if desired. The approach of mixing text with graphics allows programmers to switch flexibly between direct manipulation and keyboard entry. Another example of this flexible mixture is the fact that the textual operations often seen in the formulas are actually optional

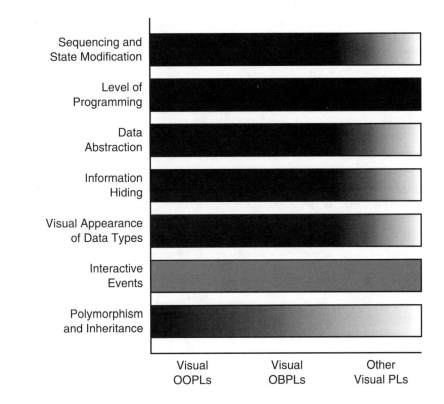

Figure 8.2   This figure summarizes the issues discussed in this chapter, and compares their presence in visual object-oriented programming languages with other kinds of visual programming languages. Intensity of shading reflects the extent to which a language is affected. For example, information hiding is an issue for all visual object-oriented programming languages (Visual OOPLs in the figure), all visual object-based programming languages (Visual OBPLs), and some other visual programming languages.

shortcuts (reminiscent of keyboard shortcuts for menu items) for pointing at cells on primitive forms defining these operations. There are also purely visual facets of Forms/3, including continuous visual feedback, scope rules that are defined and communicated entirely through visual mechanisms, and graphical data types.

Research prototypes of Forms/3 have been implemented for Sun 3/160s and SPARCstation color workstations using Lucid Common Lisp and the CLX interface to X Windows. The user interface described here was not present in these early prototypes, and a new implementation of the system that includes this user interface is currently being developed using the Garnet system [Myers et al. 1990].

8.1.3 The Issues

In considering how to design a visual language based on OOP concepts, a number of programming language issues arise. We explore seven such issues, listed in Figure 8.2 and briefly stated here:

- *Sequencing and state modification*   How can visual OOP languages provide visual ways to specify the semantics of message sends, ways that help programmers determine the correct sequence of messages that create the desired system state?

- *Programming at both high and low levels*   How can new artifacts—that require new system parts—be defined in a way that is perceived to be as straightforward and mechanically as simple as visual construction with existing parts?

- *Data abstraction*   Many VPLs employ concreteness. But how can abstract data types be specified in a concrete way?

- *Information hiding*   How can the principles of information hiding be preserved while at the same time providing the visibility of objects and their private data needed to program using direct manipulation?

- *Visual appearance of data types*   How should objects in a visual OOP language—from inherently visual widgets to abstract, user-defined objects—be displayed on the screen?

- *Interactive events*   How can a visual OOP language support event handling—needed to allow programmers to express the system's response to user actions—in a way that meshes well with the conceptual simplicity sought by many visual OOP language designers?

- *Polymorphism and inheritance*   Can a visual OOP language provide explicit visual representations that aid the programmer both in keeping track of the messages to which an object responds, and in finding the method in the inheritance hierarchy that is (dynamically) bound to a given message send?

8.2 ISSUE 1: SEQUENCING AND STATE MODIFICATION

One of the areas of programming that has historically caused problems for programmers is sequencing of instructions or messages that perform state modification. Since incorrect sequencing of state modifications produces incorrect behavior and results, it is important for programmers to be able to understand and track these sequences. In visual OOP languages, visual techniques are needed that help programmers understand how messages causing state changes affect later object interactions.

One approach to tracking sequences of messages is to make message-passing explicit, as in visual OOP languages such as MFL [Cox and Pietrzykowski 1992] that are based on message-flow diagrams. Another successful approach eliminates the need to track either sequencing or state modification by eliminating the programmer's involvement with their semantics. This is handled through a declarative approach. Basically, state modification is avoided by using single assignment: the programmer creates a new object copied from an existing one with the desired differences, rather than modifying the existing object's state. Also, instead of specifying state change sequences, the programmer defines operations by specifying object dependencies. For example, if the programmer defines Y to be $X + 1$, this explicitly states that Y is to be computed using the object residing in X, which allows the system to infer that X's value must be computed before Y. Since circular definitions are not allowed in most declarative languages, the system will always be able to derive a legal sequence of computations from these stated dependencies that produces answers to the programmer's specifications. Thus sequence is present, but must be derived by the system rather than by the programmer.

Although on the surface this approach seems simpler in many ways than approaches based on state modification, the declarative notion of single assignment is sometimes cumbersome, particularly in complex applications. Visual representations, if not carefully structured, exacerbate this complexity. As the size of a program increases, imagine the difficulty for a programmer to keep track of which of dozens of versions of an object on the screen is the most current one. There is no reason why a programmer should be burdened with this task, as it is more about mechanics than about specifying the logic needed to solve the problem.

To address the issue of mutable state in a manner that is amenable to visual techniques, Forms/3 combines declarative semantics with a time dimension in an approach that can be described as vectors in time. Each vector describes a sequence of objects that are defined for a cell.[*] Returning to the example in which $Y = X + 1$, if X defines a time vector of numeric objects such as <1 2 3 4 5>, then Y defines a time vector <2 3 4 5 6>. The programmer may move backward and forward along the time dimension using direct manipulation of a global time-index slider bar to examine the different objects in the vectors over time. Each cell's vector contains a complete and accessible history of state modifications. This technique adds consistency and structure. Consistency comes by virtue of the dependencies given in the definitions, which are automatically kept up-to-date in the usual spreadsheet-like manner. (This automatic updating is the same as the "one-way constraints" found in the OOP system Garnet [Myers et. al 1990]). Structure comes from the fact that the values for one cell are all stored together in a time vector that can be browsed, and from the fact that each object is stored in its proper context in relation to other cells' objects by virtue of its position in the time dimension. Moving through time in one cell causes the related cells to move through time synchronously.

Prior values in time can be exploited in formulating time-based solutions to problems. An example is a time-based approach to finding the nth number in the Fibonacci sequence, shown in Figure 8.3. *Earlier* is one of several time-based operators in Forms/3. These operators can be entered textually, or the programmer can point to cells on a built-in *Earlier* form.

---

[*] This approach has similarities to the dataflow and functional stream-based programming approaches, but it differs from them in that there is no notion of movement nor of values being consumed in time-based vectors.

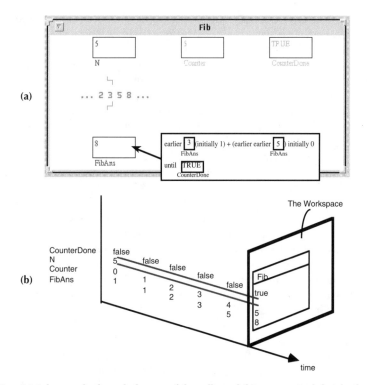

Figure 8.3   (a) A form and a formula for one of the cells, and (b) a conceptual sketch of the workspace in time

8.3 ISSUE 2: PROGRAMMING AT BOTH HIGH AND LOW LEVELS

There are a number of visual languages that are not complete programming languages—that is, it is not possible to write and maintain an entire program in these languages. Instead, the purpose is to use visual manipulation to combine textually-programmed application modules. Visual programming is done only at a high level. Examples of this approach include the visual OOP system HI-VISUAL [Hirakawa et al. 1991] and the AVS system for scientific visualization [Upson et al. 1989].

At the opposite end of the spectrum is the kind of VPL that allows programming only at the lowest level. This kind of language may have all the capabilities needed to express all the fine-grained logic needed in a program, including conditionals and repetition (recursion or iteration), but no way to organize portions of the program into modules or to create generalizations. Most VPLs of this nature are intended for very limited problem domains. They provide a number of primitives for their particular domains, thereby keeping most programs small enough to avoid the need for user-defined abstractions. One example is the NoPump system for interactive graphics [Wilde and Lewis 1990].

However, if a programming language is to scale up to large programming projects, it must support both high-level and low-level programming. Without high-level capabilities, the programmer can be quickly overwhelmed by an unstructured mass of detailed code and, without low-level capabilities, the programmer is limited to tasks that can be accomplished with prewritten modules.

In Forms/3, low-level programming is done via formulas. High-level programming equivalent to procedural abstraction is accomplished by collecting a group of related cells together on a form. Collecting cells together on a form provides a way of organizing a program. This ability is useful initially during development and testing as a way of staying organized. It is also useful later for code reuse purposes, since forms created in this way can be generalized and reused in a way analogous to the use of parameterized procedures.

At first glance, these forms may appear too concrete to be generally useful. Consider again Figure 8.3, which shows a form to compute the nth number of the Fibonacci sequence. The programmer defined N's formula to be the constant 5. This sample value 5 is important during development because it allows immediate visual feedback based on a "sample" of the Fibonacci computation. In Forms/3, cells on the screen calculate as soon as the needed data is available. Cell *FibAns*, based on N, could immediately calculate its value in the presence of the sample value 5. This helps the programmer see results and use those results to eliminate potential errors. But although they use direct manipulation and concrete sample values extensively and without restriction during development, programmers do so with the expectation that the program they enter in this concrete fashion will work the same way for any future values that might someday replace the sample values.

To fulfill this expectation of generality, the dependencies in the concrete versions of the forms are analyzed by the system to deduce which cells serve as parameters and which serve as return values [Yang and Burnett 1994]. The dependencies provide enough information to allow these deductions without inference. Because of this, the programmer does not participate in the generalization process. Instead, to reuse a form, the programmer simply copies it, enters new values or formulas on the copy via direct manipulation, and refers to cells on this new copy as needed by pointing at them with a mouse. The automatic transformation of concrete forms into generalized forms is especially important in allowing reuse of recursive forms, since otherwise some of the cell references would be overly concrete or circular.

8.4 ISSUE 3: DATA ABSTRACTION

Data abstraction is the basic concept of object-oriented programming, and is present in all OOP languages. However, supporting data abstraction in a visual OOP language must be done in a way that is consistent with the visual paradigm used in that language. Approaches such as declaring new classes using an underlying textual implementation language or generating textual code from visual specifications—while they do provide data abstraction—weaken a visual language, because they force the programmer to use a second (textual) language for part of the programming task.

In order for data abstraction to fit seamlessly into a visual OOP language, its use of visual techniques must be consistent with the rest of that language. For Forms/3, this requirement translated into the following goals: the *process* of creating, changing and debugging a new abstract data type should be as interactive and visual as the rest of the language; the *type definition* resulting from the visual process of programming should itself be visual, so that it can be reviewed and changed using the same visual techniques with which it was originally created; and the *objects* resulting from this visual definition should be visual and accessible interactively. The third characteristic implies that the appearance of such objects is visual, that a type's appearance is part of its definition, and that a type definition includes specifications about its behavior under user interaction.[*]

Forms/3's approach to providing visual support for data abstraction is based on a notion called *visual abstract data types* (VADT), combined with information hiding. A VADT conceptually is the 4-tuple: (components, operations, graphical representations, interactive behaviors). The third and fourth elements of the tuple represent the differences between the concept of a VADT and the traditional textual concept of an abstract data type, in that they require a VADT's definition to include its appearance and interactive behaviors. Although it is possible to view them both as special cases of operations, doing so ignores the fact that all objects in a visual language eventually appear on the screen. Providing for this eventuality is therefore a requirement.

Following Liskov and Guttag's lead [Liskov and Guttag 1986], we will use the term visual abstract data type for both system- and user-defined types. This emphasizes the fact that the two groups are essentially the same. Both system- and user-defined VADTs have a defined interface in which the implementation details are hidden. The only difference is that there is no mechanism that allows the programmer to find out how the system-defined VADTs are implemented; the types used in their construction are base implementation primitives (e.g., bits and pixels), and are neither included in the language definition nor apparent in any way to the programmer.

Figure 8.4 shows a copy of a form defining a Forms/3 built-in VADT. The programmer can instantiate boxes by making more copies of the box definition form, and referencing the cells on it. This approach has philosophical similarities to prototype-based languages, since the definition of a type is tightly coupled with at least one sample instance of the type.[†]

---

[*] This is a departure from approaches that advocate separating visual appearances from interactive behavior and from underlying data, such as the Model-View-Controller (MVC) paradigm [Krasner and Pope 1988].

[†] In this approach, the definition of a group of objects is done by using one concrete object (instead of a class) as a prototype. Self [Ungar and Smith 1987] is the best-known language of this kind.

```
                          1029-BOX
 ▽
 ┌──────────────┐    These cells can be used to find out
 │              │    information about aBox:
 └──────────────┘
  aBox
                    ┌──────┐ ┌──────┐ ┌────────┐ ┌────────┐
                    │70    │ │30    │ │Black   │ │        │
                    └──────┘ └──────┘ └────────┘ └────────┘
                     width?   height?  lineColor?  fillColor?


                    ABox appears on the screen like this:

                                     ┌──────────┐
                                     │          │
                                     └──────────┘
                                        image


 ┌──────────────┐    These cells can be used to set
 │              │    certain attributes of anotherBox.
 │              │    Any attributes not set by your
 │              │    program will be the same as those of
 └──────────────┘    aBox:
  anotherBox
                    ┌──────┐ ┌──────┐ ┌────────┐ ┌────────┐
                    │100   │ │50    │ │Black   │ │Red     │
                    └──────┘ └──────┘ └────────┘ └────────┘
                     width    height   lineColor   fillColor
```

Figure 8.4   This copy of the built-in form *Box* contains two atomic box objects (in cells *aBox* and *anotherBox*). Every operation is located in a cell that both defines a behavior and produces a new object. For example, an operation such as *width?* (top of the form) reports information about the box in *aBox*, but also produces the number 70. An operation such as *width* (bottom of the form) affects the construction of the box in *anotherBox* because of the underlying implementation of *anotherBox*, but also produces the number 100. The form title *1029-Box* reflects the fact that this form is a copy of the original *Box* form.

8.4.1 Programming a New Visual Abstract Data Type in Forms/3

In the same manner that all programming is done in Forms/3, a new VADT is defined by placing cells and groups of cells on a form. A form defining a VADT is termed a *VADT definition form*. Each cell on a VADT definition form defines an operation and also produces an object. The only difference between a VADT definition form and other forms is that a VADT definition form contains two distinguished items. One of these defines in detail the physical parts of the type via an *abstraction box*, and the other is a distinguished cell—called the *image cell*—whose formula defines the appearance of all objects of the new type. The formula

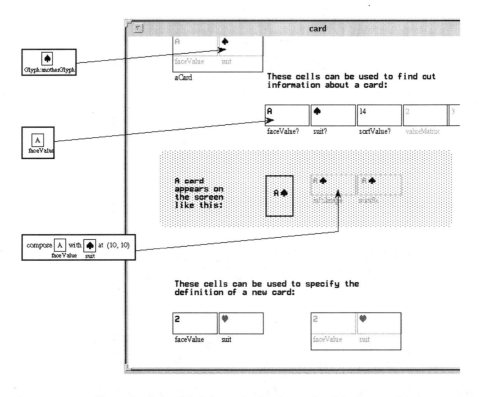

Figure 8.5   *Card* form. The distinguished abstraction box is *aCard,* and the image cell is the unnamed cell in the shaded area of the figure to the right of the phrase "A card appears on the screen like this:"

that defines the appearance can contain as complex behavior specifications as desired, resulting in graphical, textual, or even animated appearances. An abstraction box contains a number of cells, each of whose formula defines some part of the object. It can be described as the equivalent of a record or structure definition because it defines all the slots of the VADT, or it can be described as a constructor operator because it produces an atomic object of the VADT. The programmer defines additional operations by adding more cells and abstraction boxes to the form.

We demonstrate the use of these devices with a simple example in which the programmer will visually create a card VADT. To create a new card VADT, the programmer starts by creating a new VADT definition form (via button selection), naming it "card." The distinguished abstraction box and the image cell are automatically created by the system and placed on the form (as shown in Figure 8.5). The programmer defines formulas for these cells and places additional cells on the form, defining their formulas as needed. The distinguished abstraction box *aCard* contains two cells, *faceValue* and *suit.* The programmer chose sample values for these cells by providing a constant formula *A* for cell *faceValue,* and a reference to a pixmap for cell *suit.* Pixmaps are called *glyphs* in Forms/3. Like the box type shown earlier, the glyph is a built-in type defined by a built-in form. The desired shape of the glyph is hand-drawn by the programmer with a simple bitmap editor. The pixmap that results is stored in a cell on a copy of the definition form for glyphs, and is referenced in the formula for cell *suit.*

Continuing with the definition of operations for cards, the programmer adds another abstraction box near the bottom of the form. Such additional abstraction boxes on a form must have the same structure as the distinguished abstraction box (*aCard*). Each abstraction box on form *card*, by virtue of its presence on that form, results in an instance of type "card." The purpose of the second abstraction box is to define a card based upon the original card (*aCard*), but with a different face value and suit. This example is a bit contrived, but it is included here to demonstrate an operation that declaratively creates a new object from an existing one.

8.5 ISSUE 4: INFORMATION HIDING

Information hiding means that the internal implementation details of an abstract data type are not accessible to the rest of the program. Information hiding is an inherent part of data abstraction, but it is presented here as an issue in its own right because of the conflict it raises with the visibility of VPLs. Forms/3's strategy for addressing this conflict is to use physical visibility both to communicate and to enforce logical visibility. In Forms/3, a cell can be referenced by the programmer only if it can be seen. The inspiration for this approach comes from the "in the wings" performers of the visual OOP system Rehearsal World [Finzer and Gould 1984]. In the "wings" approach, the programmer restricts access by moving an object to a special location. Forms/3 has no special location. Rather, the visibility of each cell is an attribute of that cell, that can be specified either by the programmer or by the system. The system then uses this information to control when the cell is accessible.

To briefly summarize how this technique works, every cell can be seen at all times unless it is *hidden.* In Figure 8.3, the two cells *Counter* and *CounterDone* are hidden cells. The fact that they are hidden is reflected in the figure by their lighter colors. (Depending on the capabilities of the workstation, other devices such as dotted borders depict that the cell is hidden.) These two cells were hidden by the programmer because they contain computations that are necessary to the implementation but are not necessary to the use of the *Fibonacci* form. Hidden cells can be referenced only after they are made visible. Figure 8.6 shows the same form as Figure 8.3 without the hidden cells visible, which is the way the form would normally appear to the application user.

8.5.1 Cells That are Hidden by Definition

Any cell can be designated hidden by the programmer. There are also two kinds of cells that are hidden by definition—those located inside abstraction boxes, and

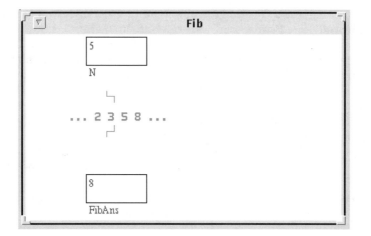

Figure 8.6   In contrast to the same form shown in Figure 8.3, the hidden cells are not visible here.

those located on attached subforms. An *attached subform* is a form that has been attached to supplement the calculations of another form. Attached subforms are similar to local subroutines in procedural languages in that they provide a way to further modularize the computations being performed on the form to which they are attached.

8.5.2 How a Hidden Cell Becomes Visible

Hidden cells are automatically made visible by the system when the programmer is defining a formula for another cell on the same form or on a subform attached to it. They cannot be seen at any other time. Thus, they are accessible only in the context of the implementation.

Hidden cells can also be made visible by the programmer on an ad hoc basis, to allow investigation into the workings of the code for debugging. To do this, the programmer requests (via checkbox selection) a temporary display of the hidden cells on a form. When the programmer makes a hidden cell visible in this fashion, it can be referenced from other forms on the screen, but these references are valid only as long as the hidden cell remains on the screen. Ad hoc calculations can thus be done as flexibly for a hidden cell as for any other kind of cell, despite their inaccessibility during normal usage. Ad hoc calculations do *not* provide a general mechanism for circumventing information hiding, because the only way to perform these calculations is via direct manipulation of cells currently on the screen. There is no way for such calculations to become a permanent part of a program. An advantage of this approach is that it does not rely on "debugging modes" or independent debugging tools.

8.6 ISSUE 5: THE RUNTIME VISUAL APPEARANCE OF OBJECTS

How an object can be viewed occupies a central role in visual languages. In Forms/3, the visual appearance of a VADT is included in its definition. The way a Forms/3 object appears is entirely flexible. It can be based on any combination of objects in the system. The specification of this appearance is a simple matter of providing a formula that defines the desired visual arrangement of objects in the image cell. The image cell is distinguished, and must be present on every VADT definition form, as it dictates the way all instances of the type appear on the screen.

In the card example presented earlier, the image cell specifies the appearance of *all* cards. Suppose the formula for some *cellX* on the screen results in a card. This means that the system must consult the image formula to decide how to display the object in *cellX*. To accomplish this, the system internally reuses or creates an instance of form *card* in which cell *aCard* is a reference to *cellX*, and calculates the image cell on that form instance. The result of that evaluation is used to display the contents of *cellX*. (The new form instance is not itself automatically displayed, but it is possible for the programmer to select it for viewing from the list of forms.)

In Forms/3, evaluation is done lazily, and an object is computed only if needed. Computation takes place if an object that has not been computed before is needed for display on the screen, or if the object is needed to finish computing something else that is needed. Because of this lazy approach, only the image cell on the new copy is calculated, along with the other cells needed by the image cell's formula. The other cells on the new copy such as *faceValue?* are not needed and therefore not evaluated.

The image cell is entirely flexible. There are no restrictions on which operators to use, or on what kinds of objects to compose. The images can be any arbitrary combination of text and graphics. If the programmer wants to have alternative displays, the formula for the image cell would include a conditional expression such as:

if <circumstances> then *anotherGlyph* else...

In the card examples, cards have been displayed by composing their face value, suit, and a box. To conditionally display cards face down, cell *anotherGlyph* on one of the *Glyph* form instances would contain a pixmap designed to look like the flip side of a card. Although this example is very simple, the image formula can be arbitrarily complex, including conditional compositions of images predicated on many different combinations of objects.

The declarative aspect of the Forms/3 model means that a cell does not change state per se, but its time-based vector of components represents a sequence of objects over time. Since the formula of the image cell is normally based on the current object in that vector, a rudimentary form of animation is inherent in the approach.

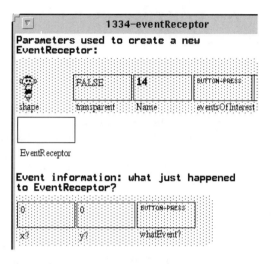

Figure 8.7   **The event receptor built-in type**

8.7 ISSUE 6: INTERACTIVE EVENTS

In visual OOP languages, the programmer may quite reasonably expect to be able to write programs in which the user can interact with the objects displayed on the screen. To accomplish this, the programmer must be able to specify interactive user events. This requires language support for event-handling. This support must be provided in a way that is consistent with the other goals of the language. It must also be high-level, because otherwise a program of any size could easily become overcrowded with low-level, event-handling detail.

To support high-level event handling in Forms/3, event detection, events themselves, and other objects, are all computable objects—no different from any other kinds of objects. There is no distinction between event-based programming and any other kind of programming. Formulas that use event objects to produce their results contain the desired response to the events. Forms/3 builds this approach on a primitive VADT called an event receptor (displayed in Figure 8.7). It is the only kind of object in the language capable of receiving interactive events, and can be composed with other VADTs to construct complex interactive VADTs.

The VADT form in Figure 8.8 defines an abstract data type called a Window. The definitions of each cell are very simple. For example, the appearance of any instance of a window is defined by the window's image cell (bottom of Figure 8.8), and is simply the composition of a box with all the objects on the window at their computed x- and y-positions. The objects composing the window (middle of the form) are references to as many other objects as desired (three sample values are shown here), and their x- and y-positions. The objects on the window are instances of a user-defined VADT called an imageMover, which have been defined to include event receptors so that interactive operations—such as dragging them about on the window with the mouse—are possible. Abstractions such as dragging are

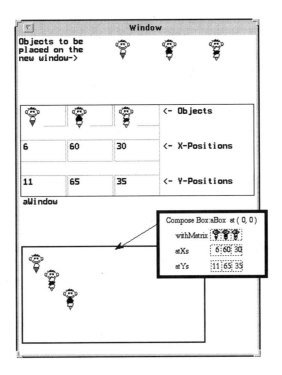

Figure 8.8   Three objects in a window

defined by the programmer using formulas built up from primitive event information reported by the event receptor. Figure 8.9 shows the time-history data of moving such an object on the window. Since the window's image is defined in terms of
each object, changes to an object's position also cause changes to the image as
shown in the figure.

There are two important differences that this approach has from approaches to
event-handling in textual OOP languages. First, there is no event loop from the
point of view of the Forms/3 programmer. Instead, all event-related programming
is done the same way nonevent-related programming is done—no paradigm shift
is required. Second, the data and operations are not separated from interactive
behavior or from appearance. These are integrated in a VADT's definition. The
code is still well modularized because all interactive behavior is handled by the
event receptors incorporated in the type definition, and because the specification
of visual appearance is always encapsulated in the image cell.

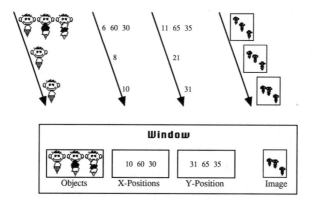

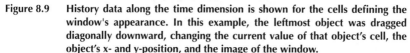

Figure 8.9   **History data along the time dimension is shown for the cells defining the window's appearance. In this example, the leftmost object was dragged diagonally downward, changing the current value of that object's cell, the object's x- and y-position, and the image of the window.**

8.8 ISSUE 7: POLYMORPHISM AND INHERITANCE

Polymorphism has long been a strength of OOP. There are several different kinds of polymorphism, but they share a common goal—writing code that is applicable to more than one type. Polymorphism is supported in OOP by inheritance and by dynamic binding. This combination provides the benefits of expressive power, especially during program construction, but can detract from programmer understanding during program maintenance.

The kind of polymorphism in OOP that comes from inheritance is called *inclusion polymorphism*. For example, in Smalltalk-80 [Goldberg and Robson 1986], if a class *SortedList* is defined as a subclass of *List*, *SortedList* reuses the messages originally specified for *List* by virtue of inheritance. A second kind of polymorphism comes from dynamic binding—an operation that involves sending messages to each element of a list is polymorphic when all the elements in the list can respond to the same enumerated message. This kind of polymorphism exists, for example, if *SortedList* can contain any kind of element that responds to the messages < and =. The kind of polymorphism in which the arguments of a message can be objects of multiple types is called *parametric polymorphism*. For example, in CLOS [Keene 1989], arguments of an if-then-else message—a "then" expression and an "else" expression—can be any type.

Hierarchies of classes are intentionally abstract. And dynamic binding, without static type-checking, does not allow immediate feedback at program-entry time as to whether the code will execute. These factors lead to the well-known *yo-yo* problem, in which the programmer must exert considerable effort traveling up and down the inheritance tree to track down exactly *which* set of methods will be invoked in responding to a polymorphic message (c.f. [Budd 1990]). The alternative to classes and inheritance—delegation and prototypes—avoids the abstractness of class hierarchies but still does not solve the yo-yo problem. Although some environments offer debugging tools to help programmers with this problem, such tools do not solve the problem, they merely provide access to information for the programmer who is attempting to track down methods. The issue in visual OOP languages is to maintain the polymorphism needed in OOP, while at the same time providing the programmer with concrete information and immediate feedback.

Forms/3 offers a partial solution to the need for concrete communication with the programmer about polymorphic types in its approach to parametric polymorphism. To provide immediate feedback to the programmer, static type-checking is used to verify the type safety of a formula, as soon as it is entered. Because of this, only type-correct formulas may be entered, which prevents errors such as arithmetic operations on nonnumeric objects. However, the programmer does not enter type declarations; instead, the system automatically gathers type information via incremental type inference, which is performed immediately whenever the programmer enters a new formula. This approach to type-checking builds upon recent research in the functional and object-oriented programming language arenas. However, Forms/3 uses a more concrete type system than is found in these languages to avoid requiring that the programmer grapple with type-theoretic concepts such as function types, subtypes, recursive types, and the like [Burnett 1993]. Fabrik [Ingalls et al. 1988; Ludolph et al. 1988] and Visa-Vis [Poswig and Moraga 1993] are other examples of VPLs with type systems supported by type inference.

8.9 SUMMARY

We have explored seven programming language issues that are critical to visual OOP languages, and we have presented approaches that address some of these issues in the VPL Forms/3. The characteristics of immediate visual feedback, concreteness, explicitness, and conceptual simplicity are used by VPLs to improve the programmer's ability to express, see, and understand a program. The challenge to visual OOP language designers is to maintain these characteristics when providing support for the features needed for OOP, such as data abstraction, polymorphism, and inheritance. The result of meeting this challenge may be that, by using these characteristics to improve the areas where OOP has been most abstract and complex, and by using OOP's strengths in enabling VPLs to scale up to large problems, new programming languages will emerge that are better than either OOP or visual programming alone.

ACKNOWLEDGEMENTS

I would like to thank the referees for their helpful comments on earlier drafts. I especially thank Adele Goldberg and Marla Baker for their help in improving and editing this chapter.

REFERENCES

[Budd 1990] T. Budd, *An Introduction to Object-Oriented Programming*, Addison-Wesley, Reading, MA, 1990.

[Burnett 1991] M. M. Burnett, *Abstraction in the Demand-Driven, Temporal-Assignment, Visual Language Model*, PhD thesis, University of Kansas Computer Science Department, August 1991.

[Burnett 1993] M. M. Burnett, "Types and type inference in a visual programming language," *1993 IEEE Symposium on Visual Languages*, Bergen, Norway, August 24–27, 1993, pp. 238–243.

[Burnett and Ambler 1994] M. M. Burnett and A. L. Ambler, "Interactive visual data abstraction in a declarative visual programming language," *Journal of Visual Languages and Computing*, Vol. 5., No. 1, March 1994, pp. 29–60.

[Cox and Pietrzykowski 1992] P. Cox and T. Pietrzykowski, "Visual message flow language MFL and its interface," in *Proceedings of the Interantional Workshop AVI'92: Advanced Visual Interfaces* (T. Catarci, M. Costabile, and S. Levialdi), World Scientific Press, Singapore, 1992.

[Finzer and Gould 1984] W. Finzer and L. Gould, "Programming by rehearsal," *Byte*, Vol. 9, No. 6, June 1984, pp. 187–210.

[Goldberg and Robson 1986] A. Goldberg and D. Robson, *Smalltalk-80: The Language,* Addison-Wesley, Reading, MA, 1986.

[Hirakawa et al. 1991] M. Hirakawa, Y. Nishimura, M. Kado, and T. Ichikawa, "Interpretation of icon overlapping in iconic programming," *Proceedings of the 1991 IEEE Workshop on Visual Languages*, Kobe, Japan, October 8–11, 1991, pp. 254–259.

[Ingalls et al. 1988] D. Ingalls, S. Wallace, Y.-Y. Chow, F. Ludolph, and K. Doyle, "Fabrik, a visual programming environment," *Proceedings of OOPSLA 88*, San Diego, also *ACM SIGPLAN Notices*, Vol. 23, No. 11, November 1988, pp. 176–190.

[Keene 1989] S. E. Keene, *Object-Oriented Programming in Common Lisp: A Programmer's Guide to CLOS*, Addison-Wesley, Reading, MA, 1989.

[Krasner and Pope 1988] G. E. Krasner and S. T. Pope, "A cookbook for using the model-view-controller user interface paradigm in Smalltalk-80," *Journal of Object-Oriented Programming*, Vol. 1, No. 3, August 1988, pp. 26–49.

[Liskov and Guttag 1986] B. Liskov and J. Guttag, *Abstraction and Specification in Program Development*, MIT Press and McGraw-Hill, New York, 1986.

[Ludolph et al. 1988] F. Ludolph, Y.-Y. Chow, D. Ingalls, S. Wallace, K. Doyle, "The Fabrik programming environment," *1988 IEEE Workshop on Visual Languages*, Pittsburgh, PA, October 1988, pp. 222–230.

[Myers et al. 1990] B. Myers, D. Guise, R. Dannenberg, B. Vander Zanden, D. Kosbie, E. Pervin, A. Mickish, and P. Marchal, "Garnet: Comprehensive support for graphical, highly interactive user interfaces," *Computer*, November 1990, pp. 71–85.

[Poswig and Moraga 1993] J. Poswig and C. Moraga, "Incremental type systems and implicit parametric overloading in visual languages," *1993 IEEE Symposium on Visual Languages*, Bergen, Norway, August 24–27, 1993, pp. 126–133.

[Tanimoto 1990] S. L. Tanimoto, "Towards a theory of progressive operators for live visual programming environments," *1990 IEEE Computer Society Workshop on Visual Languages*, Skokie, Illinois, October 4–6, 1990, pp. 80–85.

[Ungar and Smith 1987] D. Ungar and R. Smith, "Self: The power of simplicity," *ACM SIGPLAN Notices (OOPSLA'87 Proceedings)*, Vol. 22, No. 12, 1987, pp. 227–242.

[Upson et al. 1989] C. Upson, T. Faulhaver, D. Kamins, D. Laidlaw, D. Schlegel, J. Vroom, R. Gurwitz, and A. Van Dam, "The application visualization system: A computational environment for scientific visualization," *IEEE Computer Graphics and Applications*, Vol. 9, No. 7, July 1989, pp. 30–42.

[Wilde and Lewis 1990] N. Wilde and C. Lewis, "Spreadsheet-based interactive graphics: From prototype to tool," *ACM SIGCHI Special Issue, CHI '90 Proceedings*, April 1990, pp. 153–159.

[Yang and Burnett 1994] S. Yang and M. Burnett, "From concrete forms to generalized abstractions through perspective-oriented analysis of logical relationships," *IEEE Symposium on Visual Languages*, St. Louis, Missouri, October 1994.

PART III

THE VISUAL
ENVIRONMENT

CHAPTER 9 ❏ ❏ ❏ ❏

Getting Close to Objects

BAY-WEI CHANG, DAVID UNGAR, AND
RANDALL B. SMITH

CONTENTS

185

We begin Section III on visual environments with a discussion of the visual environment for the Self object-oriented programming language. This chapter illustrates an emerging trend in visual programming environments, in which the environment is becoming so closely integrated with the language itself, it is hard to discern where one ends and the other begins. While most other environments have focused on the use of views and tools to present views of objects, the environment described in this chapter is object-focused, and attempts to foster the notion that objects themselves are directly available for interaction. Two principles are presented that allow object-focused environments to match the functionality of view-focused environments. The principle of availability makes the functionality of objects accessible across contexts, and the principle of liveliness allows objects to participate in multiple contexts while retaining concreteness. By presenting objects concretely, the environment encourages programmers to focus on the program objects themselves rather than on the trappings of the interface.

9.1 INTRODUCTION

Visual programming's attractiveness stems in large part from its immediacy—programmers directly interact with program elements as if they were physical objects. These concrete visualizations of the program on the computer screen shape how programmers visualize the program within their mind, and may give them a foothold from which to think about the program: people find it easier to deal with the concrete than with the abstract. Object-oriented programming languages (even those that rely primarily on textual representations) strive toward the same end by providing objects as the fundamental elements in the program. Objects encapsulate and make concrete the elements of the program, including the data to be manipulated and the behavior to be applied to that data. Again, this paradigm works because most people find it easier to deal with the concrete than with the abstract.

Yet while object-oriented programming languages assist the programmer by providing a concrete notion of objects, most programming environments for these languages push the programmer in the opposite direction, back toward the abstraction of objects. Rather than presenting objects directly, the environments present intermediaries that show certain aspects of the object—for example, an inspector shows instance variables but cannot show all references to the object without launching another tool. This approach has the effect either of fragmenting the object into many different aspects, weakening the sense of a single unified object, or of distancing the object deep in the recesses of the computer, making it reachable only through intermediaries acting to show aspects of it.

Our premise is that a visual programming environment that closely matches the programming language can lessen the cognitive load of programming, by reducing the distance from the programmer's model of the object to the programming environment's model of it. We propose that programming environments employ the principles of *immediacy* and *primacy* to present objects as concrete entities that are the primary loci of action, rather than as abstract entities which are secondary to the tools and views used to examine and manipulate them.

But by eschewing conventional views and tools in favor of direct interaction with objects, it may seem that we must also give up the functionality that views and tools provide. For example, views show multiple representations of the object, allow separate instances of the object on the screen, and are gathered together into useful tools, like browsers and debuggers. However, by taking the idea of independent, individual objects very seriously, we have discovered two principles, *availability* and *liveliness*, which enable us to attain similar levels of functionality in a concrete world.

We begin by discussing the differences between conventional view-focused environments and the proposed object-focused paradigm, concentrating on the nature and identity of objects in those environments. The Seity interface, an experimental browsing user interface for the programming language Self, is used as an example of a visual environment that focuses on objects rather than on views and tools. Within Seity, Self code is still represented textually, but the objects of the language are presented directly as concrete entities.

9.2 VIEW-FOCUSED VERSUS OBJECT-FOCUSED ENVIRONMENTS

Most current programming environments for object-oriented languages are *view-focused*: objects are examined and manipulated through intermediaries, each of which permit a certain view of the objects (Figure 9.1).

The Smalltalk-80 environment [Goldberg 1984] is the seminal object-oriented exploratory programming environment. Tools like class browsers, method browsers, protocol browsers, and inspectors provide various perspectives of the objects in the system. Tools are associated with objects, but the same object may be shown by many tools, and the same tool may show different objects over its lifetime. The tools are concrete—they are the things that are manipulated in the environment— but, in a formal sense at least, the objects are abstracted, distanced, and secondary. The objects are abstracted because they reveal different parts of themselves within multiple, separate forums (the tools) and because they maintain no central locus of existence or manifest identity. The objects are distanced because they cannot be reached directly by the programmer, but must be viewed through tools. The objects are secondary because the tools are manipulated as the primary action (Figure 9.2).

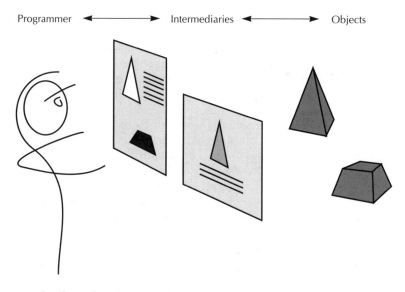

Figure 9.1   In a view-focused environment, the programmer interacts with intermediaries (tools), which present views of the objects.

However, this is the most formal interpretation of tools in a view-focused environment. The programmer can come to identify tools with the object, as the tools become transparent with frequent use. Thus a Smalltalk inspector is thought of as the object which it inspects, thereby pushing the object to the forefront and eliminating the distance to it. The *object-focused* model takes this concept as a starting point, attempting to eliminate the sense of an intermediary from the first (Figure 9.3). The object in the interface is intended to be concrete, immediate, and primary. For example, Seity [Chang 1994], an experimental user interface for the prototype-based object-oriented programming language Self [Ungar and Smith 1987], presents a Self object as a box with a column of slots on its face (Figure 9.4).

Seity currently represents all Self objects in the same way. This is consistent with the Self object model: Self is prototype-based, meaning it has no classes. New objects are created by cloning existing objects; shared behavior (for example, methods that would reside in the class for a class-based language) is inherited from other objects. The uniformity of this model encourages a uniform way of looking at any object, hence the basic set-of-slots representation in Seity. However, the object-focused model is not only applicable to prototype-based languages. There is no reason why class-based languages like Smalltalk and C++ cannot be supported by an object-focused programming environment. While in Self there is only one kind of object, in Smalltalk there are instances, classes, and metaclasses. These objects would appear in the environment with different representations, each showing appropriate information about itself. The non-object constructs in languages like C++ would also appear in the environment, with identities appropriate to their function. The important thing is not that a particular object model exists

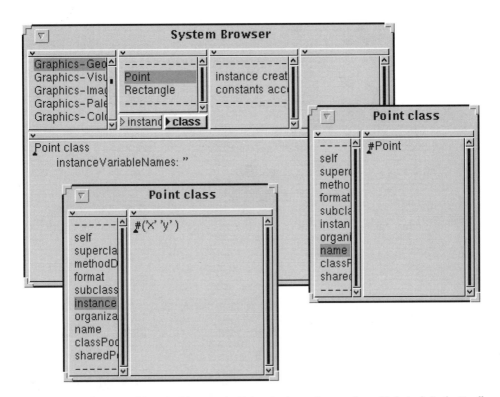

Figure 9.2   The same object (in this case, the Point class) can show up in multiple tools in the Small-talk environment; the same system browser can view many different classes and methods.

for the language (a non-object-oriented language could also be represented), but that the language be divided into logical units to be mapped to on-screen objects. When the division is a useful way of conceptualizing the program elements, the units will be able to function effectively in the object-focused programming environment. There will be no need for other windows, browsers, or other such tools with which to view objects, because the programmer can already see and interact with the objects themselves.

But what does the phrase *the objects themselves* actually mean? After all, the object is simply a mutually agreed upon notion between the programmer and the computer, based on the programming language. This raises two issues: first, whether a concrete representation can be chosen for the object that not only can stand for the object, but in fact can come to be accepted as the object itself (the principle of *immediacy*); and second, what that representation should be.

In the object-focused model the on-screen representation of the object is considered to represent the object itself, not merely a singular tool through which the object shows itself. To this end, there is never more than one such representation of any given object (though this representation can be malleable). In addition, this particular on-screen representation is never associated with any other object. Since there is a one-to-one mapping between the representation and the object, it

Programmer ◄————► Objects

Figure 9.3   **The object-focused environment fosters the notion that the programmer is interacting directly with the objects.**

is a small step to discard the strictly accurate notion that the representation is an intermediary separate from the object, and to consider the concrete representation to actually *be* the object. While the programmer does not truly believe that the on-screen representation is the object, it is convenient and natural to act as if it were—the offered concrete manifestation is easier to embrace than an abstract

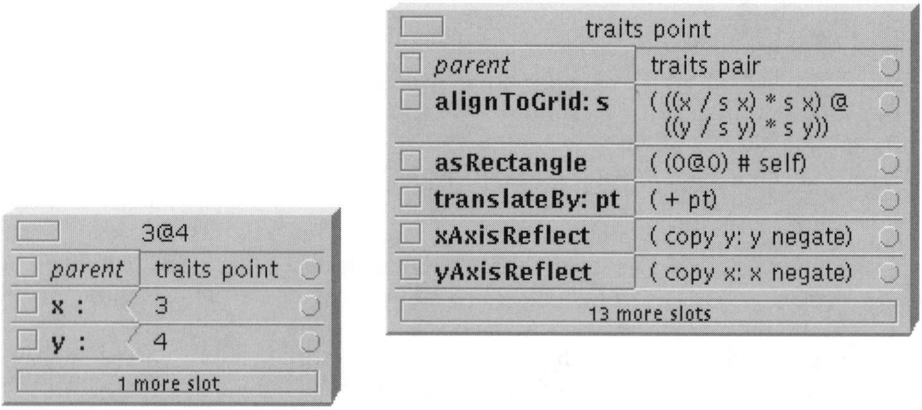

	traits point	
parent	traits pair	○
alignToGrid: s	(((x / s x) * s x) @ ((y / s y) * s y))	○
asRectangle	((0@0) # self)	○
translateBy: pt	(+ pt)	○
xAxisReflect	(copy y: y negate)	○
yAxisReflect	(copy x: x negate)	○
	13 more slots	

	3@4	
parent	traits point	○
x :	3	○
y :	4	○
	1 more slot	

Figure 9.4   **Two Self objects in Seity**

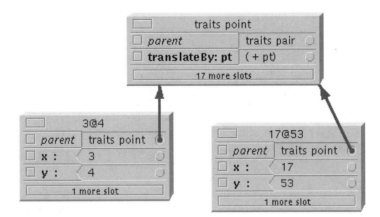

Figure 9.5   Objects in Seity maintain their identity by not appearing more than once on the screen.

one, and the object is at hand to be examined and manipulated. This identification encourages programmers to feel as if they are directly dealing with the objects of the language. Hutchins et al. [Hutchins et al. 1986] refer to this sense of immediacy with the semantic objects of interest as *direct engagement*. Direct engagement is achieved in view-focused environments when tools become transparent; by eliminating the levels of indirection introduced by view-focused tools, object-focused environments may increase the frequency of direct engagement.

The constraint in choosing the representation itself is that it must match the model of objects in the language. An object in Seity, for example, is presented essentially as a set of name–value pairs, which corresponds precisely with a Self object. This of course leaves wide latitude in the details of the representation—the Seity representation could have as easily been a simple rectangle instead of a 3D slab. But these details are important, for the programmer will come to identify the representation with the language object, and it will shape his or her mental model of objects. The concrete representation informs the programmer of the nature of the objects, and the more accurately it can reflect a useful model of them, the more likely the programmer will feel comfortable working with such representations in the environment.

The concreteness of Self objects is heightened in Seity by making it seem as if those objects are physical, real-world things. Thus their concreteness is not only one of spatial localization and identity, but also one of image and behavior—the objects look like 3D slabs, and they move solidly. An object has an identity; it never appears more than once on the screen. Instead, multiple references to it refer (via arrows) to the same instance (Figure 9.5). Furthermore, the objects are placed in an environment that can be called an artificial reality, a world that has some features reminiscent of the real world but is primarily a consistent, individual universe unto itself. In the Seity Self reality, objects move smoothly with the use of animation, employing cartoon-inspired techniques to make their movements seem lively, engaging, and realistic [Chang and Ungar 1993]. The use of visual solidity and animation helps make objects seem real, furthering the illusion that these are indeed the objects in the program.

The overall effect of making objects immediate is, in fact, to make them seem real. Our goal is to create the sense that the object is directly available to the programmer: the object is the thing right there on the screen.

9.3   OBJECTS AT THE CENTER OF ACTION

Of course, just seeing the object isn't enough to give it a complete sense of identity. It must also have appropriate properties associated with it, just as real-world objects have properties. That is, just as the properties of real-world objects define, individualize, and unify them, the properties and behavior of objects in the programming environment ought to do the same. Since its properties and behavior are properly owned by the object, the programmer must go to the object to get at them—the principle of *primacy*. Consolidating the functionality needed of the object within itself serves to centralize focus on the object, rather than on outside view-focused tools that have traditionally encapsulated areas of functionality. Again, this makes the objects primary in the environment, which in turn brings the programmer closer to the objects. But can all the functionality of traditional view-focused tools be preserved in the object-focused model?

9.3.1 Views and Tools Revisited

For the purposes of this discussion, the term *view* will be used to mean a particular way of presenting some subset of information within an object. Views allow an object to be understood from defined perspectives, carving up the large semantic space of the object and packaging up the chunks in useful and comprehensible configurations. They specialize the presentation of the object for a particular task— for example, showing the values of variables, the code of methods, or the place on a stack. Each view is a discrete unit of functionality.

Tools, as used in this discussion, are objects in the interface that centralize functionality for a given activity. They are a conglomeration of views, with ways to manipulate those views. A debugger tool, for instance, might show the current stack, with ways to look at activations on that stack and objects involved in those activations. Several views of different objects would be involved in a single debugger tool. What the views have in common is that the functionality they provide is needed in this one activity: debugging.

View-focused tools for programming emphasize the activities the programmer engages in. There are tools for browsing objects, for writing code, for debugging, and for presenting inheritance hierarchies. View-focused environments make the programming activity explicit, but at the expense of somewhat distancing the targets of that programming activity, the objects with which one is working. (This has also been called the activity-focused model [Hedin and Magnusson 1988].) The objects are somewhat subordinated to the operations on them and the ways of looking at them.

9.3.2 Object-Focused Functionality

Object-focused environments achieve functionality by giving objects the behavior needed for studying and changing them. Properties of the object are part of the object, so we just need to know how to get at them—perhaps by pressing a button, choosing a menu item, or selecting an option from a pull-out drawer. The same kind of direct manipulation techniques used to manipulate view-focused tools can be applied to manipulate the objects themselves. The difference is that the result affects the object itself, not a disconnected intermediary. The object may show more information, change aspects of its presentation, or even radically transform its representation. In each manifestation, however, it is clear that the object itself is being manipulated and examined.

A Self object in Seity, for example, is a complete entity. No separate browser or inspector is needed to examine it—the object itself serves that purpose. Poking a button gets the contents of a slot (the object in the slot grows from a dot within the button to a full-sized 3D slab, see Figure 9.6). Poking other buttons can remove the object from the screen (it falls off the bottom of the screen), or hide a slot from view (the slot slides out from the slab and get sucked into the bottom of the slab). Other actions, like finding all the references to the object, are initiated from menus integrated into the object (Figure 9.7).

While view-focused environments make the programming activity explicit, the object-focused model incorporates the manipulation of the objects as the general activity; programming activities are implicit within those manipulations. Rather than centralizing functionality into a monolithic tool, smaller chunks of functionality are coupled to the object, so that any functionality can be invoked at any time on the object, not only when it is being viewed by a particular kind of tool. This principle of *availability* frees the programmer from modes in which limited portions of object functionality are available at any one time—for example, within a view-focused debugger tool it might be possible to inspect an object's slots, but it might not be possible to find all references to that object without going to a separate tool. In addition, object-focused functionality naturally shares functionality across conceptual domains of activity. The activities of debugging, browsing, and creating objects might all require inspecting the contents of slots, or finding all senders of a message. Rather than distribute this functionality of the object in many places as discrete tools would, objects in the programming environment implement it as part of themselves. When objects are concrete, their behavior is always available. The principle of availability is a natural consequence of the object-focused model.

9.3.3 View Functionality for Concrete Objects

Clear benefits accrue from the ability to view an object in more than one respect, and it would be a loss if they were sacrificed on the altar of concreteness. Luckily, concrete objects in the object-focused model can indeed have multiple views—by

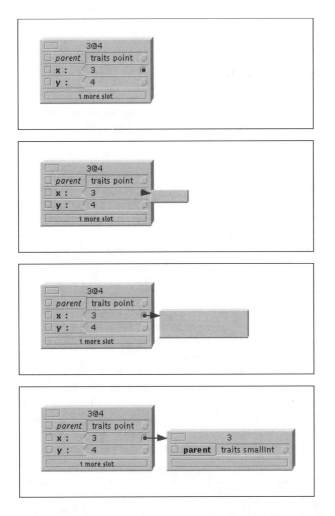

Figure 9.6   Seity allows examination of the contents of a slot by poking directly on the slot to get the object inside.

transforming themselves into different visual representations when requested. Like a view in a view-focused tool, the object is specialized for the current task; but unlike the view-focused tool, it is implicit that the thing on the screen is still the same object, just showing a different face. The concreteness is retained because the view is not decoupled from the object.

Multiple simultaneous views, which are useful for comparing disjunct aspects of the object at the same time, can also be handled. Objects show the two representations at once, but in keeping with the goal of concreteness, the object remains connected and solid. When multiple simultaneous views of an object are needed in separated locations, the object-focused model potentially runs into trouble. The

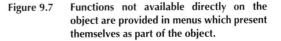

Figure 9.7   Functions not available directly on the object are provided in menus which present themselves as part of the object.

essence of the object-focused model is that objects have a single identity. The single strongest cue that objects are concrete is that like real-world objects, they cannot be in two places at one time. Disjoint instances of the same object would destroy the illusion of the identity of the object, weakening the sense that the things on the screen are the objects in the program. This functionality could still be provided by reifying the remote views as view objects, but there may be a better way.

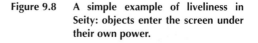

Figure 9.8   A simple example of liveliness in Seity: objects enter the screen under their own power.

We suggest that the principle of *liveliness* can at once provide much of the functionality of disjoint views while increasing the sense of concreteness of objects. A *lively* interface allows objects to move, change, and interact under their own power. The programmer still controlls what happens, but the interface is no longer a static environment, passive until the programmer reaches out and grabs an object or pushes a button. Objects go where they are needed, when they are needed.

We have experimented with liveliness in the Seity interface: objects enter and leave by moving on and off screen under their own power; self-dismissing notifiers simply drop off the screen if they have not been handled; and an object can be arranged to come to the cursor on the click of a mouse button (Figure 9.8).

Liveliness mitigates the need for disjoint views by letting objects move from one place to another and transform themselves along the way if necessary. If an object is needed in multiple places, it can move to those places when it is needed, depending on the programmer's desire or the environment's needs. The objects are in collaboration, not competition, with the programmer.

9.3.4 Tools—Cooperating Concrete Objects

Tools, in the traditional view-focused environment, bring together multiple objects in order to operate on several at once, or to show relationships among them. The object-focused environment needs the ability to work with multiple objects at once as well. In fact, we need not give up the formal notion of a tool, if we recast it as an organizer and coordinator of multiple objects, rather than as a repository for remote views of objects. The role of the coordinator is then played by an object intimately connected with the activity, not an outside presence.

For example, consider the activity of debugging. An object-focused environment can present the process object, which has a button that will show the current stack. Pressing the button begins assembling the stack, which calls in the activation objects. The objects may simply gather in a column, connected to one another by arrows, or the process object might sprout a shelf and the activations will align themselves in a tower on that surface. Just like in a traditional view of a stack, the result is a list of activation frames, but the frames feel more like the activation objects themselves than they might in a traditional view. Because they are *lively*, we can pull activations off the stack, confident that when we want to look at the stack as a whole again, the unglued activations will remember their role and return. Because they are *available*, any browsing, searching, or modifying—any functionality ever available in the object—can be performed on the activation objects without going elsewhere or changing modes. This debugging "tool" is merely the conglomeration of lively, available, concrete objects cooperating under the direction of another, the process object. It can be seen as a whole unit, or as a momentary collaboration between many different objects. The participating objects are free to be coaxed out and individually manipulated at any time, and can even participate in more than one activity at one time, by shuttling themselves around when necessary.

Cooperating concrete objects can mimic any view-focused tool to provide a locus in which several objects are acted on or show their relationships to one another. But concreteness increases the utility of this locus over that of a view-focused tool by maintaining the individuality and usefulness of each participating object.

Currently, Seity does not have facilities for multiple views of objects or object-focused debugging such as that described above. However, our experience with the object-focused browsing environment suggests that a full object-focused programming environment could be both effective and pleasing to use.

9.4 SUMMARY

Object-oriented programming languages present an opportunity to break out of the largely text-oriented environments of conventional languages. We propose the object-focused model of an object-oriented programming environment, in contrast to the traditional view-focused model. In the object-focused model, objects are made concrete by enforcing their unique identities; they are made immediate by showing directly manipulable representations unfettered by intermediaries; and they are made primary as the source of action by basing functionality on the objects rather than on remote tools. In addition, the object-focused model achieves most of the functionality natural to a view-focused environment by applying the principle of availability, which makes available all the functionality of objects in any context, and the principle of liveliness, which allows them to move and change under their own power.

The resulting object-focused programming environment can make objects seem more real, potentially lessening some of the cognitive burden of programming by reducing the distance between the programmer's mental model of objects and the environment's representation of them. Programmers can get the sense that the objects on the screen *are* the objects in the program, and thus can think about working with objects rather than about manipulating the environment.

REFERENCES

[Chang and Ungar 1993] B. Chang and D. Ungar, "Animation: From cartoons to the user interface," in *UIST'93 Conference Proceedings*, Atlanta, November 1993, pp. 45–55.

[Chang 1994] B. Chang, *Seity: Object-Focused Interaction in the Self User Interface*, Ph.D. dissertation in preparation, Stanford University, 1994.

[Goldberg 1984] A. Goldberg, *Smalltalk-80: The Interactive Programming Environment*, Addison-Wesley, Reading, 1984.

[Hedin and Magnusson 1988] G. Hedin and B. Magnusson, "The Mjølner environment: Direct interaction with abstractions," in *ECOOP'88 Conference Proceedings*, published as *Lecture Notes in Computer Science #322*, Springer-Verlag, New York, 1988, pp. 41–54.

[Hutchins et al. 1986] E.L. Hutchins, J.D. Hollan, and D.A. Norman, "Direct manipulation interfaces," in *User Centered System Design* (D. Norman and S. Draper, eds.), Lawrence Erlbaum, Hillsdale, 1986, pp. 87–124.

[Ungar and Smith 1987] D. Ungar and R. Smith, "Self: The power of simplicity," in *OOPSLA'87 Conference Proceedings*, published as *SIGPLAN Notices*, 1987, Vol. 22, No. 2, pp. 227–241.

Visual Programming and Software Engineering with Vista

STEFAN SCHIFFER AND JOACHIM HANS FRÖHLICH

CONTENTS

199

Many visual programming efforts have been focused primarily on providing support for programmers who have a clear vision of their program's design before they enter the visual environment. In the environment presented in this chapter, however, both design and implementation tasks are supported. These features are tightly integrated at a fine-grained level in the visual environment, and are supported by a flexible mix of graphical and textual notations. Vista's intended audience is the software engineer, and its goal is to support fundamental software engineering principles in the design and implementation of nontrivial, high-quality Smalltalk programs.

10.1 INTRODUCTION

Within the past few years visual programming (VP) has been increasingly attracting attention, mainly because of its promise to make programming easier, thus allowing not only computer experts but also novices to solve problems using the computer. This revives the expectations of over 30 years ago, when programming languages such as Cobol where supposed to make the programmer obsolete by providing a new natural way for every English-speaking professional to communicate with data processing machines. In fact, programmers did not lose their jobs because of Cobol, and VP will also not leave them unemployed.

However, the market has already discovered the fascination of VP, and various new programming environments have been declared to be "visual." A closer look at some of those products (e.g., Visual C++ and VisualWorks) shows that they typically consist of browsers for manipulating text, combined with a GUI editor and a rudimentary application skeleton generator. Although it may be right to call such environments visual, that is not what we mean by VP. In our understanding, VP has to offer substantially higher expressiveness than conventional textual programming by means of software visualization and a visual programming language. Systems such as LabView [VW86], PARTS [Digitalk 1992], Prograph [Gunakara 1992], and Serius [Serius 1992] fall into this category. (For definitions and taxonomies of VP see [Ambler and Burnett 1989, Chang 1990, Glinert 1992, Myers 1986, Shu 1988, Selker and Koved 1988, and Price et al. 1993].)

This chapter describes Vista, a visual multiparadigm language integrated within a comfortable development environment. In our opinion, Vista provides substantial expressiveness at the visual layer, as well as concepts necessary to build real applications. Vista supports fundamental software engineering principles during programming, such as adequate notation, modularization, and weak coupling. Vista augments the object-oriented programming paradigm by signal-flow and data-flow based programming. It provides capabilities for the construction of event-driven and data-transformation systems. Characteristic features of Vista are especially aimed at the combination of high-level and easy-to-use building blocks that are hierarchically organized. In constructing an application with Vista, visual as well as textual means can be used.

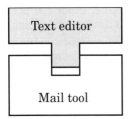

Figure 10.1   A naive approach: plugging a text editor into a mail tool

10.1.1 Visual Programming and Software Engineering

VP addresses two key issues of software engineering: mastering complexity and increasing productivity. Complexity can be reduced by offering concepts which raise the abstraction to the visual level. Such high-level abstractions reveal semantic relationships among program entities that otherwise would remain hidden. Productivity can be improved by what Shneiderman calls the central features that produce enthusiasm in using interactive systems [Shneiderman 1983]: "visibility of the object of interest; rapid, reversible, incremental actions; and replacement of complex command language syntax by direct manipulation of the object of interest."

With regard to abstraction, building blocks like classes and modules have proven their worth. Well-specified, tested components are a prerequisite when manufacturing high-quality applications. But in spite of this indisputable fact, it is a misleading notion that software systems might be built almost solely by assembling building blocks. Captivating, simplistic pictures like Figure 10.1 are intended to convince the observer how easy programming could be if only the right visualization and assembly tools were available for powerful building blocks. (It is sometimes argued that graphical user interface editors, which are supposed to be usable by nonprogrammers, follow a similar approach. What usually remains concealed is that problems arise as soon as a nonprogrammer has to bring the user interface to life.)

Programming based solely on assembling building blocks is relevant only if static structures with fixed operations are the foundation of the system under construction. This is rarely true and should be called *configuration*, not programming. Software engineers design reactive systems where components are created, changed, and destroyed at run time. The specification and implementation of the behavior of such dynamic systems is a difficult task that cannot be handled by merely plugging components together, but requires the definition of the right control structures. Even application frameworks [Pirklbauer et al. 1992 and Weinand et al. 1989] or design patterns [Gamma 1992] do not make control structures obsolete.

Object-oriented programming (OOP) as the state of the art in software engineering provides good concepts for writing high-quality programs. Nevertheless, there is a lack of concepts and tools that help the programmer to cope with the complexity of OOP. A few exceptions exist, e.g., the object-oriented VP environment *Prograph* [Gunakara 1992 and Cox and Pietrzykowski 1988], which represents an exemplary step toward promoting OOP by visual means. Prograph is a complete software development tool set based on a visual data-flow language. Though the data-flow paradigm is well suited for transformational systems and a very natural base for VP (by means of lines and boxes), it is not appropriate when designing reactive systems. The modeling process of reactive systems has to cover complex sequences of events, actions, time constraints, etc., which lead to systems with interactive behavior. By contrast, transformational systems convert data by applying functions without the notion of state or time. Although there exist extensions to the pure data-flow model for handling control flow, synchronization or state (e.g., Prograph includes case windows, synchro links, and object attributes), modeling systems solely based on the data-flow paradigm is not always suitable. Such inappropriateness of the modeling language induces what we call a *semantic break*.

Our efforts focus on how to enrich OOP by means of a visual model without causing a semantic break. In this context we think that it is important to support more than one paradigm. Because we know the potency of OOP and the strength of control-flow programming, as well as the declarative power of data-flow programming, we want to harmoniously integrate them all under a visual layer. Moreover, we are convinced that constructing nontrivial, high-quality software requires special knowledge and skills. VP supports, but cannot replace, these human dimensions. Therefore we concentrate our research on how VP techniques can aid software engineers, rather than on the empowerment of lay persons.

10.2 VISTA—A VISUAL SOFTWARE TECHNIQUE APPROACH

It is our firm conviction that the design of a feasible VP environment should rely on well-founded software engineering concepts and programming paradigms. Unfortunately, too few publications on VP have dealt with software engineering principles. The assumption that pictures are natural, so VP is good per se, may be one reason for the lack of research. We are convinced that practical software projects require the application of principles like information hiding and weak coupling for VP as much as for any other programming paradigm; thus strong efforts should be made to incorporate them into VP.

Our approach for a VP environment is to join object-oriented programming based on Objectworks\Smalltalk [ParcPlace 1992a] and programming with signal flow and data flow. We call the model and its programming environment Vista. The name Vista is an acronym for *visual software technique approach,* with equal emphasis on *visual* and *software technique*. The model, together with the environment, offers the following features:

- It provides a visual language for defining signal and data networks.
- It supports the visual design of encapsulated and weakly coupled components.
- It offers full access to the Smalltalk class library.

- It supports visual interaction by direct manipulation of components.
- It avoids visual overload by permitting text input whenever useful.

Vista promotes evolutionary prototypical development of object-oriented software systems but does not support the whole software life cycle. It is intended to be used during the design and implementation steps. We have tried to rigorously obey software engineering principles for the conception of the model as well as for the implementation of the environment.

In the following we introduce Vista's programming model and explain how this adheres to the basic requirements for the construction of quality software. We do not describe the visual language formally, because in our opinion that is of less value in a truly visual environment such as Vista, where a distinction between the language and the environment is somewhat artificial. Instead, we give a complete example in Section 10.4, showing how a thermo-alarm system can be build with Vista.

10.2.1 The Programming Model

Entities called *processors* constitute the central computational components of the Vista programming model. Processors are high-level objects constructed by visual or textual means. Textually defined processors (simple processors) are programmed in Smalltalk; they establish the set of Vista primitives. Visually constructed processors (compound processors) are implemented by direct manipulation of visible objects; they make up the programmer-defined library of building blocks.

On the programming surface, visual and tangible representations of processors are exposed and various accesses are granted by Vista, depending on the intended manipulation: if a processor is to be redesigned, the programmer has full access to all aspects of its structure and behavior; if a processor is to be used for construction of another processor, only an external (black box) view of the used processor is given. Interaction between processors is carried out via messages and tokens. As usual in Smalltalk, messages sent to processors (synchronously) activate methods and return values.

An additional communication mechanism is provided by token passing, for which processors have input and output ports to receive and send tokens. Processors are visually linked by these ports with *connections*. A collection of interconnected processors is called a *network*. In the following we discuss each of these components in more detail.

Processors   Processors are objects with distinguishing structure and communication facilities. Before explaining the internal structure of a processor, we will discuss how processors communicate. This should help the reader to understand what makes them unique compared to ordinary objects.

A processor's operations are usually triggered by tokens. Generally a processor receives tokens at input ports, performs operations bound to these ports, and can emit new tokens via output ports. Emitted tokens are passed over connections to other processors. A token may carry event information (signal token) or data objects (data token). Each transported item is stored in a slot from which it can be retrieved by the components to which the token is passed.

Before a token is handed over to a processor, it is checked by the receiving input port. If the input port awaits event information or data objects, it searches for the items at the expected slots. If items of the right type are found, no further setup actions are performed; if no suitable data is detected, the port substitutes default values for items with illegal types. The programmer may override the port's default values with an expression. This can be either a simple literal or a sequence of statements.

The fallback scheme for data acquisition (1. token-defined, 2. user-defined, 3. default) greatly contributes to the flexibility of Vista. Due to this *modus operandi,* arbitrary processors can be connected. An output port is not required to deliver a token satisfying the expectations of the connected input ports as long as either the programmer supplies meaningful data or a suitable default value is available. This feature stresses the special communication mechanism of processors, in contrast to common message passing, where the sending object has to know about the services offered by the receiver.

Beyond their special interaction, processors have a distinctive makeup, too. This arises from the hybrid nature of Vista, which integrates a conventional class-based programming system with the interactive manipulation of visible and "living" objects. On the one hand, processors are objects in the sense of prototypes, with behavior modifiable on a per-object basis. This is true for compound processors, which themselves contain networks (behavior). On the other hand, processors share characteristics with objects of class-based, object-oriented languages whose behavior is defined by the class to which they belong. This applies to the method interface of both compound and simple processors. The same ambiguity concerning where behavior is defined applies for a processor's structure, too. Simple processors are objects with instance variables defined by their class. Compound processors consist of inner processors which principally can be added to and removed from each individual processor.

No principle distinction exists between typical objects and processors regarding encapsulation. A processor is divided into an interface part which is accessible from outside and an interior part which can only be accessed by the processor itself. Figure 10.2 shows the overall architecture of a processor with its interface (ports and dashed boxes) and interior (anything else).

The interface of a processor consists of input and output ports as well as public methods and public processors. Access to a processor is provided only via this interface.[*] Public processors are designated to be replaced by other processors having the same interface. One can image the substitution of public processors as the exchange of a chip on a digital board with a newer, better, or otherwise more suitable version. This feature is extremely important, as it allows the construction of frameworks as well as convenient customizing (see also Section 10.3.2).

---

[*] It should be noted that the privacy of processors can be violated by low-level programming. Since we did not make any changes to the Smalltalk language, which protects only instance variables from public access, the notion of privacy is not recognized by the compiler. For instance, although hidden by browsers of Vista, private methods are still accessible from Smalltalk code.

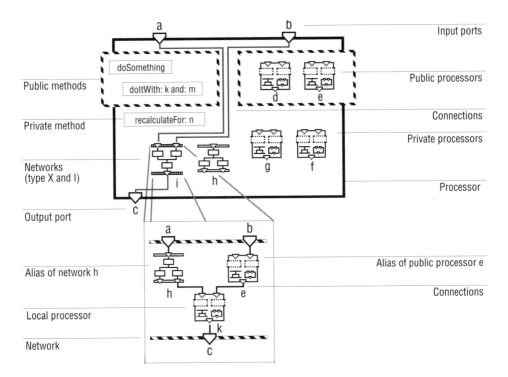

Figure 10.2   Principal structure of a processor

The interior appearance of a processor depends on whether it is simple or compound. The interior of simple processors consists of instance variables and methods, just as with any class in Smalltalk. This need not be discussed further. Of greater interest are compound processors. Such visually defined processors encapsulate private processors (simple or compound), methods, and networks.

Private processors represent the constituent components of a compound processor and therefore conform to the is-part-of relationship of objects. Installing them inside a processor also manifests this relationship topologically. Private processors may be considered as internal devices used to perform the enclosing processor's task. To hold atomic attributes such as characters, numbers, and color values, private processors have to be used, too. There is no other construct besides processors for this purpose.

Processors are part of inheritance hierarchies. When defining a new kind of compound processor, the programmer has to subclass the general class which is the root of all compound processors. The new subclass provides an empty template for the prototypical instance to be defined in the sequel. Further manipulations (adding new ports, defining networks, etc.) affect only the prototypical processor, not the class. An exception is the definition of methods; they are installed directly in the class. After having finished the prototypical processor, the programmer generates the complete class definition from it. The processor thereby becomes part of the library of reusable components. The same procedure may applied in order to subclass existing processors. So, specialized subprocessors inherit the properties of their ancestors and represent extensions or adaptations of them as needed.

Methods and Networks   Methods and networks define the behavior of processors. Methods are written in ordinary Smalltalk code by means of text editors, whereas networks are graphically composed in two-dimensional diagrams. As methods in Vista are the same as those of Smalltalk, we will not explain them further but rather focus on the notion of networks.

Networks are ensembles of linked processors or other networks. Vista provides only networks for joining components. Like processors, networks have ports to receive and send tokens. The ports of a network are collected by *terminals* (input and output bars) which constitute the interface of the network. The interior consists of interconnected processors and other networks, which are either locally defined objects or references to objects defined elsewhere (aliases). Local processors and networks are internal to the enclosing network, just like a method's local variables. All components of networks have unique names which are used when sending messages.

The presence of processors inside a network constitutes an important difference between networks and methods. Methods represent *code*. When a method is called, its parameters and local variables are pushed on to the execution stack, and are removed from there when control returns to the caller. Networks represent interconnected objects, not code. When a token arrives at an input port, these objects are already alive. The sequence by which objects gain control is defined by the way the token moves through the network. When the token eventually leaves the network at an output port, the network's objects remain alive, ready to process the next token.

We distinguish two categories of networks which provide connection points for the enclosing processor's ports and a means of network sharing, respectively:

- *X-networks* link the interior of a processor with its exterior. They either interconnect the processor's input and output ports or join internally known entities (sources of control) with the processor's output ports. Terminals of X-networks are dashed.

- *I-networks* are internal to the enclosing processor or network. They can be used within other networks, similar to subroutines. Terminals of I-networks are solid.

The distinction between these two sorts of networks is especially important regarding execution. Each processor may contain the source of a control flow. Using X-networks, control stemming for an internal source can be passed on to connected processors via a token. Thus an output port of an X-network may trigger without the preceding activation of an input port. For the purpose of network sharing it is not desirable to have sources of control flow inside a dynamically invoked network. This would violate input/output causality, which says that every outgoing token must first be fed into a network. For this reason we have introduced I-networks, which ensure exactly this behavior.

To keep the model simple, Vista currently supports only synchronous forwarding of tokens. If an output port is connected to more than one input port, tokens are transmitted with a depth-first strategy; i.e., a token is passed down along the chain of linked processors rooted at the first connection before the second connection is used. Usually the ordering of connections is defined by the sequence in which the programmer draws them. Explicitly assigned priorities may alter the default order.

Aliases   In Vista, a programming entity is usually defined at the location where it is seen. A programmer looking at an object sees the original. However, sometimes we need to use the same object several times in distinct places. Evident examples include processors shared among different networks or networks used like subroutines within other networks. For these cases Vista provides special components called aliases.

Aliases are surrogates of processors or networks. A token passed to an alias is forwarded to the original, and tokens emitted by the original are sent to its aliases. Aliases can reference only objects of the same or an outer scope. This rule avoids obscure cross references and enforces proper structuring. Aliases are tightly bound to their originals. Manipulations on the interface of the original object are immediately reflected in its aliases. Deleting the original object removes all of its aliases, too.

10.2.2 Construction of Reactive and Transformational Systems

In the previous section we explained the basic entities of Vista's programming model at a rather abstract level. For a more detailed discussion we now introduce three kinds of processors, namely *signal, data,* and *coupler processors.* All these processors handle *signal* or *data tokens*, which pass control or data from one processor to the next.

By making a distinction between signal and data processing, Vista provides thought models for the construction of reactive (event-driven) as well as for transformational (data-converting) systems, depending on what is more appropriate for the system under development. Coupler processors combine these two kinds of systems explicitly. This is close to reality, where reactive and transformational systems can often be identified as subsystems of larger systems. They do not exist independently, but are coupled at particular points. A radio, e.g., includes the transformational subsystems receiver and amplifier, which make sound out of radiowaves; the controls that switch the channels may be regarded as a reactive subsystem since they react to the station selected by the listener. A coupling point might be the electronic circuit which turns the channel selection signal from the controls into a new frequency of the receiver's quartz. Shell languages of UNIX systems which integrate control and data-flow constructs in a really elegant way (ignoring the drawbacks of cryptic textual languages) have also inspired the idea behind the multiparadigm programming aspects of Vista.

Reactive systems are preeminent in Vista, while transformational systems are considered to be part of them. We made this decision because we assume that in most cases looking on the problem domain from a reactive point of view leads to a better model. In our opinion this is apparent when applying object-oriented design methods. We prefer to view an object as a minisystem with an internal state defined by its instance variables. We see messages to this object as signals or events which change the state.*

Reactive Systems   A reactive system is an event-driven ensemble of cooperating components which respond to a stream of internal and external stimuli. Depending on certain conditions, these stimuli trigger actions which in turn produce cascades of new events. Examples include traffic control systems, computer networks, operating systems, and interactive graphical user interfaces of many kinds of modern software. Harel et al. state [Harel et al. 1990],

> Common to all of these is the notion of reactive behavior, whereby the system is not adequately described by a simple relationship that specifies outputs as a function of inputs, but, rather, requires relating outputs to inputs through their allowed combinations in time. Typically, such descriptions involve complex sequences of events, actions, conditions and information flow, often with explicit timing constraints, that combine to form the system's overall behavior.

A lot of effort has been invested in developing methods and tools for specifying, designing, and implementing such systems, among them module-oriented development environments [Harel et al. 1990] as well as object-oriented approaches [Shlaer and Mellor 1992 and Jacobson et al. 1992]. On the one hand, a particular method for the specification and design of reactive systems should allow a very natural mapping of the problem domain to the computer model and implementation; on the other hand, formal means should be used to achieve secured statements about the system's conformance with the requirements and the expected behavior over time.

Vista does not compete with such complex and comprehensive methods, and certainly is not intended to cope with real-time embedded systems. Formal methods and explicit modeling of concurrency or distribution are beyond the project's present scope (but see Section 10.5). Instead, we have designed an environment for the quick assembly of limited reactive software systems by means of encapsulated components. Examples of such components embrace Boolean switches, number calculators, alarm clocks, document processors, email servers, and operating-system components. We call these building blocks *signal processors*, which, as the name suggest, are intended to react to events, called *signals* in our terminology.

Signal Processors   Signal processors send signal tokens whenever a certain task has been completed or their state changes in a way that may be interesting to the environment. We distinguish active and passive signal processors. Active processors emit signals asynchronously at arbitrary times. Passive processors produce signal tokens only when they receive a message or a signal token from another processor. All activities which are triggered by the flow of signal tokens form a process. The source of a process is always an active signal processor or an external entity like the operating system. Multiple signal flows may be active at the same time; thus processes conceptually execute in parallel. This

---

* We recognize the controversy of such statements. Proponents of data-flow languages might argue that exactly the opposite approach yields more natural models. Maybe this is a philosophical question only; however, we adhere to the notion of messages sent to objects instead of objects being piped through operations (in most cases).

statement is important when considering networks, as it says that more than one signal token might be on its way through a particular network simultaneously.

Transformational Systems   We outline a transformational system as a data-converting ensemble of components that either generates or transforms data [Harel 1987]. The computational process usually does not depend on particular conditions but only on the available data flowing through the system on predefined paths. Thus the relationship of input to output of such a system is a function with no side effects.

As with reactive systems, we do not claim that Vista's model for transformational systems comprises all aspects of data processing systems. Our model supports pure data-flow semantics with no additional control-flow structures, sequential execution constructs, or other augmentations. These features are covered by the reactive model, and thus have been left out of the transformational one. Examples where the application of Vista's data-flow model seems to be well suited are noninteractive, batch-oriented problems like data filtering, image processing, and format conversion.

Data Processors   Data processors form the basis of Vista's transformational model. In contrast to signal processors, data processors do not inform their environment about state changes, but transform input data via internal machinery to output data—a style of computation well known from many data-flow languages. A data processor can execute only if all required data have arrived, i.e., if all its ports hold a token. When this condition is true, the processor performs its *sole* data conversion operation. This behavior is fundamentally different from that of signal processors, where ports are mutually independent and trigger different actions when different signals arrive.

Unlike signal processors, data processors are always passive; i.e., they perform operations only if new data come in. That is due to the execution model which is solely based on step-by-step forwarding of data tokens. Active sources of data have to be simulated by asynchronously triggered signal/data couplers.

Combining Reactive and Transformational Systems   A network may contain an arbitrary mix of signal and data subnetworks. *Coupler processors* are the designated link points for the joining of signal and data networks. Within Vista two types of coupler processors exist: *signal/data couplers* are triggered by signals and produce data, whereas *data/signal couplers* collect data and send out signals.

Figure 10.3 shows examples of signal, data, and coupler processors as well as diagrams of signal and data networks. The left diagram shows a signal network consisting of a timer and a speaker. When a signal arrives at port *testAlarm*, the speaker is switched on (connection 1) and then the timer is requested to count down for 10 seconds (connection 2). When the timer expires, it emits a signal at port *expired*, which switches off the speaker.

The right diagram depicts a data network which performs the task of a file chooser. If a user changes the file name pattern in order to get a new filtered list of directory entries, the port *fileNameChanged:* is triggered. The given pattern is then fed into the network, piped through the signal/data coupler *fileName* (which extracts the signals token's item at slot 1), and passed on to the left port of the data processor *matchPatternInList*. This processor checks each element of the list

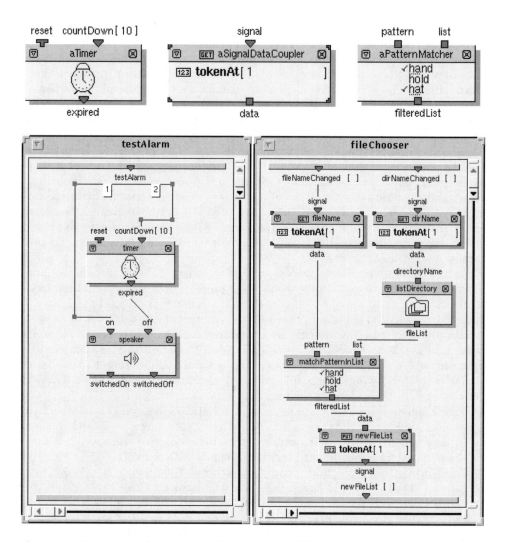

Figure 10.3   Processors and networks: signal processor, signal/data coupler, data processor, signal network, and data network

at its right port against the pattern and produces a filtered list of all matching entries. The filtered list is given to the data/signal coupler *newFileList*, which makes a signal token out of it. When invoking file chooser for the first time, signals both on ports *fileNameChanged*: and *dirNameChanged:* are required before *matchPatternInList* can start processing. Later on, each signal token produces a new filtered directory list as old data are remembered by ports of data processors.

10.3 SOFTWARE ENGINEERING ISSUES

In order to give the programmer the ability to build high-quality software, Vista's concepts are based on a number of fundamental principles of software engineering. Particular determining factors in the design of Vista were the support of:

- *Mastery of complexity* by adequate notation and modularization.
- *Reuse of components* by abstraction and weak coupling.
- *Safety in programming* by analysis of type information.

In the following we will give a short overview of the mapping of these principles onto Vista's concepts.

10.3.1 Adequate Notation

To enhance the comprehension of a complex software system, the right representation of both the system's structure and the execution process is of central importance. Ideally it should be possible to look at the system from different points of view; for an outline of the overall design, a coarse-grained view would be quite suitable, whereas detailed insights have to be provided to focus on a single component with all its relationships.

It is not always easy to find the right visualization because different views require different notations. As experience with visual programming has shown, the role of graphics should not be overrated in the search for the right representation. Early approaches in visual programming which totally banned text are considered to have failed because pure pictorial representations lack abstracting power. If the depicted system is not absolutely trivial, it is inevitable that important aspects will remain in the dark; these eventually have to be unveiled by textual means. We are convinced that pictures alone are insufficient to promote understanding of even a moderately complex system.

In Vista the same rank is assigned to graphics and text. Graphics is used for the representation of directly manipulated objects, for overview representations, and for the definition of high-level operations. Text is used for naming objects, for comments, and for writing algorithms.

Objects are depicted either as icons or in an expanded form. Icons show only a typical picture along with the object's name, whereas the expanded representation exposes all accessible properties. Those objects constituting the Vista programming model can be annotated. Annotations have two parts: a brief textual comment and a hypertext document. The hypertext document is a standardized form which contains the specification of the object, including examples of how to use it, a dynamically created catalog of current instances with the ability to inspect them, cross-references to other documents, etc.

Lines characterize various kinds of relationships among objects, e.g., hierarchical organization or communication channels. Currently, spatial relationships are not used to convey semantics. Thus it is not important whether an object is near another object or if two icons overlap.

Colors and grays display the state of objects (executing states are shown in green, blocked states are shown in red, and disabled states are shown in gray). Shadows of different brightness indicate whether an object is the original one (dark shadow) or an alias (light shadow).

Objects are usually kept in lists and registers. From there, objects can be dragged with the mouse to destinations where they are needed. All visible objects are alive and offer a menu containing generic commands, such as browse, edit, inspect, and annotate, along with special operations depending on the current context.

As a concluding remark on the issue of adequate notation, we once again outline the role of graphics versus text: although Vista's visual programming language is computationally complete (offering sequential execution, conditional branching, and recursion), it is not intended to be used for writing algorithms. Despite the fact that one could define the faculty function or sorting procedures by interconnecting processors, nobody should do so. Such algorithms can usually be found in the Smalltalk library; if nothing from there seems to be suitable, the programmer should write an ordinary Smalltalk method to obtain what is needed.

The visual capabilities of Vista were designed with the task of system construction in mind. As a rule of thumb, Vista's visual programming capabilities are perfectly suitable if the collaboration of processors has to be specified; e.g., if the sum of an array of integers is to be the result of processor collaboration, the statement *sum := array inject: 0 into: [:s :i | s + i]* will do the job better.

10.3.2 Abstraction

It seems to be a contradiction to try to incorporate abstraction into the visual programming environment, which draws its power from the objective of making all objects visible and concrete. Distinguishing between the representation of abstraction, and the abstraction of concepts resolves this discrepancy. Vista supports three kinds of abstraction:

- Separation of interface and implementation.
- Substitution of processors.
- Inheritance hierarchies.

In the following we will explain each of these in more detail.

Separation of interface and implementation   When designing a software component, one has to decide, among other things, what the functional level of the component should be, how much flexibility should be built-in, and how the particular component will communicate with other components. On the last point, the only way communication within a modular system can take place is via the interfaces of its components. The consequence of this is that using a component requires only knowledge about the specification of the interface; the component's internal structure does not matter and even need not be available when referencing the interface. This fundamental principle is called *information hiding*.

Vista strictly separates the interface and the interior at the visual layer. As soon as the interface is defined, its associated component is virtually available: the programmer can see it, touch it, drag it out of the component catalog, and drop it onto the programming area. Of course, nothing will happen if performance of an operation is requested from a component which is not yet implemented, but all communication connections can already be established. When the implementation eventually becomes available, things start working automatically. This supports the top-down approach of system decomposition and fits into what Richard P. Gabriel means by abstraction in programming [Gabriel 1993]: "An abstraction facilitates separation of concerns: the implementor of an abstraction can ignore the exact uses or instances of the abstraction, and the user of the abstraction can forget the details of the implementation of the abstraction, so long as the implementation fulfils its intention or specification."

Substitution   Regarding functionality and flexibility, there is a strong correlation between the capabilities of a component and its range of applications in different contexts. In general, it can be said that increasing functionality decreases flexibility. That is because a high-level component depends on other high-level components and a number of base modules, with the connections among them mostly hard-wired. Substitution, which also may be called configuration or customizing, can help to overcome this dilemma.

By substitution in the context of Vista, we mean that parts of a processor may be replaced with parts having a compatible interface. It is important to note that some or all of the parts being anticipated for exchange may offer unimplemented operations in their interface. Such parts must be replaced in order to make the containing processor fully functional.

Parts intended for exchange are called public processors, as their replacement is performed from the outside. They should not be confused with parameters of methods as they are more than just objects; they are full-fledged processors. Being processors, they have the ability to directly control the flow of tokens inside the processor of which they are parts. Controlling the receiver is not possible for ordinary objects passed to methods as parameters.

Substitution can take place either statically or dynamically. Static substitution happens when a programmer uses a processor in a particular context and customizes it in order to achieve the desired behavior. For this purpose one or more of the processor's public processors are superseded. The static replacement of public processors resembles the exchange of chips on a digital board. Dynamic substitution is possible, too. Here a message is sent to the processor whose public processor is to be exchanged. The name of the message is the same as that of the processor to be replaced, and the message's sole parameter is the substitute (see also Figure 10.7)

Because public processors can be replaced by all compatible processors and not only by those of exactly the same type, substitution allows higher abstractions than the simple separation of interfaces and implementations. Substitution abstracts from the implementation of a group of classes of objects, whereas the separation of interfaces and implementations hides only the implementation aspects of a single class.

Inheritance hierarchies   Vista is a true object-oriented programming environment: it offers all common features of object-oriented programming languages like inheritance, polymorphism, and dynamic binding. We presume that the reader is familiar with the basic concepts of OOP, and therefore omit a broader discussion of these terms. Furthermore, we will concentrate on Vista's inheritance mechanism, since polymorphism and dynamic binding are essentially a side effect of Vista's Smalltalk-based implementation.

In object-oriented languages like Smalltalk, classes are organized in an inheritance hierarchy. A subclass inherits attributes (instance variables) and methods from its superclass. Processors of Vista are also organized in such a hierarchy. Actually this is a subtree of the Smalltalk class tree rooted at the abstract class *CompoundProcessor* (for visually defined processors). Inheritance of a processor involves all its properties, namely public and private processors, public and private methods, ports and networks. For all these properties, with the exception of networks, Vista does not care about inheritance but relies on the standard mechanism of Smalltalk. Networks are treated specially because they implement instance-based behavior (in contrast to methods, which are classed based). Hence we have written our own dynamic binding mechanism, which finds the appropriate network when a token arrives at an input port.

Inheritance provides an excellent means for abstraction. It permits the implementation of abstract processors that are semifinished components. An abstract processor defines a general interface of its subprocessors and factors out common behavior into nonempty networks and methods. Empty networks and methods are placeholders for unique behavior and have to be overridden in subprocessors in order to make them usable.

Inheritance together with substitution provides an excellent means to build object-oriented frameworks. This is a superior technique that codes common patterns of a certain problem domain into highly reusable abstractions [Stritzinger 1991]. Vista's support for the construction of frameworks is perhaps its greatest strength, besides its visual facilities.

10.3.3 Weakest Coupling

Bertrand Meyer defines the *weak coupling* or *small interfaces principle* as follows [Meyer 1988]: "If any of two modules communicate at all, they should exchange as little information as possible."

He justifies this principle in particular by the criterion of continuity and protection, which demands that changing a small part of a module's interface should result in little modification of other parts of the system. But that is not the only advantage. Weak coupling also ensures the composability of software components, because a small communication channel increases the probability of finding components that are able to participate in communication. An example is the toolbox of UNIX commands. A lot of UNIX commands can work on a stream of bytes; they read bytes from a default input channel, process them, and write them to a default output channel. These channels form a very narrow interface. Consequently UNIX commands adhering to this standard can be combined in thousands of ways.

The UNIX toolbox example shows that there is something beyond weak coupling, which we call weakest coupling. Using the terminology of Vista, we outline the *weakest coupling principle* as follows: "For a signal processor to inform any other processors about anything, it should not address these processors explicitly but should broadcast a signal together with a minimum amount of related data."

With this principle we expect to obtain maximum composability even for building blocks that were never planned to work together. There is a good chance that unforeseen combinations of building blocks are possible if data received or transmitted are simple, and if the sender or receiver of the information need not be known in order to process the data.

The elegance of data-flow languages is founded on point two of this observation. The implementor of a functional block for a data-flow language has to think only about the input/output channels, whereas the user of such blocks may combine them in arbitrary ways, provided that data types match.

It was an incentive for us to apply the principle of weakest coupling for an object-oriented visual language that encourages the combination of high-level building blocks instead of focusing on algorithmic aspects. The search for an appropriate construct eventually led to Vista's signal processor, an object that mainly communicates with the environment through signal tokens instead of by sending and receiving messages (see Section 10.2.2).

Observance of weakest coupling leads to one-way communication relationships where the sending processor need not care about the receiver, and the receiver may react to the signal without being aware of where it comes from. Vista is not the originator of such interobject communication. The change-and-update mechanism of Smalltalk [Goldberg and Robson 1983] is based on a similar concept. One difference between Smalltalk's mechanism and Vista's signal metaphor is that the change-and-update mechanism is used for certain design patterns only, e.g., within the MVC architecture, whereas in Vista one would not program without signals. Another difference is that change-and-update relationships are invisible, whereas in Vista signal connections are concrete and visible objects.

We cannot predict how much productivity can be increased using weakest component coupling or what the penalty will be in terms of performance or efficient use of resources. Empirical results will emerge over time and with the construction of larger, nontrivial software.

10.3.4 Analysis of Type Information

Preferences for static or dynamic typing fuel a never ending dispute among committed proponents of the respective points of view. In object-oriented languages like C++ and Eiffel [Ellis and Stroustrup 1990, and Meyer 1988], the compiler can detect whether a message sent to an object is recognized by this object (i.e., if the object is of the right type), whereas in languages like Smalltalk and Self [Ungar and Smith 1987] this can be determined only at run time.

Both kinds of type checking have their advantages and disadvantages. Dynamic type checking offers a maximum of flexibility and simple declaration of variables, with the drawback of some uncertainty, unreadability, and inefficiency of programs. Static type checking restricts polymorphism and may force the programmer to perform obscure type casts. Nevertheless, static typing supports documentation and maintenance, offers safety guarantees, and contributes to efficiency of message passing.

Vista follows a best-effort strategy with regard to type checking according to the motto: "Never let the user provide information the system already knows." It uses all available information to detect and prevent actions which would obviously lead to type incompatibilities, but does not guarantee that every operation specified is type clean. The advantages of static type checking are reflected in Vista as follows.

- *Readability*   Since every object of Vista's programming model is visible and alive, the programmer can always recognize the type of a certain object either by looking at its external representation (layout, icon, etc.) or by inspecting its internal state and type information.

- *Efficiency*   Message passing in Vista is done exclusively by the underlying, dynamically typed Smalltalk system. Here efficiency is not improved.

- *Safety*   Actions by the programmer concerning the substitution of public processors with other processors are type safe. When such an operation takes place, Vista automatically checks whether the surrogate processor is compatible with the public processor. If this is true, the substitution is carried out; otherwise an error message is reported.

Although Vista's support of type checking is more ad hoc than rigorous, it helps the programmer to avoid unintentional errors, without any modification of the Smalltalk language.

10.4 A COMPLETE EXAMPLE

Explaining and understanding visual programming without pictures is almost impossible. In this section we give a complete example of a simple application built with Vista. We want to demonstrate how the various concepts fit together at the visual layer, and to reveal how Vista cooperates with a third-party user interface builder.

10.4.1 Task

A thermo-alarm processor (TA) is to be built that receives temperature values, compares them with a given lower and upper limit and triggers an alarm device if the temperature is out of range. The limits specifying the temperature range can be changed. The TA is to maintain the constraint that the lower limit never goes beyond the upper limit. The alarm device has to be substitutable. The TA triggers whenever the temperature goes out of range and also when temperature is normal again. The left side of Figure 10.4 shows the TA's interface with the public processors *max*, *min* and *alarmDev* for upper and lower limit, and the alarm device. Below this picture, the TA's iconic representation is shown.

For testing purposes, we need a user interface that looks like the prototype at the right side of Figure 10.4. The sliders *Temp, High,* and *Low* modify the corresponding values that the TA should watch. Temperature values are displayed numerically below the sliders (in degrees Celsius and Fahrenheit). The area labeled *Alarm* is a colored region that is green if the temperature is within the limits; else it is blinking red. This region is independent of the exchangeable alarm device, which actually is an invisible speaker.

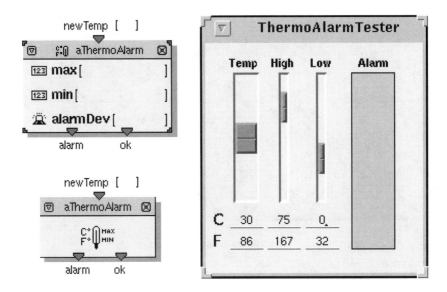

Figure 10.4 Thermo-alarm processor (left) and user interface prototype (right)

10.4.2 Building the User Interface

Vista does not provide a user interface builder itself. We use VisualWorks [Parc-Place 1992b] for building user interfaces of Vista programs. VisualWorks is built on Objectworks\Smalltalk. It provides an integrated environment for operating system independent application development. A VisualWorks application consists of

- A *user interface* built with a set of common widgets like windows, sliders, push buttons and list panes.
- An *application model*, which coordinates the effect of user input and links the user interface to the underlying domain model.
- A *domain model*, which defines the essential structure and behavior of the application (in our case, this is the TA processor).

Figure 10.5 shows this layered architecture applied to our thermo-alarm system. The application model is between the user interface on top and the domain model at bottom. It consists of a number of elements that are either value holding objects for the user interface widgets (*tempF*, *lowF*, *lowC*, and *alarmRegion*) or connectors to the domain model (*onChangedDo*, *low*, and *onTriggerDo*). The application model is sketched only partially in order to avoid clutter. Before explaining the construction of a TA processor, we show how a particular TA is connected to the application model.

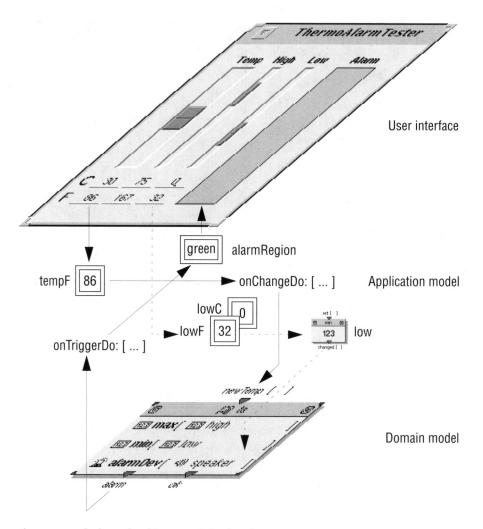

Figure 10.5   The layered architecture of VisualWorks

The dashed arrows in Figure 10.5 depict the principle flow of control when the user moves the slider for adjusting the TA's minimum temperature limit. Any movement of the slider changes *lowF*, which stores the current lower limit. This value holder forms the glue between two more objects, namely the (unnamed) visual display at the user interface and *lowC*, which holds the limit converted to Celsius. These two objects depend on *lowF*. So, whenever *lowF* changes they are updated, too. In the case of *lowC*, a conversion function is triggered that assigns the result of the formula $(lowF - 32) \times 5/9$ to *lowC*. This in turn updates *lowC*'s visual representation on the user interface.

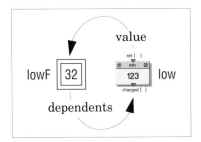

Figure 10.6   Interconnection of a value holder and a number processor

Although we have not engaged Vista so far, the thermo-alarm system is already partially functional. Moving the sliders updates the number displays accordingly, and editing any of the numbers updates the corresponding slider as well as their Celsius and Fahrenheit displays.

The alarm region is still dead, as the necessary logic is not connected yet. This leads us to Vista and to the embedding of the TA. First, we create a new TA from class *ThermoAlarm* (see Section 10.4.3). Then we link the TA's public processors with the related objects of the application model. As the TA expects processors at its interface, we have to convert the value holders *lowF* and *highF* into number processors. We do this by sending them the message *asProcessor*. Figure 10.6 shows the situation after the message has been sent to *lowF,* which currently holds the value 32.

The underlying mechanism that creates the object relations shown in Figure 10.6 does the following: first, it instantiates the number processor *low* from class *NumberProcessor*, which belongs to the set of Vista's primitives. This processor does not directly store the associated number, but maintains a reference to the value holder *lowF*. Second, the created processor is added to the list of objects dependent on *lowF*. Thus the value holder *lowF* automatically informs the processor *low* about changes.

The number processors *high* and *low* are plugged into the corresponding slots *max* and *min* of the TA. In addition the TA's abstract alarm device is replaced by a concrete speaker object.

Next we send the value holder *tempF* the message *onChangeDo:*, thus connecting the TA's input port *newTemp* to *tempF*. The block parameter supplied by the message specifies that whenever *tempF* changes, the current temperature is passed to *newTemp*. Linking the TA's output ports with the alarm region is the final action in order to fully connect the TA to the application model. To achieve this, the message *onTriggerDo:* with a block parameter is sent to ports *alarm* and *ok*. Each time one of these ports triggers, the statements inside the blocks are executed, thus updating the alarm region. Figure 10.7 outlines the method *initialize* of class *TATester* that is necessary for proper initialization of the TA.

Now the user interface has been built and the code to couple it with TA has been written. The next step is to implement the TA by means of the visual part of Vista.

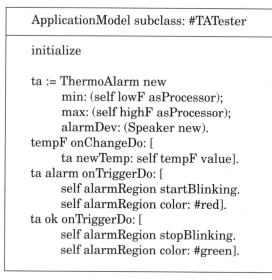

```
ApplicationModel subclass: #TATester

initialize

ta := ThermoAlarm new
        min: (self lowF asProcessor);
        max: (self highF asProcessor);
        alarmDev: (Speaker new).
tempF onChangeDo: [
        ta newTemp: self tempF value].
ta alarm onTriggerDo: [
        self alarmRegion startBlinking.
        self alarmRegion color: #red].
ta ok onTriggerDo: [
        self alarmRegion stopBlinking.
        self alarmRegion color: #green].
```

Figure 10.7   Initialization of the thermo-alarm processor

10.4.3 Building the Thermo-Alarm Processor

To ease the description of the construction process, let us build the TA from scratch, assuming that it has nothing in common with any existing processor. When building a new processor, at first we get two templates, one for the processor's interface, another for its implementation. These templates are to be filled with ports, processors, methods, and networks.

Defining the Interface   The interface of a processor consists of input and output ports, public processors, and public methods. For the TA we need an input port and two output ports which we name *newTemp, alarm,* and *ok*. After naming and typing, the ports immediately show up in the template. Next we select the required public processors from Vista's processor register, where all processors are organized in categories. We do so by dragging two number processors and one alarm device to the section *Public Processors* of the interface template. Afterwards we name them *min, max,* and *alarmDev*. We do not need any public methods, and therefore leave the corresponding section blank.

The interface is now complete and we are able to catalog (install) the TA processor in Vista's register. By that action the interface is turned into the Smalltalk class *ThermoAlarm*. The new processor is yet not functional, but is ready to be

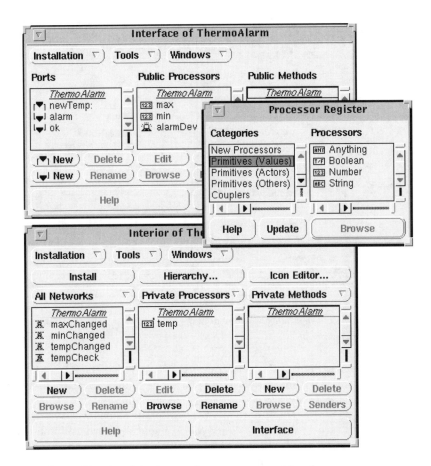

Figure 10.8 Interface and interior of the thermo-alarm processor, register of processors

used anywhere. The top of Figure 10.8 depicts the TA's complete interface and the processor register.

Defining the Interior Considering its task, the interior of the TA can be kept quite simple. A private processor named *temp* holds the last reported temperature. Additionally, we need three X-networks, namely *tempChanged, minChanged,* and *maxChanged,* which handle changes of the temperature, and the lower and upper limits. A fourth internal network comprises the common part of all X-networks. It is used to test if a temperature value violates the limits. We name that network *tempCheck.* Figure 10.8 depicts the interior template after the creation of processor *temp* and all networks. Let us now consider each particular network.

The network *tempChanged* (see Figure 10.9) contains only aliases of the private processor *temp* and the internal network *tempCheck.* The brackets attached to the input port *newTemp* indicate that signals arriving at this ports carry one data item (i.e., the new temperature value). After storing the new temperature in *temp* (connection 1) *tempCheck* tests if the temperature exceeds the limits (connection 2).

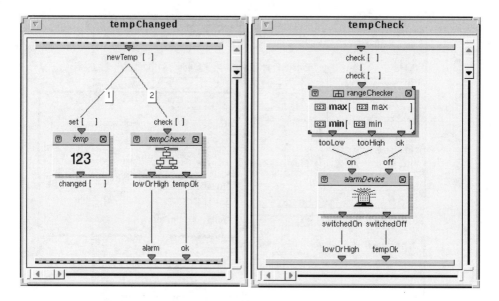

Figure 10.9   Networks *tempChanged* and *tempCheck*

Figure 10.9 also depicts the network *tempCheck*. This network is shared among the other networks. Its input and output bars are solid, indicating its special purpose. Inside the network we see a local processor named *rangeChecker* and the public processor *alarmDev*. If port *check* of processor *rangeChecker* triggers, a signal is emitted at one of the output ports *tooLow*, *tooHigh*, or *ok*. Which port is actually triggered depends on whether the current temperature violates the limits. A signal emitted by either of the ports *tooLow* or *tooHigh* switches on the alarm device and is further routed to the network's port *lowOrHigh*. A signal emitted by port *ok* turns off the alarm and eventually triggers port *tempOk*.

Figure 10.10 shows the networks *minChanged* and *maxChanged*. These networks are activated whenever the value of *min* or *max* changes. Network *minChanged* is fully exposed, whereas parts of *maxChanged* have been collapsed into the local network *testAndAdjustMin*. The network *maxChanged* works analogously to *minChanged*; hence we will explain only the expanded network.

The switcher within the network *minChanged* first checks whether *min* > *max*. If so, *max* is set to *min* in order to ensure the integrity of the temperature range. Afterwards *tempCheck* is activated just as within the network *tempChanged*. The two processors *portier1* and *portier2* are of particular interest. These processors temporarily prevent port *changed* of processor *max* from sending out a signal. This is necessary because otherwise the operation that sets *max* to *min* would have a side effect on the network *maxChanged*.

Now the TA processor is finished. Installing the interior in class *ThermoAlarm* is the final step required in order to turn the networks into methods of this class.

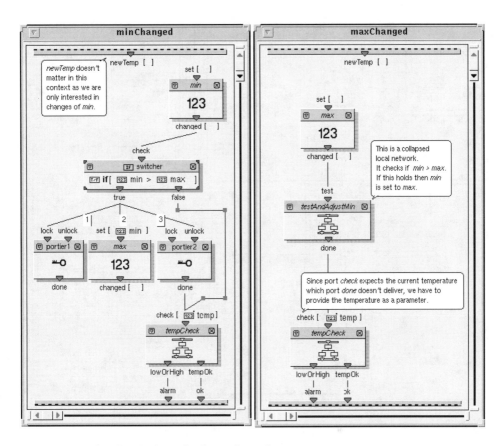

Figure 10.10 Networks *minChanged* and *maxChanged*

Figure 10.11 shows a snapshot of the Vista programming environment during the construction of the TA. The Vista workbench consists of a variety of tools which are designed to offer visual interaction at a level suitable for the supported task. Currently available are

- Registers for organizing and storing objects.

- Browsers, editors, and inspectors for exploring and manipulating objects and relationships among them.

- Animators and debuggers for the interactive execution of signal and data networks.

- On-line help for most parts of the environment.

- An annotation facility, which lets the user attach arbitrary information to any object.

We believe that these tools strike the right balance between graphical and textual representation, hence saving screen space and avoiding visual overload. A preliminary version of the Vista programming environment is available on Sparc-Stations, on the Macintosh, and under MS-Windows.

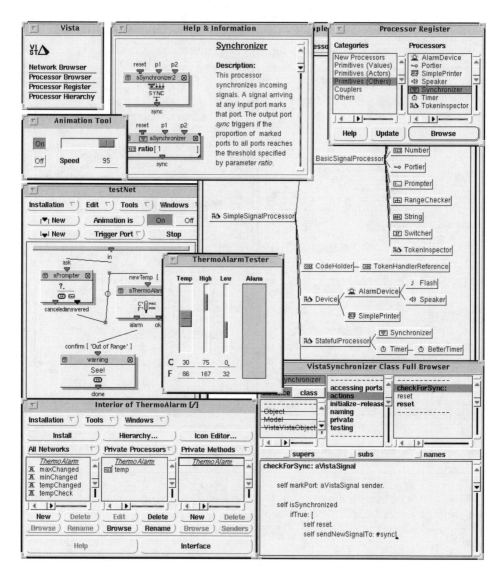

Figure 10.11 Snapshot of the Vista programming environment

10.5 FURTHER WORK

Several redesign cycles were needed to simplify and clarify the key concepts of Vista, but so far the final stage has not been reached. Our current work on Vista covers concurrency, distribution, and performance issues.

A problem which remains conceptually unsolved concerns the indeterministic behavior of Vista programs if asynchronous forwarding of tokens is allowed. In this case one token may pass another, thus causing unexpected and undesirable side effects. We are currently exploring several formalisms and strategies to cope with this problem. One of the decisions we will have to make will be whether mechanisms which deal with these aspect of concurrency should be built into Vista or provided by special processors.

In addition, we are facing problems concerning execution speed and memory requirements. Vista's communication mechanism, based on token passing, is sluggish even compared to the execution of Smalltalk methods. We feel that the use of optimization heuristics as well as compiler techniques are needed in order to obtain better performance. With respect to memory requirements the prototypical characteristics of processors leads to heavy objects. For instance, every processor has to instantiate each of its own networks, even if there is no structural difference among networks belonging to the same class of processors. Despite the advantage of this approach, which allows self-modifying objects (processors that modify their subprocessors and networks dynamically), in many cases such capabilities are not needed but introduce a remarkable overhead. Whether the interesting possibilities offered by prototypes is worth the additional complexity needs careful justification.

Improving Vista's performance is the most important next step, as this is the precondition for programming real-world applications with Vista. Gathering experience with the implementation of large systems will help to advance the conceptional work. Additionally, this work will indicate whether Vista has the potential for significant rationalization of the software development process—the global goal of software engineering.

10.6 SUMMARY

This chapter has outlined concepts and application issues of Vista—a multiparadigm system that supports the construction of semifinished components in the realm of reactive and transformational systems.

Various kinds of processors (signal processors, data processors, and couplers) are central concepts to Vista. Usually processors communicate with each other by means of tokens that are either signals or data items. Token routing networks combine processors. This communication mechanism leads to weakly coupled, high-level building blocks.

Within the Vista project we have strived to master the complexity of larger visual programs by obeying such important software engineering principles as

- Weak coupling of building blocks.
- Functional and data abstraction.
- Security by introducing an elementary type system.
- Component reuse.
- Direct integration of documentation parts in visual programs.

Visual programming has become increasingly attractive in recent years. A discussion on how to incorporate software engineering principles has to take place to make visual programming relevant for professional software production. We are convinced that combining visual with object-oriented programming is a step in the right direction. Vista follows that approach. One hopes that it will make programming less frustrating and more productive.

REFERENCES

[Ambler and Burnett 1989] A. L. Ambler and M. M. Burnett, "Influence of Visual Technology on the Evolution of Language Environments," *Computer*, Vol. 22, No. 10, October 1989, pp. 9–22.

[Chang 1990] S. K. Chang, Ed., *Principles of Visual Programming Systems*, Prentice Hall, New Jersey, 1990.

[Cox and Pietrzykowski 1988] P. T. Cox and T. Pietrzykowski, "Using a Pictorial Representation to Combine Dataflow and Object-Orientation in a Language Independent Programming Mechanism," *Proceedings of the International Computer Science Conference*, 1988, pp. 695–704.

[Digitalk 92] *PARTS Workbench User's Guide*, Digitalk Inc., 1992.

[Ellis and Stroustrup 1990] M. A. Ellis and B. Stroustrup, *The Annotated C++ Reference Manual*, Addison-Wesley, Reading, 1990.

[Gabriel 1993] Richard P. Gabriel, "Abstraction descant, part I," *Journal of Object-Oriented Programming*, Vol. 6, No. 1, March/April 1993, pp. 10–14.

[Gamma 1992] E. Gamma, *Objektorientierte Software-Entwicklung am Beispiel von ET++ Design-Muster, Klassenbibliothek, Werkzeuge* (in German), Springer, Berlin, 1992.

[Glinert 1992] E. P. Glinert, "Visual Programming Environments and Graphical Interfaces: Where We Are Now, Where We're Headed," *Tutorial notes at the 1992 IEEE Workshop on Visual Languages*, Seattle, Washington, 1992.

[Goldberg and Robson 1983] A. Goldberg and D. Robson, *Smalltalk-80, The Language and its Implementation*, Addison-Wesley, Reading, 1983.

[Harel 1987] D. Harel, "Statecharts. A visual formalism for complex system," *Science of Computer Programming*, Vol. 8, No. 3, June 1987, pp. 231–274.

[Harel et al. 1990] D. Harel, H. Lachover, A. Naamad, A. Pnueli, M. Politi, R. Sherman, and A. Shtul-Trauring, "STATEMATE: A Working Environment for the Development of Complex Reactive Systems," in *Software State-of-the-Art: Selected Papers* (Tom DeMarco and Timothy Lister, Eds.), Dorset House Publishing, New York, 1990, pp. 322–338.

[Jacobson et al. 1992] I. Jacobson, M. Christerson, P. Jonsson, and G. Oevergaard, *Object-Oriented Software Engineering—A Use Case Driven Approach*, Addison-Wesley, Wokingham, 1992.

[Meyer 1988] B. Meyer, *Object-oriented Software Construction*, Prentice Hall, New York, 1988.

[Myers 1986] B. A. Myers, "Visual Programming, Programming by Example, and Program Visualization: A Taxonomy," *Conference Proceedings, CHI'86: Human Factors in Computing Systems*, Boston, April 13–17, pp. 59–66.

[ParcPlace 1992a] *Objectworks\Smalltalk Release 4.1, User's Guide*, ParcPlace Systems Inc., 1992.

[ParcPlace 1992b] *VisualWorks Release 1.0, User's Guide*, ParcPlace Systems Inc., 1992.

[Price et al. 1993] B. A. Price, Ronald M. Baecker, and Ian S. Small, "A principled taxonomy of software visualization," *Journal of Visual Languages and Computing*, Vol. 4, No. 3, September 1993, pp. 211–266.

[Pirklbauer et al. 1992] K. Pirklbauer, R. Plösch, and R. Weinreich. "ProcessTalk: An Object-Oriented Framework for Distributed Automation Software," *Proceedings of the 4th International Symposium on Systems Analysis and Simulation*, Elsevier, 1992, pp. 363–368.

[Selker and Koved 1988] T. Selker and L. Koved, "Elements of Visual Lamguages," Proceedings of the 1988 Workshop on Visual Languages, Pittsburgh, Pennsylvania, 1988, pp. 38–44.

[Serius 92] *Serius Programmer User's Guide*, Serius Corporation, 1992.

[Shneiderman 1983] Ben Shneiderman, "Direct Manipulation: A Step Beyond Programming Language," *Computer*, August 1983, pp. 57–69.

[Shu88] N. C. Shu, *Visual Programming*, Van Nostrand, 1988.

[Stritzinger 1991] A. Stritzinger, "Reusable Software Components and Application Frameworks, Concepts, Design Principles and Implications," PhD thesis, University of Linz, Austria, 1991.

[Shlaer and Mellor 1992] S. Shlaer and S. J. Mellor, *Object Lifecycles—Modelling the World in States*, Yourdon Press Prentice Hall, Englewood Cliffs, 1992.

[Gunakara 1992] *Prograph Reference Manual*, The Gunakara Sun Systems Ltd., 1992.

[Ungar and Smith 1987] D. Ungar, R. Smith, "Self: The Power of Simplicity," *Proceedings of the OOPSLA 87 Conference*, Paris, Vol. 22, No. 12, December 1987, pp. 227–242.

[Weinand et al. 1989] A. Weinand, E. Gamma, and R. Marty, "Design and Implementation of ET++, a Seamless Object-Oriented Application Framework," *Structured Programming*, Vol. 10, No. 2, 1989, pp. 63–87.

CHAPTER 11

Connecting the Pieces

JOHN GRUNDY, JOHN HOSKING,
STEPHEN FENWICK, AND WARWICK MUGRIDGE

CONTENTS

This chapter presents a holistic approach to the integration of the capabilities needed in all phases of software development into a single visual environment. The intent of the approach is to support both visual and textual representations, but a key feature is that the choice between a visual and textual approach for any given task can often be left to the programmer, rather than to the designer of the environment. With this feature in mind, the environment described here provides editing capabilities and multidirectional consistency among all views (textual and visual). The resulting fluidity among the views and tasks supports exploratory programming and an evolutionary approach to object-oriented software development.

11.1   INTRODUCTION

The aim of this work is to provide an integrated, yet extensible, environment for constructing object-oriented software. Many useful tools have been developed to support various parts of the object-oriented development cycle. There is, however, a need for a suitable collection of tools that not only provide support for each phase of software development but also communicate with each other in a transparent manner [Meyers 1991]. We believe that such a collection requires an environment supporting multiple visual and textual views, each of which can be used to either visualize or construct a program, and which are kept consistent with one another in as automatic a fashion as possible.

In this chapter, we will describe SPE (the Snart Programming Environment), which has been developed to meet this. SPE provides an environment for programming in Snart, an object-oriented extension to Prolog [Grundy 1993]. It should be stressed that although SPE is tailored for Snart, the ideas are applicable to object-oriented software development in general. In particular, the notations used are not as important as the general ideas of consistent multiple visual and textual view support.

The chapter commences with a discussion of desirable features of an integrated software development environment for object oriented systems, before reviewing existing work in this area. This is followed by a description of SPE, and its approach to fulfilling these features. We then describe Cerno, a counterpart to SPE that provides execution-time support, before discussing current work and conclusions.

11.2   DESIRABLE FEATURES OF AN INTEGRATED ENVIRONMENT

For an individual programmer, a useful environment capable of supporting integrated object-oriented software development should include at least the following features:

- **Support for visual representations**   It is hard to imagine constructing or maintaining an object-oriented program without diagrammatic aids,
  even if these amount to simple inheritance graphs. The various competing
  object-oriented analysis and design methodologies [e.g., Booch 1991, Coad
  and Yourdon 1991, Henderson-Sellers and Edwards 1990, or Wasserman et
  al. 1990] provide a wealth of diagrammatic techniques and notations to
  support object-oriented development. These range from depictions of structural relationships, such as inheritance and aggregation graphs, to depictions of more dynamic relationships, such as call graphs, dataflow graphs,
  scenario diagrams, and "timing" diagrams. Variations of these are also
  available to support analysis or overview documentation, detailed low-level
  design, implementation, and debugging.

- **Support for textual representation**   While visual representations are
  good for expressing high-level relationships, it is the authors' opinion that
  text is better for representing program detail compactly yet understand-
  ably. For example, the authors prefer a textual style for representing
  expressions over visual approaches, such as Prograph's dataflow graphs
  [Cox et al. 1989] or forms-based approaches such as that used in Forms3
  [Burnett and Ambler 1994]. Documentation, too, requires a mixture of textual and diagrammatic forms. In this regard, we are not "radically visual,"
  to use the terminology of [Furnas 1993], but acknowledge that different
  programmers have different "visual literacy." Hence environments should
  support programmers in using whatever representations with which they
  feel comfortable, and in whatever way.

- **Support for both visualization and construction**   Different visual
  and textual representations should be available to both visualize object-oriented programs and to visually or textually construct them. For example,
  drawing an inheritance arc in an inheritance diagram should create that
  inheritance relationship in the program. Support for construction at a variety of levels is needed: analysis and design tools help "construct" abstract
  program entities, to be refined into more concrete entities using design and
  implementation tools.

- **Consistent views**   Each *view* of a program, i.e., a diagrammatic or textual representation of part of the program, must be consistent with all
  other views [Meyers 1991]. A corollary of the discussion about visual literacy above is that it is undesirable to have any one view type as the "master
  view" with other views being for visualization only. Thus all types of program view should be editable in ways sensible to their semantics, with any
  changes propagated to other affected views. However, there may be only
  partial mappings between views. This is particularly likely in the earlier
  phases of program construction, and when transferring between phases,
  where more detail may be needed to suitably implement an analysis or
  design decision. Partial consistency is an important problem that must be
  addressed by any integrated environment.

- **Support for many views of software systems**   An environment must
  support many views of the software under development. This means supporting not only multiple view types, such as inheritance graphs and call

graphs, but multiple views of each type. This allows views to be created which focus on limited aspects of the software's structure or functionality, for example just the inheritance relationships between the figure classes in a geometric application. Allowing multiple views can avoid the difficulty of large, unwieldy visual views.

- **User control of view contents and layout**   Users must be able to specify what they want to see in each view. This implies the need for simple ways of selecting (for visualization) or constructing information to be displayed. Users should also be able to lay out views in the way they want so that, for example, locality in diagrams can be exploited. In addition, users should be able to mix representations, possibly in controlled ways, within each view. Thus, for example, to explain the operation of the rendering services in a drawing application, it may be useful to include elements of call graphs, inheritance graphs, and whole part graphs, together with textual annotations, all on one diagram. In this latter respect we have similar aims to those of the literate programming community [Knuth 1992], but without the dual straight jackets of a fixed linearization of the program, and limitation to only textual representation.

- **Fuzzy phase boundaries**   Easy flow is needed between phases, given that phases in object-oriented programming are far less distinct than in conventional system development [Coad and Yourdon 1991]. The development process tends to be more of a continuum, with additional notation and syntax available in later phases. The development process also tends to be more evolutionary [Henderson-Sellers and Edwards 1990, Booch 1991], with many small cycles of analysis-design-implementation, rather than one large one. Environments that impose rigid phase boundaries work against this flexible approach to programming.

- **Simple view navigation**   Supporting many small views of a program implies a local reduction of complexity, as each view focuses on a small part of the system; but global complexity then becomes a problem. Thus simple and intuitive ways of navigating to any view of relevance plus the ability to have several views displayed at once are needed. A program could be thought of as a hyperdocument, with navigation via (automatically constructed) hyperlinks connecting relevant views together. Navigation facilities should also extend to program execution views as well, to support rapid debugging and maintenance.

- **Traceable effects of design decisions**   It should be possible to trace how requirements are fulfilled by design and implementation decisions, and vice versa [Boehm 1984]. The lack of support for traceability is one of the most critical failings of existing CASE tools. Traceability is closely related to the issue of partial consistency noted above: solving the partial consistency problem should provide leverage in traceability support. Traceability, in turn, provides support for impact analysis [Pfleeger 1991].

In addition to the requirements of the individual programmer, tool support is needed for team development of large systems. This includes version control, libraries, code "ownership," security, transaction control and locking, project management, testing, metrics and other collaborative software development tools. In this chapter we will focus mainly on the single programmer issues, but will briefly discuss issues of multiuser support and versioning in the section on current work.

11.3 EXISTING WORK

There have been many approaches to the development of integrated development environments for textual programming. These include: the Gandalf project [Habermann and Notkin 1982], Centaur [Borras et al. 1988], MELD [Kaiser and Garlan 1987], and Mjølner/ORM environments [Magnusson et al. 1990]. While these systems support many of the requirements listed in the previous section, they lack integrated support for visual programming.

CASE tools provide graphical editors supporting the construction of analysis and design diagrams [Chikofsky and Rubenstein 1988]. They usually provide consistency management between different views to ensure that a software developer has a consistent view of the software system under construction. Software through Pictures [Wasserman and Pircher 1987] provides various views which support dataflow analysis, structured analysis, and detailed object-oriented design. The OOATool [Coad and Yourdon 1991] supports Coad and Yourdon Object-Oriented Analysis. TurboCASE [StructSoft 1992] supports entity–relationship modeling, structured analysis and design methodologies, and object-oriented analysis and design methodologies.

Most CASE tools do not support complete program implementation. A common approach is to generate program fragments from a design and allow programmers to incorporate these into their own programs. A major drawback of this approach is the problem of *CASE-gap*, where modifications to the design or implementation lead to inconsistencies between them.

CASE tools are often incorporated into software development environments to provide analysis and design capabilities [Reiss 1990a, Reiss 1990b]. One problem is that their data storage and user interfaces are difficult to integrate, especially when CASE tools are developed separately from the environment into which they will be integrated.

A variety of object-oriented Visual Programming languages exist, which unlike CASE tools, extend the visual paradigm to program implementation, and in some cases, to execution. For example, Prograph [Cox et al. 1989] uses dataflow diagrams to specify programs and provides an object-oriented structure in which methods are implemented as dataflow diagrams. An interface builder allows programmers to specify user interface components diagrammatically, and to specify user interface semantics using dataflow diagrams. Prograph's dataflow diagrams are "reused" during execution to visualize program behavior. As another example, the Forms languages [Burnett and Ambler 1994] use a form-based paradigm for visually programming abstract data types. While these languages are important and useful in their own right, and while they provide very good integration between implementation and execution, none yet provides an "all-phases" solution to software development. In addition, these languages tend to adopt a completely visual approach, which is at odds with the arguments in the previous section for textual representation support.

FIELD environments [Reiss 1990a, Reiss 1990b] provide the appearance of an integrated programming environment built on top of distinct Unix tools. Program representation is usually as text files, with each tool supporting its own semantics (with conventional compilers and debuggers). Views are not directly supported, but tool communication via selective broadcasting [Reiss 1990a] allows changes in one tool "view" (for example, an editor) to be sent to another tool "view" (for example, the debugger or compiler). Free-edited textual program views are supported, but these text views cannot contain over-lapping information. Graphical representations are generated from cross-reference information, but a lack of user-defined layout and view composition for these graphical views is a problem [Reiss 1990b]. Data storage is via Unix text files and a simple relational database (for cross referenced information). Data integration is thus not directly supported, but tools can implement translators, driven by selective broadcasting, to allow data from one tool to be used by another.

Dora environments [Ratcliffe et al. 1992] support multiple textual and graphical views of software development; all editing is structure-oriented. Dora uses the Portable Common Tool Environment (PCTE) [Wang et al. 1992] to store program data, and uses PCTE view schemas to provide selective tool interfaces to these programs. Dora supports the construction of analysis and design views, as well as implementation code views, but assumes that these views are updated by structure-oriented editing of base program data. It is not clear what the effect is on an abstract, design-level structure when a corresponding code-level structure is updated.

While each of these systems implements portions of the requirements listed above, there is still a need for a more holistic approach to the integration problem. In the following sections we will introduce SPE and its approach to satisfying the requirements of Section 11.2, based on the mechanism of update record propagation to achieve view consistency.

11.4 VIEWS AND VIEW TYPES IN SPE

Figure 11.1 is a screen dump of SPE, showing two visual and three textual views of a program implementing a simple drawing package. This example illustrates some of the types of view available with SPE. The *window-root class* view shows several of the inheritance and abstract aggregation relationships between various classes. The *figure-Drawing* view shows method-calling protocols related to rendering figures in a drawing window. The *window-Class Definition* and *figure::hide-Method* views are textual views showing a class and method implementation, respectively, while the *window-Documentation* view is a textual view serving to document the window class. These views together provide analysis, design, implementation, and documentation views of the drawing package, all within the one environment. The addition of Cerno, described in Section 11.8, extends this to visualization of program execution as well.

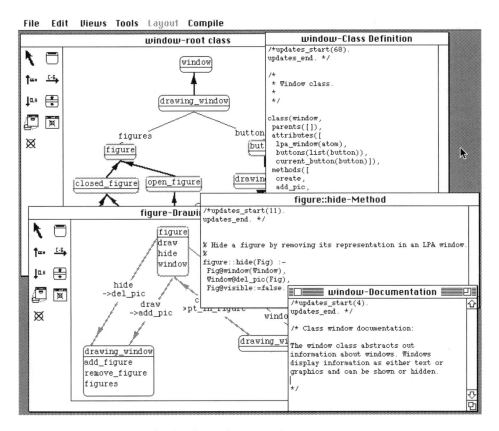

Figure 11.1   Sample SPE graphical and textual program views

In the visual views, classes are represented as icons, with textual annotations for the class name, and (a selection of) its features. Various types of, possibly annotated, connectors are used to depict interclass relationships. For example, bold arrows represent inheritance (e.g., closed_figure inherits from figure), thin annotated lines represent aggregation relationships (drawing_window has a feature, figures, which is a collection of figures) and annotated grey arrows represent method calls (e.g., the hide method of figure calls the del_pic method of drawing_window). The amount of annotation varies depending on the "abstractness" of the relationship: at the analysis level, classes are simply related together in an abstract way; at the design and implementation level, annotations detail how the relationship is implemented. As mentioned in the introduction, the particular notations used are unimportant for the purposes of this chapter. SPE could readily be adapted to suit the reader's favorite diagramming notations; tailoring SPE to support other notations or languages is not demanding.*

---

* For example, a specialization of SPE has been developed to provide an environment for constructing models in the object-oriented specification language EXPRESS and its graphical variant EXPRESS-G [Amor et al. 94].

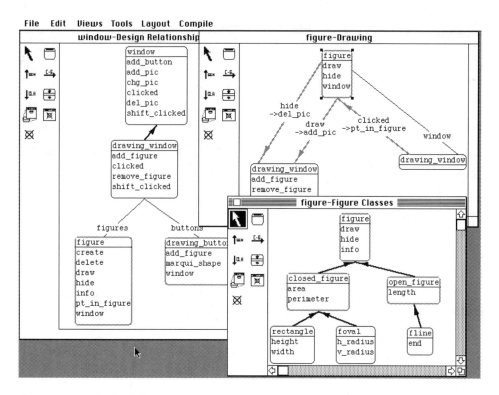

Figure 11.2   Design level diagrams

Information in a view may overlap with information in other views. For example, the figure and drawing window classes appear in both graphical views, and the drawing window class appears twice in the *figure-Drawing* view. An underlying *base view* integrates all the information from each view, defining the program as a whole. If shared information is modified in one of the views, the effects of the modification are propagated, via the base view, to all other interested views to maintain consistency, as described in Section 11.7.

11.5 VIEW CONSTRUCTION AND VIEW NAVIGATION

The user of SPE may construct any number of views of a program. Figure 11.2, for example, shows several additional design level views used in constructing the drawing program example of Figure 11.1. Each view may be hidden or displayed using the navigation tools described below. Elements may be added to a view using a variety of tools, with an arbitrary depth undo/redo facility. We distinguish between two types of view and element addition: the *extension* of a view to incorporate program elements already defined in another view (i.e., browser construction and static program visualization); and the *addition* of new program elements (i.e., visual programming).

Each graphical view has a palette of "drawing" tools which are primarily used for element addition. Tools are provided for the addition of classes, class features (added to the class icon), and generalization and client-supplier relationships. For the latter, additional information about the relationship (name, arity, whether it is inherited, and type-call, aggregate, abstract) is specified by dialog box. Class icons can be selected and dragged (using a selection tool) in a similar manner to figures in a drawing package. Tools are also provided for creating new views and removing elements from a view, or completely from the program.

Mouse operations on class icons allow views to be extended to include feature names, generalizations, specializations, and the various forms of client supplier relationships defined in other views. This allows specialized views of an existing or partially developed program to be rapidly constructed, focusing on one or more aspects of that program. The view may then be used to modify the program using the visual programming tools. The *figure-Drawing* view in Figure 11.1, for example, has been created to show the interaction of methods in each of the figure and drawing_window classes. Programmers lay out views themselves to obtain the most useful visualization of programs. SPE automatically lays out view extension information, but programmers are able to move these extra objects to suit their needs.

Textual views are created in a similar manner to visual views, but consist of one or more *text forms* (class definitions, method implementations, or documentation), rather than icons and connectors. Textual views are manipulated by typing text in a normal manner, i.e., a *free-edit* mode of operation, in contrast to the *structure-edit* approach of the graphical tools,* and then parsed to update base program information. This is in contrast to most other environments, such as Dora [Ratcliff et al. 1992], Mjølner [Magnusson et al. 1990], and PECAN [Reiss 1985], which use structure-editors for both graphics and text. Structure-edited approaches for text tend to be quite restrictive on the user [Arefi et al. 1990, Welsh et al. 1991]. Methods can be added to the same textual view as a class definition, or can have their own views (and windows). Class definition and method textual views may be typed in from scratch, or may, more typically, be generated by extension from other views and then modified in a free-edit fashion. In addition, existing textual programs may be imported into SPE. Textual views for imported programs are automatically constructed, and corresponding visual views can be simply constructed by extension from the textually derived information.

As described in Section 11.2, programmers need to locate information easily from a large number of views and to be able to gain a high-level overview of different program aspects. SPE's approach is to use the program views themselves in a hypertext-like fashion as the basis for browsing. Class icons in graphical views have a number of active regions, or *click-points*, which cause predetermined actions to be carried out (similar to Prograph's dataflow entities [Cox et al. 1989]). Click points allow rapid navigation to any other views (textual or graphical)

---

* Text forms can also be edited using an alternative menu-driven, structure-oriented style of editing.

containing the class or individual features of the class. Menus in textual views provide similar functionality to click points, but based on the currently selected piece of text. Programmers can construct additional views, textual or visual, primarily for program browsing, based on information selected from other views.

11.6 PHASES AND MODES OF CONSTRUCTION

SPE makes little distinction between the different phases of the design cycle, in keeping with the philosophy of Section 11.2. There are no special view types for each of the phases. The palette of tools in the visual views can be used to define analysis, design, and implementation level view elements. The one-client supplier tool, for example, can be used to specify abstract class relationships, abstract or concrete aggregate relationships, and abstract or concrete method calling protocols by a combination of click and drag mouse operations and an auxiliary dialog box. It is left to the user to decide what information is to be placed in each view. Thus, the user may choose to have separate analysis, design, and implementation views, or may mix several phases in the one view. Relationships initially specified as abstract may be refined to more concrete implementations either within the current view, or by creating a new view and specializing the relationships there.

The lack of distinction between tools for use in various phases is deliberate. It would be fairly straightforward to define specialized SPE view types for the different design phases [e.g., Wasserman and Pircher 1987], providing limits on what can be specified in each phase. This would, however, run counter to the rather fluid, evolutionary way in which object-oriented systems tend to be developed.

Users are not constrained to program only in a single mode (textual or visual). More visually literate programmers can construct their programs mostly via visual views. Most of the important inter- and intra-class relationships (e.g., inheritance, method, and attribute declaration, and method call protocols) can be defined visually. Currently, textual views are required only for detailed method implementation and textual documentation. More textually literate programmers can develop their programs using textual views, creating visual views by extension for purposes of documentation, browsing, and static program visualization, and for communication with their more visually literate colleagues.

There is, however, some distinction between the different view types. Detailed method implementation may only be done within textual views, as there is no corresponding visual representation.* Some of the high level relationships expressible in visual views have no corresponding representation in textual views, other than as comments. Two specialized textual view types are provided in SPE: canonical textual views for class definition and for method implementation. These views provide a textual rendering of the underlying base view of the program. They can

---

* We are currently implementing a dataflow-style visual tool, similar to Prograph [Cox et al. 1989], to also permit the complete visual construction of systems.

be edited and manipulated just like any other textual view but also serve to specify what the language compiler will "see" of the program. They also have a special significance with respect to view consistency, as described in the following section.

11.7 VIEW CONSISTENCY AND TRACEABILITY USING UPDATE RECORDS

The requirements, analysis, design, and implementation of a program may change many times during its development. Thus a mechanism is needed for managing changes, maintaining consistency between views after a change, and recording the fact that a change has taken place. Many CASE tools and programming environments provide facilities for generating code based on a design [Coad and Yourdon 1991, Wasserman and Pircher 1987], and some support reverse engineering, such as the C Development Environment [IDE 92], updating design from code. A few provide complete consistency management when code or design are changed, such as Dora [Ratcliffe et al. 92], but they can not propagate "fuzzy" updates between design and implementation views (i.e., updates which don't have a one-to-one correspondence from one level to the next, such as client–supplier relationships).

In addition, the ability to trace requirements and design decisions is important [Boehm 1984, Pfleeger 1991]. Modifying a requirement implies the need to trace through the design and implementation decisions made to support that requirement and to update them appropriately. Similarly, if code implementing a requirement is modified, it is important to be able to trace back to the requirement to check if it is still met.

SPE uses *update records* for consistency management. When a change takes place (for example, a feature is renamed, or a generalization relationship is removed from a class) the modification is recorded as an update record against the class (and possibly some of its subcomponents). Update records contain a complete specification of the change made, and form the basis of the undo/redo facility.

Update records are propagated from the view that is the source of a modification to all other views affected by the modification. The views affected by a change are automatically determined from the semantics of the element modified. Thus deletion of a method of a class will cause update records to be propagated to any view containing either the method or the class (and possibly subclasses).

What is done with a propagated update record depends on the view to which the record is sent. Consider the case of a method deletion update record. It is ignored if it does not affect the view, for example, if the deleted method is not shown in the class' icon. Alternatively, there may be sufficient information for the view to be modified immediately; for example, the method name can be removed from a class icon without additional information being required. In this case, however, it is often useful to have a visual indication that a change has occurred as a result of work done in another view. This is done in a number of ways, depending on

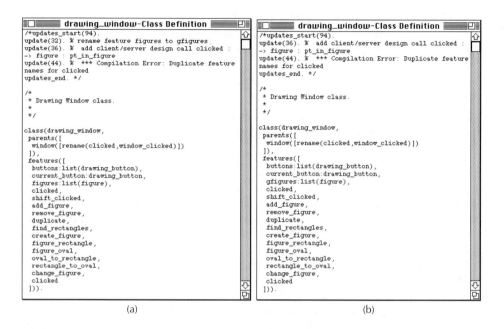

<table>
<tr><td>

```
╔═▣═════ drawing_window-Class Definition ═════╗
/*updates_start(94).
update(32). % rename feature figures to gfigures
update(36). % add client/server design call clicked :
-> figure : pt_in_figure
update(44). % *** Compilation Error: Duplicate feature
names for clicked
updates_end. */

/*
 * Drawing Window class.
 *
 */

class(drawing_window,
  parents([
    window([rename(clicked,window_clicked)])
  ]),
  features([
    buttons:list(drawing_button),
    current_button:drawing_button,
    figures:list(figure),
    clicked,
    shift_clicked,
    add_figure,
    remove_figure,
    duplicate,
    find_rectangles,
    create_figure,
    figure_rectangle,
    figure_oval,
    oval_to_rectangle,
    rectangle_to_oval,
    change_figure,
    clicked
  ])).
```

</td><td>

```
╔═▣═════ drawing_window-Class Definition ═════╗
/*updates_start(94).
update(36). % add client/server design call clicked :
-> figure : pt_in_figure
update(44). % *** Compilation Error: Duplicate feature
names for clicked
updates_end. */

/*
 * Drawing Window class.
 *
 */

class(drawing_window,
  parents([
    window([rename(clicked,window_clicked)])
  ]),
  features([
    buttons:list(drawing_button),
    current_button:drawing_button,
    gfigures:list(figure),
    clicked,
    shift_clicked,
    add_figure,
    remove_figure,
    duplicate,
    find_rectangles,
    create_figure,
    figure_rectangle,
    figure_oval,
    oval_to_rectangle,
    rectangle_to_oval,
    change_figure,
    clicked
  ])).
```

</td></tr>
<tr><td align="center">(a)</td><td align="center">(b)</td></tr>
</table>

Figure 11.3   (a) Updates expanded in a textual view, (b) first update applied

whether the view is graphical or textual. In SPE visual views, elements deleted by another view are shown *grayed out*, to provide the appropriate visual clue. If the user, on reviewing the effect of the change, is unhappy with the change, it can be simply reversed by manipulating the grayed-out element, which acts as an interface to the undo/redo facility. In textual views, the update record is *unparsed* into a human readable form and included as a pseudo comment in the view. Figure 11.3a, for example, shows a textual class definition view with three update records unparsed at the beginning of the text.

As a special case, canonical textual views display every update record prior to its "implementation," so that the user has a final chance to review the changes before "committal." Thus, the first update record in Figure 11.3a indicates that the figures feature of the drawing_window class has had its name changed (in another view) to gfigures. The user may commit the changes by selecting the update records and requesting the changes to be effected. Figure 11.3b shows the same view after automatically effecting the first update record.

In many cases, however, there is insufficient information for the view to be updated adequately, as there is only a partial mapping between representations. For example, the second update record in Figure 11.3a indicates that there has been an addition of a method call client–supplier relationship to a visual view. This addition contains insufficient information to directly modify the implementation. Missing are parameter information, and the exact location within the calling method where the call is to be made. Similarly, a compilation error record (as shown in the third update record of Figure 11.3a) does not contain sufficient information to automatically infer the appropriate correction. In these cases, the update records serve to show that the view or program is (potentially) inconsistent or erroneous, and that the programmer may need to make an appropriate change. These fuzzy update records are an important and novel contribution of the work presented here. Recognizing that automatic consistency is impossible, these update records provide a means for the environment to interact with the creative element (the programmer) responsible for achieving complete consistency.

A special case of fuzzy updates occurs in textual documentation views. These receive and display every update record relating to the program entity being documented (class or method), providing a partially automatic documentation revision facility. The textual contents of the update records can be cut and pasted by the programmer into the body of the documentation in an appropriate way to complete the documentation revision.

SPE's view consistency mechanism provides support for the evolutionary, iterative refinement approach to software development typical of object-oriented programming. For example, if the drawing program requirements are extended so that wedge-shaped figures and arbitrary polygon figures are supported, these changes are made incrementally at each stage. Analysis views are extended to incorporate new figure and button classes, and new features are added to classes. Design level views are extended to support the requirements of each new type of figure and implementation level views are added or modified to implement these changes. At each stage, update records are used to notify views of changes that have been, or need to be made, to keep the entire design consistent. Similarly, if changes are made to an implementation or design view, update records are propagated to relevant design and analysis views, thus supporting bidirectional consistency between programming phases.

Update records provide more than a consistency mechanism. Update records are persistent, providing a permanent history of program modification, and may be viewed, for any program component, via a menu option. User-defined updates may be added to document change at a high level of abstraction. Users may also textually annotate an individual update, such as to explain why the change was made, by whom, and when. This mechanism provides documentation support addition to the automatic inclusion of fuzzy updates in documentation views.

The update record mechanism currently provides only partial support for tracing requirements through design and implementation (and vice versa). Yet to be implemented is a mechanism whereby changes manually made as a result of an update record can be associated with that update record. This is conceptually fairly straightforward, but requires careful implementation, as such changes may be spread across a number of views and places within a view. Such an extension, together with the ability to navigate via the persistent update records would give full support for traceability.

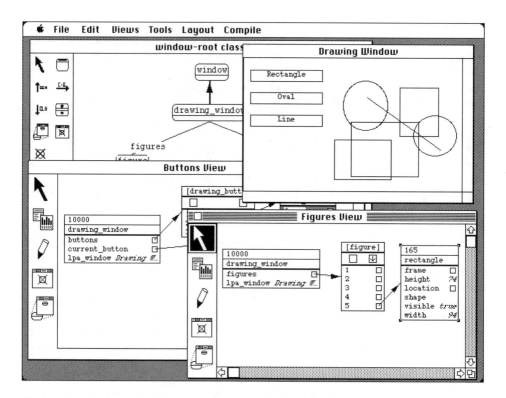

Figure 11.4   Cerno in use with SPE debugging the drawing program

11.8 BRIDGING THE GAP TO EXECUTION—CERNO

Multiple program views, at different levels of abstraction, are also beneficial at execution time. Cerno is a visual debugging system for the Snart language which provides multiple views of an executing Snart program [Fenwick et al. 1994]. Each view is kept consistent with the underlying program execution state. A Cerno view is composed of a number of *displays* for objects, together with connectors representing relationships between the objects, such as object references. A display is an iconic depiction of the state of an object or a higher level abstraction of a collection of objects. The contents of a view and the way in which the view is laid out are under the user's control.

Figure 11.4 shows Cerno in use, with SPE debugging and visualizing the drawing program. In the background is an SPE view. In the foreground is a drawing window, generated by the application, and two Cerno views, one focusing on the button objects and one on the figure objects associated with the drawing window. As with SPE, a Cerno view includes a tool palette (the array of iconic buttons to the left of the Cerno views). Tools include an icon layout editor, an object value editor to modify the underlying program execution state, and a view creation tool. Additional functionality is provided via menus.

The form and contents of a display can be quite flexibly defined and layed out. Filters select specific attributes to display or those that satisfy specified criteria. Layout of information can be done using predefined object view types (such as a vertical list of features plus values, or a bar graph for collections of numbers). New filters and view types can be defined using a simple, but powerful and extensible, icon layout language.

Rather than accessing and manipulating the underlying object state directly, Cerno's display level interacts with a layer of *abstractors*, which, in turn, interact with low level object-tracing facilities.* Abstractors present a uniform interface to the display level. An abstractor provides a display with a list of (attribute, type, value) triples and informs the display whenever any values in that list change (making use of update records). The display uses the list to construct the iconic representation.

Simple abstractors perform a direct translation from the actual object state to the list of triples. More complex abstractors may be constructed to aggregate information from a number of simple abstractors in a similar fashion to the encapsulators of Noble and Groves [Noble and Groves 1992]. For example, abstractors for viewing collections abstractly in a variety of forms, e.g., linked lists of nodes, abstracted lists of values, etc., are provided. Similarly abstractors may be used to disaggregate information from lower level abstractors; for example, Cerno allows records embedded in objects to be viewed as pseudo objects through the use of appropriate abstractors.

Figure 11.5 illustrates the use of complex abstractors in Cerno. At the top of the view, a box and connector view of a linked list containing integer values are shown. This uses simple object abstractors, one for each list element. The central display is a high level view of the same list showing the list as a sequence of (element number, value pairs), abstracting away the list links. The list abstractor gathers information from the individual object abstractors, and presents this to the display level as a single list of (element number, type, value) triples, which are displayed as shown. The bottom display uses the same high level list abstractor, but the icon display language has been used to construct a display showing two subviews of the list: as a vertical list of element numbers, types and values, and as a vertical bar graph of values. This complex list view is specified with a line of icon layout language code:

(horizontal([features(long,all),vline(1),features(vertical_graph(–10,10,100),all)])).

Abstractors can also be used to provide views of the dynamic calling structure of an executing program. Figure 11.6, for example, shows object displays which include both the data relationships between objects and the current method stack. Active methods are listed at the bottom of each object display (with vertical bars at the left to distinguish them from attributes), while method calls are shown as arrows connecting the methods. Figure 11.7 shows a "timing diagram" (similar to

---

* The Snart language provides object-spying facilities which allow any object's execution state to be monitored transparently without program code modification. These facilities provide standard breakpoint insertion, spypoints, and single step execution capabilities.

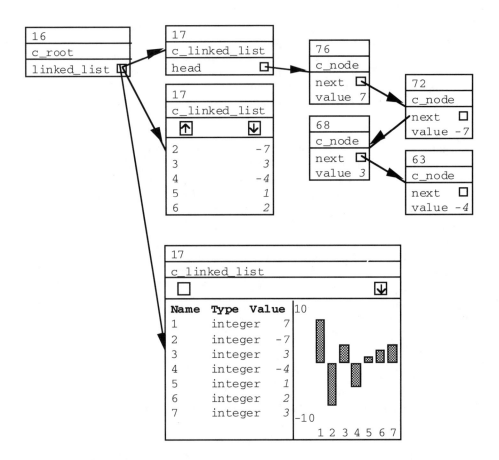

Figure 11.5   Three Cerno views of a linked list

those of [Booch 1991]), visually illustrating the history of method calls during the execution of a program. This display makes use of a history abstractor, which gathers information from each method call, and provides it to a display view to depict the time and duration* of each method call with bar graphs.

Interesting program views can be saved as templates, to be reused during later executions of the same (or a similar) program. When applied to an object, a template attempts to reconstruct as similar a view as possible to the view used to construct the template. The views will differ, however, owing to the different objects, object references, and attribute values involved. In addition to their reuse in fault finding, templates allow execution time views to be reused for dynamic documentation; a program, template and suitable test data can be used to illustrate important aspects of the program's behavior.

---

* In terms of the number of other method calls made between the call and return of a method.

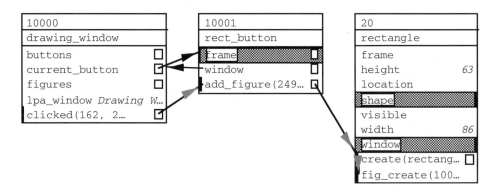

Figure 11.6 Cerno View showing object references (dark arrows) and active method calls (grey arrows). The hashed background on some attributes indicate their value is incompatible with their declared type.

Currently, SPE and Cerno interact in a simple manner: it is possible to navigate from Cerno views to SPE views and vice versa. This allows the definitions of the classes of an object (and related class diagrams) or method implementations to be accessed directly from the object, and for execution views and templates related to a class to be accessed from a class view. Both of these are done in a similar hypertext style manner to the SPE inter-view navigation capabilities. Current work aimed at improving the integration is described in Section 11.11.

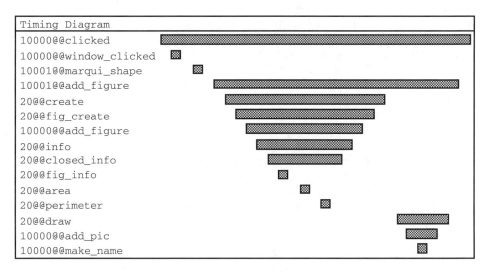

Figure 11.7 Cerno timing diagram, showing time and duration of method calls (listed as objectid@@methodname labels to the left). The time is given in terms of numbers of method calls, and increases to the right.

SPE already provides a fairly fluid program development environment, permitting boundaries between different phases of software development to be easily bridged. The integration of Cerno and SPE extends this to include debugging and dynamic program visualization, providing "cradle-to-the-grave" support for software development.

11.9 IMPLEMENTATION—MVIEWS

Both SPE and Cerno are implemented as specializations of MViews, a generic object-oriented framework for developing multiple-view based programming environments described in the literature [Grundy and Hosking 1993]. MViews provides base support for multiple textual and graphical views, consistency management via the update record mechanism, undo and redo facilities using update records, and program and view persistence. MViews is implemented in Snart, the object-oriented Prolog for which SPE provides a programming environment. Snart's combination of object-orientation and logic programming provides a powerful prototyping language, incorporating support for object persistence, object version spaces, declarative and procedural programming styles, and ready access to the powerful graphics capabilities of LPA Prolog [LPA 1992]. Construction of SPE proceeded much faster with Snart than with earlier prototypes of SPE that used Eiffel [Meyer 1992] and C++ [Stroustrup 1984].

Specialization of MViews to SPE is in two steps. IspelM is a generic specialization of MViews for object-oriented programming. It provides most of the graphical tool support used by SPE, together with other language-independent facilities. SPE specializes IspelM further for programming in Snart, through provision of Snart-specific facilities, such as parsers, unparsers, compiler integration, and Snart object management.

The approach of using multiple layers of frameworks added extra complexity to the initial construction of SPE. Some careful design was required to cope with the multistep specializations. Building in useful reusability almost always results in additional costs in terms of the time taken to sort out suitable general purpose abstractions. However, we believe the additional costs are worthwhile, as they have led to a much more flexible product.

As an indication of the reusability of the base MViews framework, a system for multiple-view entity–relationship diagramming plus relational schema editing, required less than 1 person-week to design and implement. Extension of IspelM to support other diagramming notations and object-oriented languages is a straightforward task of appropriately specializing the generic framework. Modifying an icon shape to support an alternative notation, compatible with the programmer's preferred object-oriented analysis and design methodology for example, amounts to a few lines of code. Adding an additional graphical tool involves specialization of the appropriate window class, the addition of a method for tool invocation, and possibly redefinition of generic routines for mouse handling, line drawing, etc.

SPE makes use of a preexisting language compiler for Snart.* Modification of SPE to support other languages, such as C++ [Stroustrup 1984], mostly impacts on the textual view handling components, as the graphical tools are just as applicable to other (class-based) object-oriented languages. Textual views require parsers and unparsers to match the language syntax, and the availability of an existing C++ compiler to use for semantic processing. The parsers and unparsers can be written directly in Snart (or Prolog), or implemented using Yacc or other parser generators. Additional textual forms may also be required. For example, C++ could usefully make use of .h forms, while class contract forms for pre and post conditions and class invariants are desirable for Eiffel [Meyer 1992]. To give an indication of the likely costs involved, the specialization of IspelM to support programming in the Express and Express-G textual and graphical object-oriented specification languages [ISO 1992] (together with use of Snart and Cerno to prototype and visualize implementations of the resulting Express schema) took only 2–3 person-weeks to yield a usable system [Amor et al. 1994].

Cerno too, is fairly generic in its approach, and could be used to visualize other object-oriented execution environments. The principal requirement is access to the underlying object states, with appropriate events indicating change of state. This involves modification of the simple object abstractor classes, but very little in the way of modification is required for the rest of the system (including the higher level abstractors). Modifying Cerno to support new display abstractions involves specializing or creating new abstractor classes (written in Snart), while new display visualizations can be simply developed using the icon layout language.

11.10 EXPERIENCE

SPE has, to date, been applied to two substantial projects. In one, two existing object oriented systems were integrated together using high level SPE analysis views to perform the initial schema integration, and design and implementation views to implement the interschema mappings [Mugridge and Hosking 1994]. This involved use of SPE's textual import capabilities, to load the environment with the legacy systems, and consequent construction of abstract visual views by extension from the textual information. Use of multiple views to manage the complexity of integrating the two large systems was invaluable in completing this project. In particular, the ability to rapidly create abstract visual views from the original textual program was important for the early stages of schema integration [Mugridge and Hosking 1994].

Both SPE and Cerno have been adapted and used extensively in a project for constructing object oriented models of buildings (SPE), using Snart to represent the building schema, and navigable and editable instances of the models (Cerno) [Amor and Hosking 1993]. Here, the view consistency provided by SPE is critically

---

* Allowing the environment to make use of an existing compiler has obvious advantages over constructing a special-purpose compiler.

important, as it allows views of the building schema tailored for different building professionals to be kept consistent with one another.

SPE has been used to develop and visualize both the MViews framework, and SPE itself [Grundy 1993]. Use of SPE has enabled us to better visualize the inter-relationhips of MViews components, and hence it has assisted in both maintaining MViews and SPE and in making design improvements for future versions of these systems. The multiple views of these complex object-oriented frameworks, particularly the provision of graphical and textual views with bidirectional consistency management, has made their maintenance easier. We are able to make design changes via visual programming or textual programming, whichever is most appropriate. More formal user testing of SPE, comparing the ease of development of given systems with and without SPE, is planned.

SPE can represent large, complex graphs within one view. A zoom facility is supported which shows an overview of the whole graph structure and allows programmers to zoom in on specific parts of the graph as required. However, we have found multiple views to be a more useful approach to representing and manipulating such complex visual program structures. A large graph is better split into multiple views, with each view focusing on specific classes and class relationships. This allows programmers to more easily understand the complex structures, as many relationships and classes can be removed from a diagram and shown in a separate view. This approach allows for either hierarchical views, as found in many dataflow systems, like Prograph [Cox et al. 89], or many overlapping views. This means that the view navigation facilities of SPE are essential to managing these multiple aspects of a complex software system.

The MViews framework underlying SPE has application beyond the realm of object-oriented programming environments. MViews has been used to develop a multiple-view entity–relationship diagrammer, a dialog box painter/editor, and is currently being used to implement a visual-Pascal [Lyons et al. 1993] and to implement an environment for parallel programming.

11.11 FUTURE WORK

While there is much to be done to fully meet the requirements listed in Section 11.2, a substantial start has been made. Current work is aimed at traceability support, tools for large scale software development including multi-user program construction support (moderated by update records), version control and macroediting operations using update records, and improving the crossover between Cerno and SPE. An interesting extension, which we are currently tackling, is to permit translation from Cerno templates into SPE class diagram views and vice versa. Thus, an interesting execution time view of a program could be translated into a class diagram, useful for documentation purposes or static browsing. Likewise, program design and implementation views can be translated into templates that can be used to view actual program state. The MViews update record mechanism could also potentially be used to maintain a "pointing finger," or similar, approach to highlight the source code of the currently executing method in an appropriate SPE textual view. There is also potential in adapting Cerno's icon layout language for use in defining SPE's icons. Other extensions to Cerno planned include the creation of "replayable" program animations, and experimentation with new higher level abstractors. There is also scope for adding more specialized view types to both SPE and Cerno, such as the dynamic views of De Pauw [De Pauw et al. 1993].

11.12 SUMMARY

We have described SPE, an environment for object-oriented programming, and its execution time companion Cerno. Together these implement most of the requirements specified in Section 11.2. In this summary we will review those requirements and the means by which SPE and Cerno implement them.

Visual representations of abstract interclass relationships and more concrete instantiations of those relationships are provided in SPE. Textual representation in the form of class interface, method implementation, and documentation views are supported. The textual and visual views can be used to both visualize parts of the program, by extension from information supplied in other views, and to construct, by direct manipulation and free form editing, new parts of the program. Visual and textual representation of the execution state of the program is provided by Cerno. Cerno views are also editable, and hence can be used to modify the execution state of the program.

All SPE and Cerno views are kept consistent with one another using the update record mechanism. Where automatic view consistency is not possible, such as changes propagated between SPE views showing different levels of abstraction or programming phases, views are visually annotated to indicate that programmer modifications are required to maintain the consistency. This fuzzy update support is a particularly novel feature of the work presented here. A special, and important, example of the latter is in the partially automatic revision of documentation views in SPE. The viewable, editable, persistent history mechanism is another useful and novel byproduct of the update record mechanism.

There is no limit to the number of views that can be constructed in either SPE or Cerno, and users are free to choose both the contents and layout of views. This permits users to construct views that focus on either small parts of the system, or to abstract away detail to provide system overview views. Simple view navigation, via automatically constructed hypertext links, allows users ready access to desired information. The access links between Cerno and SPE bridge the gap between program specification and program execution and testing.

Boundaries between programming phases in SPE are deliberately kept vague (or more precisely there is no enforcement of which relationships can be specified in which type of view). This supports exploratory programming and an evolutionary approach to software development. The proposed facilities for mapping between SPE views and Cerno templates will also assist in breaking the barrier between phases.

Traceability is not yet well supported. The mechanism of expansion of fuzzy update records as readable text provides partial support, but extra facilities are required to associate update records propagated from changes made in early phase views with implementations of those changes made in later phase views. A navigation facility using this traceability information will also enhance software development which uses visual techniques. Work is in progress to provide such facilities.

ACKNOWLEDGMENTS

We gratefully acknowledge the financial support of the University of Auckland Research Committee. John Grundy has been supported by an IBM Postgraduate Scholarship, a William Georgetti Scholarship, and a New Zealand Universities Postgraduate Scholarship. Stephen Fenwick has been supported by a University of Auckland Graduate Scholarship. John Hosking acknowledges the assistance of the EEE Department of Imperial College of Science Technology and Medicine in the preparation of this manuscript.

REFERENCES

[Amor and Hosking 1993] R.A. Amor and J.G. Hosking, "Multidisciplinary views for integrated and concurrent design," in *Selected (refereed) Papers from the Proc of the First International Conference on Management of Information Technology for Construction* (K.S. Mathur, M.P. Betts, and K.W. Tham, eds.), Singapore, 1993, pp. 255–267.

[Amor et al. 1994] R. Amor, G. Augenbroe, J. Hosking, W. Rombouts, J. Grundy, *Directions in Modelling Environments*, Technical report, Technical University of Delft, Department of Civil Engineering, 1994.

[Arefi et al. 1990] F. Arefi, C.E. Hughes and D.A. Workman, "Automatically generating visual syntax-directed editors," *Communications of the ACM*, Vol. 33, No. 3, 1990, pp. 349–360.

[Boehm 1984] B.W. Boehm, "Verifying and validating software requirements and design specifications," *IEEE Software*, Vol. 2, 1984, pp. 75–88.

[Booch 1991] G. Booch, *Object-Oriented Design with Applications*, Benjamin/ Cummings, Menlo Park, 1991.

[Borras 1988] P. Borras, D. Clement, T. Despeyroux, J. Incerpi, G. Kahn, B. Lang, and V. Pascual, "CENTAUR: the system," in *Proceedings of ACM SIGSOFT '88: Third Symposium on Software Development Environments*, Boston, 1988, pp. 131–142.

[Burnett and Ambler 1994] M. Burnett and A. Ambler, "Interactive visual data abstraction in a declarative visual programming language," *Journal of Visual Languages and Computing*, March 1994, pp. 29–60.

[Chikofsky and Rubenstein 1988] E.T. Chikofsky and B.L. Rubenstein, "CASE: Reliability engineering for information systems," *IEEE Software*, Vol. 5, 1988, pp. 11–16.

[Coad and Yourdon 1991] P. Coad, and E. Yourdon, *Object-Oriented Analysis*, Second Edition, Yourdon Press, Englewood Cliffs, 1991.

[Cox et al. 1989] P.T. Cox, F.R. Giles, and T. Pietrzykowski, "Prograph: a step towards liberating programming from textual conditioning," in *Proceedings 1989 IEEE Workshop on Visual Languages*, Rome, 1989, pp. 150–156.

[De Pauw et al. 1993] W. De Pauw, R. Helm, D. Kimelman, and J. Vlissides, "Visualizing the behavior of object-oriented systems," in *Proceedings OOPSLA 93*, Washington DC, September 1993, pp. 326–337.

[Fenwick et al. 1994] S. Fenwick, J.G. Hosking, and W.B. Mugridge, *Cerno-II: A Program Visualisation System*, Report No. 87, Department of Computer Science, University of Auckland, New Zeland, 1994.

[Furnas 1993] G. Furnas, "Towards radically visual computation," in *Proceedings 1993 IEEE Visual Languages Symposium*, Bergen, Norway, 1993, p. 2.

[Grundy 1993] J.C. Grundy, *Multiple textual and graphical views for interactive software development environments*, PhD thesis, Department of Computer Science, University of Auckland, Auckland, New Zealand, 1993.

[Grundy and Hosking 1993] J.C. Grundy and J.G. Hosking, "Constructing multi-view editing environments using MViews," in *Proceedings 1993 IEEE Symposium on Visual Languages*, Bergen, Norway, 1993, pp. 220–224.

[Henderson-Sellers and Edwards 1990] B. Henderson-Sellers and J.M. Edwards, "The object-oriented systems life cycle," *Communications of the ACM*, Vol. 33, No. 9, 1990, pp. 142–159.

[IDE 1993] *The C Development Environment*, Interactive Development Environments, 595 Market Street, San Francisco, CA 94105, 1993.

[ISO 1992] *ISO/TC184 1992 Part 11: The EXPRESS Language Reference Manual in Industrial automation systems and integration—Product data representation and exchange*, Draft International Standard, ISO-IEC, Geneva, Switzerland, ISO DIS 10303-11, August, 1992.

[Kaiser and Garlan 1987] G.E. Kaiser and D. Garlan, "Melding software systems from reusable blocks," *IEEE Software*, Vol. 4, No. 4, 1987, pp. 17–24.

[Knuth 1992] D.E. Knuth, *Literate Programming*, University of Chicago, Chicago, 1992.

[LPA 1992] *MacPROLOG Graphics Manual*, Logic Programming Associates, London, 1992.

[Lyons et al. 1993] P. Lyons, C. Simmons, and M. Apperley, "HyperPascal: Using visual programming to model the idea space," in *Proceedings 13th New Zealand Computer Society Conference*, Auckland, New Zealand, August 1993, pp. 492–508.

[Magnusson et al. 1990] B. Magnusson, M. Bengtsson, L. Dahlin, G. Fries, A. Gustavsson, G. Hedin, S. Minör, D. Oscarsson, and M. Taube "An overview of the Mjølner/ORM environment: incremental language and software development," in *Proceedings of TOOLS '90*, Santa Barbara, October 1990, pp. 635–646.

[Meyer 1992] B. Meyer, *Eiffel the Language*, Prentice Hall, Herts, United Kingdom, 1992.

[Meyers 1991] S. Meyers, "Difficulties in integrating multiple view editing environments," *IEEE Software*, Vol. 8, No. 1, 1991, pp. 49–57.

[Mugridge and Hosking 1994] W.B. Mugridge and J.G. Hosking, "Towards a lazy, evolutionary common building model," accepted for publication in *Building and Environment.*, 1994.

[Noble and Groves 1992] K.J. Noble and L.J. Groves, "Tarraingim—a program animation environment," *New Zealand Journal of Computing*, Vol. 4, No. 1, 1992, pp. 29–40.

[Habermann and Notkin 1982] N. Habermann, and D. Notkin, "Gandalf software development environment," in *The Second Compendium of Gandalf Documantation*, Department of Computer Science, Carnegie-Mellon University, May 1982.

[Pfleeger 1991] S.L. Pfleeger, *Software Engineering: The Production of Quality Software*, 2nd Edition, MacMillan, 1991.

[Ratcliff et al. 1992] M. Ratcliff, C. Wang, R.J. Gautier, and B.R.Whittle "Dora—a structure oriented environment generator," *Software Engineering Journal*, Vol. 7, No. 3, 1992, pp. 184–190.

[Reiss 1985] S.P. Reiss, "PECAN: Program development systems that support multiple views," *IEEE Transactions on Software Engineering*, Vol. 11, No. 3, 1985, pp. 276–285.

[Reiss 1990a] S.P. Reiss, "Connecting tools using message passing in the field environment," *IEEE Software*, Vol. 7, 1990, pp. 57–66.

[Reiss 1990b] S.P. Reiss, "Interacting with the FIELD environment," *Software—Practice and Experience*, Vol. 20, No. S1, 1990, pp. S1/89–S1/115.

[Stroustrup 1984] B. Stroustrup, *The C++ Programming Language*, Addison-Wesley, Reading, 1984.

[StructSoft Inc 1992] *TurboCASE*, StructSoft Inc, 5416 156th Ave. S.E. Bellevue, WA 98006, 1992.

[Wang et al. 1992] C. Wang, C-C. Leung, M. Ratcliffe, and F. Long, *Multiple Views of Software Development*, Technical report, Computer Science Department, University College of Wales, Aberystwyth, 1992.

[Wasserman and Pircher 1987] A.I. Wasserman and P.A. Pircher, "A graphical, extensible, integrated environment for software development," *SIGPLAN Notices*, Vol. 22, No. 1, 1987, pp. 131–142.

[Wasserman et al. 1990] A.I. Wasserman, P.A. Pircher, and R.J. Muller, "The object-oriented structured design notation for software design representation," *IEEE Computer*, Vol. 23, No. 3, March 1990, pp. 50–63.

[Welsh et al. 1991] J. Welsh, B. Broom, and D. Kiong, "A design rationale for a language-based editor," *Software—Practice and Experience*, Vol. 21, No. 9, 1991, pp. 923–948.

C H A P T E R   1 2   ❏ ❏ ❏ ❏

Framework Development and Reuse Support

WOLFGANG PREE

253

One of the benefits of object-oriented programming and design is the potential for design reuse through frameworks. A framework is a generic application that is suitable for easily creating a whole family of applications. But developing new software based on an application framework requires learning the classes and interaction protocol of that framework. This chapter discusses concepts and corresponding visual approaches to support learning, refining, and reusing frameworks.

12.1 INTRODUCTION

Concepts offered by object-oriented programming languages are often used to produce reusable single components. The concepts of inheritance and dynamic binding are sufficient to construct application frameworks, i.e., reusable semifinished architectures for various application domains. Such frameworks represent a real breakthrough in software reusability: not only single building blocks, but also the design of (sub)systems can be reused.

Application frameworks such as Smalltalk's MVC framework [Krasner 1988], MacApp [Schmucker 1986 and Wilson 1990], AppKit [NeXT 1990] and ET++ [Weinand 1988, Gamma 1992 and Eggenschwiler 1992] can be viewed as the first test bed for the development of reusable architectures by means of object-oriented concepts. These frameworks for the graphic user interface (GUI) domain have become one of the main reasons that object-oriented programming enjoys such a good reputation for promoting extensibility and reuse. Frameworks are not restricted to a narrow range of domains, but are almost universally applicable. Examples include frameworks for VLSI routing algorithms [Gossain 1989] and operating systems [Russo 1989].

Main thesis   Frameworks can amount to a real breakthrough in software reusability if they can be adapted easily to the specific needs of a domain. The interactive visual techniques discussed in this chapter help in understanding, refining, and developing frameworks.

A *framework* defines a high-level language with which applications within a domain are created through specialization. *Specialization* takes place at points of predefined refinement that we call *hot spots*. A framework-centered software development process requires the creation and reuse of frameworks. We recommend new tools—electronic books—to support this process:

- *Creation of frameworks*   Design books communicate the design of existing frameworks so that some design ideas can be reused in the creation of new frameworks.

- *Reuse of frameworks*   Design books and *active cookbooks* assist in specializing a particular framework.

Appropriate design books and active cookbooks should help an experienced programmer to understand the internal structures of frameworks, and to develop software based on these reusable architectures. Serving as an aid for programming novices to support end user computing is a secondary goal of these electronic books.

Since we can develop application frameworks for a range of domains, the concepts and tools we propose are applicable to various levels of programming. For instance, design books and active cookbooks can be provided for application frameworks dealing with low-level operating system tasks, as well as for application frameworks for high-level software, such as reservation systems.

12.2 CONCEPTUAL AND TERMINOLOGICAL FOUNDATIONS

Terms are often misused in the realm of object-oriented software development. This section builds a terminological and conceptual basis for the chapter.

Application framework   An *application framework* consists of ready-to-use and semifinished building blocks. The overall architecture, i.e., the composition and interaction of building blocks, is predefined as well. Producing specific applications usually means adapting components to specific needs by implementing some methods in subclasses of application framework classes.

In general, an application framework standardizes building blocks for a specific domain. An application framework is well-designed if it offers flexibility where required, i.e., if it can easily be adapted to domain-specific requirements. For example, ET++ is a well-designed application framework for the GUI domain. Weinand states that writing an application with a complex GUI by adapting ET++ can result in a significant reduction in source code size (i.e., the source code that has to be written by the programmer who adapts the framework), compared to software written with the support of a conventional graphic toolbox [Weinand 1989].

Usually, the term *application framework* means that its building blocks constitute a generic application for a domain. It is often hard to decide whether a framework belongs to this category. We will use the terms *framework* and *application framework* synonymously. When a distinction is necessary, we will use the term *application framework* explicitly.

Abstract classes and abstract methods   The principal idea underlying frameworks can be summarized in the following way. Semifinished components of a framework are represented by *abstract classes*. Some methods of an abstract class can be implemented, while only dummy or preliminary implementations can be provided for other methods, called *abstract methods*.

As a consequence, abstract classes are not instantiable classes. Their purpose is to *standardize the class interface* for all subclasses—subclasses can only augment the interface, but cannot change the names and parameters of methods defined in a superclass. Instances of subclasses of an abstract class will understand at least all messages that are defined in the abstract class. The term *contract* is used for this standardization property: instances of subclasses of a class A support the same contract as supported by instances of A.

The implication of abstract classes is that other semifinished or ready-to-use components of a framework can be implemented based on the contract of an abstract class. In the implementation of these components, reference variables are used that have the static type of the abstract classes on which they rely. Polymorphism allows such components to work with instances of subclasses of an abstract class. Due to dynamic binding, the concrete instances of subclasses of an abstract class bring in their specific behavior. So the behavior of framework components is ideally adapted by implementing only the abstract methods of semifinished components. The abstract methods constitute the principal *hot spots* of a framework.

Design patterns and metapatterns   It is still a matter of dispute how to describe essential design aspects in object-oriented systems. *Design pattern* approaches have recently emerged in the object-oriented community to cope with this problem. Proposed design pattern catalogs such as that of Erich Gamma et al. [Gamma 1992 and 1994] try to describe frameworks on an abstraction level higher than the corresponding code that implements these frameworks.

Design pattern catalogs essentially attempt to pick out frameworks that are not too domain-specific. Such frameworks are presented as examples of good object-oriented design that can be applied in the development of other frameworks. For example, the model/view aspect of the MVC framework constitutes a pattern in the design pattern catalog. In this miniframework, a model component notifies its dependent view components when changes occur. The view components display the data represented by the model component. Thus, view components have to be informed to update in the case of model changes.

Design pattern catalogs containing specific framework examples are useful means for constructing new frameworks. Nevertheless, a more advanced abstraction is necessary. This is useful to actively support the design pattern idea and to visualize a framework's design.

We will use the term *metapatterns* for a set of design patterns that describes how to construct frameworks that are independent of a specific domain. Metapatterns prove to be a simple yet powerful approach that can be applied to categorize and describe any specific framework pattern on a metalevel, so that the hot spots can be identified immediately.

The metapatterns presented in Section 12.3 do not replace state-of-the-art design pattern approaches; rather, metapatterns complement these approaches. The design books discussed in detail in Section 12.4 are based on metapatterns.

Design books and active cookbooks   *Design books* help the user browse through the essential design of a framework to see how semifinished components gain their flexibility. They are a way to visualize these flexible hot spots.

Design books can be viewed as advanced design pattern catalogs. Some aspects of a specific framework might be domain-independent, so that the design can be applied in the development of new frameworks. In these cases, design books serve the same purpose as design pattern catalogs. Actually, design pattern catalogs can be viewed as carefully chosen subsets of the design examples that can be captured and categorized in design books.

In addition to design pattern catalogs, design books can document the design of any domain-specific framework. Because metapattern browsers allow efficient design documentation of frameworks, they can help in adapting the hot spots of a framework to specific needs.

Application framework *cookbooks* contain numerous *recipes*. These recipes describe in an informal way how to adapt a framework to specific needs within a domain. Recipes usually do not explain internal design and implementation details of a framework.

Recipes are rather informal documents. Nevertheless, most cookbook recipes are structured roughly into the following sections:

* Purpose.

* Steps: how to do something, including references to other recipes.

* Source code examples.

A programmer has to find the recipe that is appropriate for a particular framework adaptation. This recipe is then used by simply adhering to the steps that describe how to accomplish a certain task.

We envision more active support of this typical way of developing software based on a framework, and we call the corresponding tool an *active cookbook*.

Active cookbooks and design books support the reuse and development of frameworks. We will first present metapatterns that form the conceptual basis of design books, and then will go on to discuss these electronic books.

12.3 METAPATTERNS

Metapatterns point out the few essential ideas of how to construct frameworks, i.e., reusable, flexible object-oriented software architectures, that are independent of a specific domain. They constitute an elegant and powerful approach to describe and visualize the design of a framework. Such efficient design communications help one to develop and reuse frameworks.

12.3.1 Class/Object Interface and Interaction Metapatterns

Template and hook methods represent the metapatterns required to design frameworks consisting of single classes or groups of classes together with their interactions. A template method implements a functionality in a generic way. Hook methods called from a template method form its generic parts. Subclasses of the class where a template method is defined can change the behavior of this template method at the predefined spots by implementing hook methods in a specific way.

The terms *template method* and *hook method* are commonly used by various authors [Wirfs-Brock 1990 and Gamma 1994]. We will assume that all methods are dynamically bound. (For example, this assumption is not valid for C++.) We will use the notation proposed by Rumbaugh in order to depict class diagrams [Rumbaugh 1991].

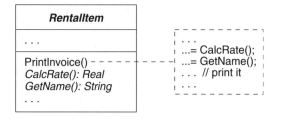

Figure 12.1   Template method *PrintInvoice* based on hook methods *CalcRate* and *GetName*

Let us take a closer look at how framework concepts are applied at the micro-level, i.e., in the implementation of methods. In order to implement frameworks, we have to consider the following kinds of methods: *template methods* that are based on *hook methods*, which are either *abstract methods*, or *template methods*.

Let us consider the example shown in Figure 12.1. We assume that an abstract class *RentalItem*, which could be part of an application framework for reservation systems, offers the three methods *PrintInvoice()*, *CalcRate()*, and *GetName()*. *PrintInvoice()* constitutes the template method based on the hook methods *CalcRate()* and *GetName()*. The hook methods are abstract methods. Abstract classes and abstract methods are written in *italic style* in the graphic representation.

The adaptation of *RentalItem* has to be done in a subclass where the abstract methods *CalcRate()* and *GetName()* of *RentalItem* are implemented. The default implementation of *PrintInvoice()* meets the requirements of the specific application under development.

The template method *PrintInvoice()* is adapted, for example, in a subclass of *RentalItem* called *HotelRoom* without changing the source code of *PrintInvoice()* (see Figure 12.2a). Figure 12.2b illustrates schematically the hook methods as hot spots of the template method *PrintInvoice()*. Framework specialization takes place at these hot spots.

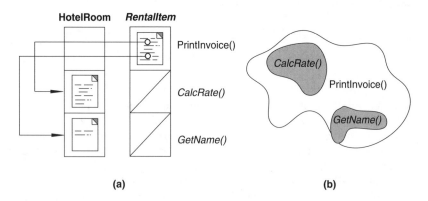

(a)   (b)

Figure 12.2   (a) Adaptation of template method *PrintInvoice()*, (b) symbolized by frozen and hot spots

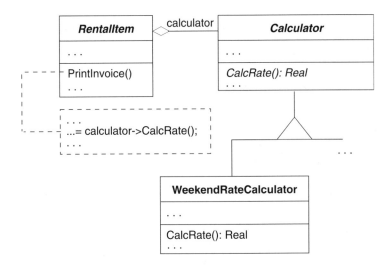

Figure 12.3   Abstract coupling based on template and hook methods

12.3.2 Class/Object Composition Metapatterns

In the example shown in Figures 12.1 and 12.2, hot spots (hook methods) and frozen spots (template methods) are unified in one class. This implies that the behavior of printing an invoice can be changed by defining a subclass and implementing
its hot spots in a specific way (see FIgure 12.2a).

In some situations, more flexibility is required to allow adaptations at run time.
In order to achieve this degree of flexibility, frozen spots and hot spots have to be
put into separate classes as explained below. In this case, the class that contains
the hook methods can be considered as the *hook class* of the class that contains the
corresponding template methods. We will call the class that contains the template
methods the *template class*. In other words, a hook class *parameterizes* the corresponding template class; the hot spots are in the hook class. We will use the letters
T for template class and H for hook class. We will refer to instances of T and H or
their subclasses as T objects and H objects.

Adaptations at run time become possible since the behavior of a T object, i.e., its
template method, can be changed by associating a different H object with it. Creating H objects and assigning references to T objects can, of course, be done at run
time.

The following example illustrates the case where class *RentalItem* is based on
the contract of class *Calculator* (see Figure 12.3). So how a rental item prints an
invoice can be changed at run time by assigning a different object to the instance
variable *calculator* of a *RentalItem* object, one that fulfills the contract of *Calculator*. The way in which *RentalItem* objects and *Calculator* objects are coupled via
calculator is called *abstract coupling*.

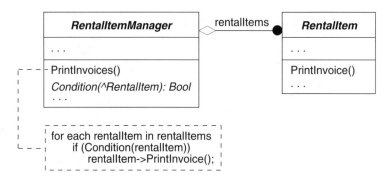

Figure 12.4   *RentalItem* **as hook class in connection with template class** *RentalItemManager*

What constitutes a template method and a hook method, and so a template class and a hook class, depends on one's point of view. A hook method is elementary compared to the template method in which the particular hook method is used. In another context, the template method can become a hook method of another template method.

For example, an instance of a class *RentalItemManager* manages an arbitrary number of *RentalItem* objects. A template method *PrintInvoices()* sends the message *PrintInvoice* to some of the managed *RentalItem* objects, depending on a certain condition. So in this context *PrintInvoice()* of class *RentalItem* becomes the hook method of the template method *PrintInvoices()* in class *RentalItemManager*. The behavior of *RentalItemManager* might be required in a hotel reservation system, for example, to print invoices for a tourist party leaving the hotel. Figure 12.4 shows the relevant aspects of the classes *RentalItemManager* and *RentalItem*.

In general, it is interesting to consider how T and H objects can be composed. We will call the few combination possibilities *composition metapatterns*.

The simplest composition metapattern is the unification of T and H in one class. This special case is termed the *Unification metapattern*, which underlies class *RentalItem* (see Figure 12.1), for example.

If T and H are separated, a T object might refer to exactly one H object or to an arbitrary number of H objects. Figure 12.5 depicts the corresponding *1:1 Connection metapattern* and the *1:N Connection metapattern*. The 1:1 Connection meta-

Figure 12.5   **(a) 1:1 Connection metapattern and (b) 1:N Connection metapattern**

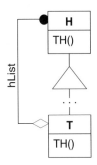

Figure 12.6   1:N Recursive Connection metapattern

pattern underlies the miniframework in Figure 12.3; the 1:N Connection metapattern the one in Figure 12.4.

If *T* is a subclass of *H*, recursive object composition becomes possible, as demonstrated in Figure 12.6 for the *1:N Recursive Connection metapattern*. Note that the names of template and hook methods are typically the same in the 1:N Recursive Connection metapattern, i.e., *TH()*.

Since *hList* manages objects of static type *H*, objects of any subclass of *H*, i.e., *T* objects, can also be handled. This allows one to build up directed graphs with *T* objects and *H* objects as nodes. Figure 12.7 shows a tree as an example.

The typical structure of *TH()* in class *T* is analogous to the template method *PrintInvoices()* shown in Figure 12.4. The message *TH* is forwarded to the managed *H* objects, probably depending on a condition. So the following characteristic of object composition based on the 1:N Recursive Connection metapattern results: A *T* object can be viewed as a place holder for all objects following that *T* object in the directed graph. Instead of sending the message *TH* to all these objects, it is sufficient to send the message to the particular *T* object. This message is then automatically forwarded to the other objects that are placed "behind" that *T* object in the directed graph.

Due to this forwarding property of typical template methods in recursive connection patterns, *a hierachy of objects* built by means of the 1:N Recursive Connection pattern *can be treated as a single object.*

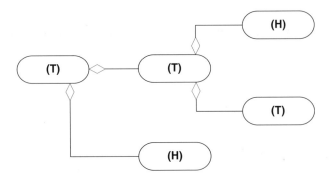

Figure 12.7   Tree hierarchy of *T* and *H* objects

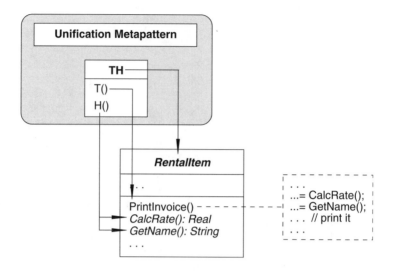

Figure 12.8 Attaching the Unification metapattern to class *RentalItem*

When to choose other recursive composition metapatterns is discussed in detail in the literature [Pree 1994].

To sum up, hook methods/classes represent the requirements necessary to produce a specific application for a domain out of a semifinished application framework. Framework-centered software development requires us to *see* these hot spots. The following section discusses how hot spots can be visualized, based on metapatterns.

12.4 METAPATTERNS AS BASIS OF DESIGN BOOKS

Each composition metapattern typically occurs several times in a framework. Only the semantic aspect of the hot spots differs. The characteristic of a metapattern, especially the offered degree of flexibility, is independent of the particular situation where a metapattern is applied.

The principal idea of a design book is to attach composition metapatterns to framework components. A design book for a framework constitutes a means to browse through its hot spots. Depending on the characteristics of a metapattern, the programmer *sees* the intended adaptations and their corresponding degree of flexibility.

For example, the Unification metapattern could be attached to various components of a framework. Figure 12.8 illustrates this for the class *RentalItem*.

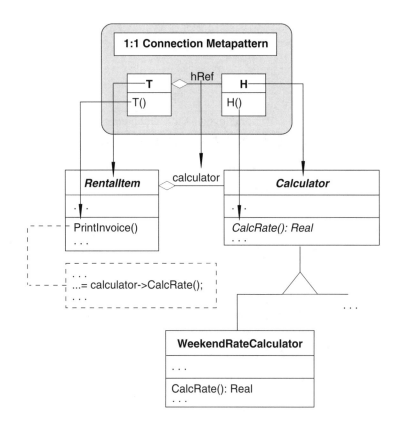

Figure 12.9   Attaching the 1:1 Connection metapattern to classes *RentalItem* and *Calculator*

Analogously, the other composition metapatterns can be attached to framework components. Figure 12.9 demonstrates this for the 1:1 Connection metapattern linked to *RentalItem* and *Calculator*.

A hypertext system is well suited for implementing a design book. The arrows in Figures 12.8 and 12.9 would be hypertext links in a design book. Figures 12.8 and 12.9 assume that there exists a class diagram for the annotated components. Thus the links refer to the corresponding items in that class diagram. If no such class diagram is available, the links could refer directly to the corresponding source code fragments.

Since a particular metapattern occurs several times in a framework, a design book has to handle this repetition in an appropriate way. Due to the fact that only the semantic aspect of a metapattern differs, we propose a solution as sketched in Figure 12.10.

A menu pops up if a design book user clicks inside the hook class of a metapattern. The hook class represents the hot spot in the pattern. The menu lists the various aspects that are kept flexible in a framework and that are based on the

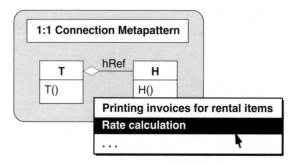

Figure 12.10 Linking specific examples to metapatterns

1:1 Connection metapattern. In our example, if the item *Rate calculation* is chosen, the corresponding example is linked to the metapattern. In this case, it would be as depicted in Figure 12.9.

An appropriate hypertext editor that lets us define links between metapatterns and source code or class diagrams forms the basis for the production of design books for any application framework. Since there will be myriads of metapatterns in (application) frameworks, programmers who know a particular framework well, especially its developers, should produce the corresponding design book.

The fact that the hot spots are visualized in a design book might not only be useful for adaptations of a particular framework. Some aspects of a framework might be pretty domain-independent, so that a programmer who grasps the design can apply it in the development of other frameworks.

12.5 ACTIVE COOKBOOK

Conceptually, an active cookbook differs from a design book in that it focuses on implementation details of an adaptation. Design books outline the hot spots for specialization on an abstraction level that is higher than the underlying implementation details.

Once the hot spots for an adequate framework specialization are identified by means of a design book, an active cookbook helps one to accomplish the adaptation steps. Though design books and active cookbooks are conceptually different, they are predestined to be integrated in one tool.

The concept of actively assisting in the adaptation of frameworks is already applied in tools in the realm of GUI application frameworks. For example, Parc-Place's VisualWorks, NeXT's InterfaceBuilder, and the "Wizard" tools of Microsoft's Foundation Classes actively support the adaptation of the corresponding GUI application framework.

The idea of actively supporting framework adaptations should be applied to application frameworks for any domain. For example, to define a subclass of *Calculator*, an active recipe would provide an editor that asks the programmer for the

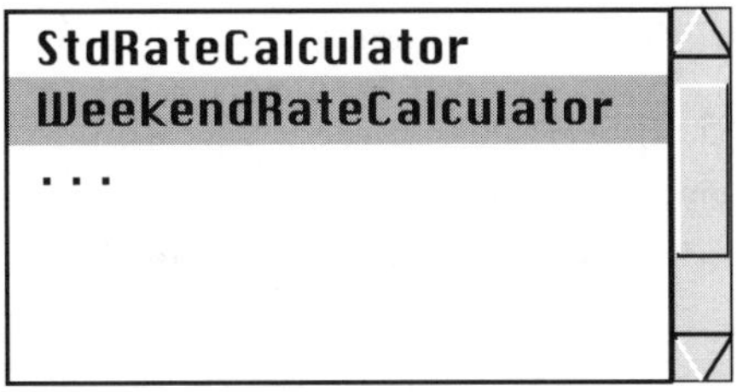

```
┌──────────────────────────────────┬──┐
│ StdRateCalculator                │▲ │
│ WeekendRateCalculator            │██│
│ ...                              │  │
│                                  │  │
│                                  │  │
│                                  │▽ │
└──────────────────────────────────┴──┘
```

Figure 12.11 Part of a configuration dialog

name of the subclass. After providing the calculation algorithm—either textually or, if appropriate, through visual manipulations—the corresponding class would be generated.

Simple configuration tasks such as choosing which *Calculator* object is combined with a *RentalItem* object could be specified by selecting from a list as shown in Figure 12.11. Note that such configuration tools can also be handled by end users. Metapatterns that allow run-time adaptations are predestined for such tools, assuming that some ready-to-use *H* components exist. In the example shown in Figure 12.11, specific subclasses of the hook class *Calculator* have already been defined and implemented.

12.6 SUMMARY

We are convinced that visually supported programming based on application frameworks should not primarily rebuild concepts already provided by textual object-oriented programming languages. A general-purpose visualization tool like a design book, together with an active cookbook that integrates specific visual manipulation editors, supports the reuse and development of application frameworks by visualizing hot spots. The textual object-oriented language is used for object definition, message passing, and control flow specification.

In order to evaluate the design book and active cookbook approach, prototypes of these tools have been implemented.* The prototypes are based on a framework that simulates an ubiquitous computing world [Weiser 1991].

Future research and hands-on experience with the design book and active cookbook prototypes will reveal pros and cons of the presented vision. Research is especially necessary to define generic editors that can be integrated into active cookbooks for several different domains.

Research and experience will also show whether a (more or less) pure visual specification of dynamic aspects of an object-oriented software system is superior to textual languages. In this case, appropriate visualization concepts could be integrated into the electronic books.

---

* This research was carried out in cooperation with Siemens Corporate Research in Munich and the PenLab at Washington University in St. Louis.

ACKNOWLEDGEMENTS

Erich Gamma, one of the developers of ET++, did pioneering work in his PhD thesis [Gamma 1992], which uses a graphic notation together with an informal textual representation as a basis for describing the design of ET++. This way of describing object-oriented design on an abstraction level higher than the underlying object-oriented programming language stimulated the search for meta-patterns.

I thank Professor Takayuki Dan Kimura from Washington University in St. Louis. During my stay at Washington University, numerous discussions on visual programming provided essential insights regarding visual programming, and especially, the motivation to find ways to combine object-oriented and visual programming paradigms.

Professor Gustav Pomberger and the team at Siemens AG Munich provided the necessary environment to discuss the presented ideas and to develop the corresponding prototypes. Albert Schappert provided helpful comments on earlier versions of this contribution.

Adele Goldberg's detailed hints helped to bring out the core points in a final revision.

REFERENCES

[Eggenschwiler 1991] T. Eggenschwiler, *Design Support in a Very Large Class Library: A Bottom-Up Approach*, Semesterarbeit, Institut für Informatik, University of Zürich, 1991. To obtain a copy write to: Institut für Informatik, Universität Zürich, Winterthurerstr. 191, CH-8057 Zürich, Switzerland.

[Eggenschwiler 1992] T. Eggenschwiler and E. Gamma, "ET++ swaps manager: using object technology in the financial engineering domain," *OOPSLA'92, Special Issue of SIGPLAN Notices*, Vol. 27, No. 10, 1992.

[Gamma 1992] E. Gamma, *Objektorientierte Software-Entwicklung am Beispiel von ET++: Klassenbibliothek, Werkzeuge, Design*, PhD thesis, University of Zürich, 1991; published by Springer Verlag, 1992.

[Gamma 1994] E. Gamma, R. Helm, R. Johnson, and J. Vlissides, *Design Patterns—Microarchitectures for Reusable Object-Oriented Software*, Addison-Wesley, 1994.

[Gossain 1989] S. Gossain and D. B. Anderson, "Designing a class hierachy for domain representation and reusability," *Proceedings of Tools '89*, Paris, France, 1989.

[Krasner 1988] G. E. Krasner and S. T. Pope, "A cookbook for using the model-view-controller user interface paradigm in Smalltalk-80," *Journal of Object-Oriented Programming*, Vol. 1, No. 3, 1988.

[NeXT 1990] NeXT, Inc., *1.0 Technical Documentation: Concepts*, NeXT, Inc., Redwood City, CA, 1990.

[Pree 1994] W. Pree, *Design Patterns for Object-Oriented Software Development*, Addison-Wesley/ACM Press, 1994.

[Rumbaugh 1991] J. Rumbaugh, M. Blaha, W. Premerlani, F. Eddy, and W. Lorensen, *Object-Oriented Modeling and Design*, Prentice Hall, Englewood Cliffs, New Jersey, 1991.

[Russo 1989] V. Russo and R. H. Campbell, "Virtual memory and backing storage management in multiprocessor operating systems using class hierachical design," in *Proceedings of OOPSLA '89*, New Orleans, Louisiana, 1989.

[Schmucker 1986] K. Schmucker, *Object-Oriented Programming for the Macintosh*, Hayden, Hasbrouck Heights, New Jersey, 1986.

[Weinand 1988] A. Weinand, E. Gamma, and R. Marty, "ET++—An object-oriented application framework in C++," *OOPSLA'88, Special Issue of SIGPLAN Notices*, Vol. 23, No. 11, 1988.

[Weinand 1989] A. Weinand, E. Gamma, and R. Marty, "Design and implementation of ET++, a seamless object-oriented application framework," in *Structured Programming,* Vol. 10, No. 2, Springer 1989.

[Weiser 1991] M. Weiser, "The computer for the 21st century," *Scientific American*, September 1991.

[Wilson 1990] D. A.Wilson, L. S. Rosenstein, and D. Shafer, *Programming with MacApp*, Addison-Wesley, 1990.

[Wirfs-Brock 1990] R. Wirfs-Brock, B. Wilkerson, and L. Wiener, *Designing Object-Oriented Software*, Prentice Hall, Englewood Cliffs, New Jersey, 1990.

Index